"Much like Edward Edinger with C. G̶ ̶ ̶ ̶ ̶ ̶ ̶ commentaries on Michael Eigen's books offer distillation, amplification, and expansion of themes that are both contemporary and timeless. I admire his deep understanding of Eigen's work and the rich and enriching way he is able to convey it. In this volume, clinical cases from Eigen's two books intertwine with universal human concerns of madness, emotional life, ethics, and creativity. With Bagai's care and illumination, Eigen's intricacies come alive again through a kindred voice, one that is both a carrier and guardian of spirit and psyche."

—Ofra Eshel, faculty, training and supervising analyst, Israel Psychoanalytic Society; head of Independent Psychoanalysis—Radical Breakthroughs postgraduate track, Tel Aviv University; author, *The Emergence of Analytic Oneness: Into the Heart of Psychoanalysis*

"Robin Bagai's commentary and introduction to Eigen's major texts reveal an approach that is heartfelt and sincere. Bagai provides a mooring at the same time as he liberates perspectives into some of Eigen's most intense and demanding passages. In many places Eigen describes psychological work as a 'digesting and opening' experience. In Bagai's hands we see this injunction in practice. His writing and own way with words demonstrates how this is to be done. With a palpable affection for Michael Eigen and an intelligent highlighting of key themes, Robin Bagai has done a great service for another generation of Eigen readers. His hermeneutic can be understood as an example of *Lectio Divina*—the reading of texts in a participatory manner which transforms the reader."

—Stephen Bloch, Jungian analyst and clinical psychologist; founding member, South African Association of Jungian Analysts; training analyst, Cape Town, South Africa; co-editor (with Loray Daws) of *Living Moments: Essays in Honor of Michael Eigen*; and (with Paul Ashton) *Music and Psyche: Contemporary Psychoanalytic Perspectives*

"Robin Bagai is a great teacher, organized and clear, able to make Eigen's writing accessible and both clinically and personally relevant. Psychosis can be frightening and confusing and it is wonderful to have a guide. Eigen's Psychotic Core is based on his experience reaching to the depths with many psychotic patients. Sometimes we encounter darkness in Eigen's writing, sometimes beauty, both in our own inner life and with our patients. Robin Bagai invites us to journey into the unknown and to find parts of ourselves still hidden. He reminds us that the beginning of learning to be a therapist may be like a musician playing scales. Only later do we learn that true psychic growth is ongoing, the psyche is vast.

Both Eigen and Bagai believe in a certain kind of faith, not a particular theory but rather belief that psychic growth can develop slowly from 'regular relational contact over time.' This type of faith is 'grounded in openness to the unknown with curiosity and respect for what arises rather than holding on to expectation or agenda.'

Bagai's book is filled with respect for Eigen and will be a trustworthy companion as you read Eigen's first book, *The Psychotic Core*, and then his turbulent *Emotional Storm*. Neither Eigen nor Bagai's commentary will disappoint."

—JoAnn Culbert-Koehn, Jungian psychoanalyst; past President, C.G. Jung Institute of Los Angeles

"Eigen's work is oxygen for the soul."

—Mark Epstein, MD; author of *The Zen of Therapy: Uncovering a Hidden Kindness in Life*

Commentaries on the Work of Michael Eigen

Commentaries on the Work of Michael Eigen is an accessible and engaging introduction to this ground-breaking psychoanalytic sage. Through exploration of Eigen's two key texts, *The Psychotic Core* and *Emotional Storm*, the author addresses universal human concerns of madness and the difficulties of our emotional life.

In conversational style, the book mirrors Eigen's chapter-by-chapter approach, focusing on and amplifying important aspects of each work. Bagai follows threads of several key themes from psychoanalysis, philosophy, literature, religious thought, and the humanities, and chapters include discussion of relevant theory from Freud, Jung, Klein, Winnicott, Bion, Buber, and Levinas, among others. Rather than a comprehensive or systematic exegesis of Eigen's work, Bagai's commentary expands nodal aspects, illuminating and probing seminal themes and ideas. Through clinical case examples, the author explores intertwining of mind and body, self and the other using an array of carefully selected quotes from Eigen's kaleidoscopic vision.

Commentaries on the Work of Michael Eigen will be essential reading for psychotherapists and psychoanalysts, as well as anyone seeking a greater understanding of Eigen's work.

Robin Bagai, Psy.D. is a clinical psychologist in Portland, Oregon, who has been practicing psychoanalytic psychotherapy for over 35 years. His work has been published in two edited collections: *The Spiritual Psyche in Psychotherapy: Mysticism, Intersubjectivity, and Psychoanalysis*; and *Healing, Rebirth, and The Work of Michael Eigen* (both Routledge). Dr. Bagai has been leading in-person and international seminars on over a dozen of Michael Eigen's books since 2014.

Commentaries on the Work of Michael Eigen

Oblivion and Wisdom, Madness and Music

Robin Bagai

Routledge
Taylor & Francis Group

LONDON AND NEW YORK

Cover image: Estela Alcaide Delgado / Getty Images

First published 2023
by Routledge
4 Park Square, Milton Park, Abingdon, Oxon OX14 4RN

and by Routledge
605 Third Avenue, New York, NY 10158

Routledge is an imprint of the Taylor & Francis Group, an informa business

British Library Cataloguing-in-Publication Data
A catalogue record for this book is available from the British Library

Library of Congress Cataloging-in-Publication Data
A catalog record has been requested for this book

ISBN: 9781032190709 (hbk)
ISBN: 9781032190716 (pbk)
ISBN: 9781003257554 (ebk)

DOI: 10.4324/9781003257554

Typeset in Times New Roman
by Newgen Publishing UK

To my grandfather Vaishno Das, whose far-reaching vision and tragic journey were not in vain;
and to all who experience the pain and suffering of being human.

Contents

Foreword

Michael Eigen

It is a pleasure to write a foreword for Dr. Robin Bagai's commentaries on my work—and more. He not only focuses on and amplifies aspects of my work but adds his own creative explorations to themes that matter and are needed. There is so much injury and inequity in life that this moment of history heightens and calls attention to in its own virulent ways. No age has had such dangerous weapons and modes of communication. We are even able to influence the very climate and possibly existence of our planet with tools we have created. And yet this very ability can be turned to well-nigh illimitable good if we continue working on what to do with ourselves, how to partner our capacities and use them less destructively. Indeed, in sectors of life we are already doing so, adding to the beauty and care of existence. To a large extent the years individuals now live has never been greater, as are many amenities of self-care and mutuality. We are even able to reach new levels of potential honesty and dialogue, ways of being together, talking together. The very existence and development of various talk and body therapies have great potential for human development and appreciation of dimensions of being and experience unfolding within and between us.

Dr. Bagai has given seminars on at least twelve of my books over the last seven years and has a profound and lucid grasp of issues and themes explored. His own family background fuses East and West and a panoply of images and presences in these pages light up transformational processes. Psychic work is mediated through the Bhagavad Gita, Socrates, Buddhism, Levinas, and Rumi as well as modern depth psychologies. He weaves threads of many schools, and with him, we feel new possibilities.

He engages both destructive and productive attitudes and capacities we need to help us go further. It is a work that spans social, personal, and spiritual dimensions that interconnect and spark each other. A sense of inspiration and deep reflection inform his writing, adding to our own faith and life.

Michael Eigen, Ph.D.
New York City

Acknowledgments

It is a great mystery how one person's insides touching another's can change the trajectory of a life. Michael Eigen's writing and person have done just that, resulting in the work you now have before you. My gratitude to Dr. Eigen is knitted into the fabric of this book. I am particularly indebted to the many local, national, and global seminar members who have accompanied me on journeys deep into Eigen's expressive portrayals of mind and psyche, heart and soul. I have included a small selection of their comments and questions in between most commentaries in the book.

Special thanks go to my local psychotherapy colleagues Kelly Bentz, Duane Dale, Selma Duckler, Mark Gundry, Rick Johnson, Stephen Kirsch, Jason Loverti, Keith Lowenstein, Willow Pearson, Donna Prinzmetal, Kelly Reams, Miriam Resnick, Willa Schneberg, Ron Sharrin, Laura Stahman, and the late Naomi Sakanoue for much support, encouragement, and thoughtful contribution throughout years of seminars when we were able to meet in person.

Particular thanks go to Lee Ann Pickrell for her skillful editing and book management, and to Ebru Salman for her careful transcription of participant comments and discussion from the recorded online videos.

Gratitude also goes to my many psychotherapy patients who have contributed to my personal growth in ways they may never realize. And to my son Coque and his family, and to my spouse Willa, who has provided much support, encouragement and care through the years.

Credits

Introduction

I begin with a plea to the reader. There is no substitute for reading Michael Eigen's words in the original. What follows is an elaboration and amplification—a wish to shine light on the intricacies of his voice and thought.

This volume is a result of my seminar talks on Eigen's work, ongoing for more than seven years. The commentaries are conversational in tone, adjusted for the book's narrative style. Eigen's first book *The Psychotic Core* (Jason Aronson 1986; Routledge 2018) and *Emotional Storm* (Wesleyan, 2005) comprise Parts One and Two, and consist of 12 and 13 commentaries, respectively. As with nearly all of Eigen's work, my talks include important aspects of Freud, Jung, Melanie Klein, Donald Winnicott, Marion Milner, Wilfred Bion, Martin Buber, Emmanuel Levinas, and others. These authors are highlighted and engaged, both within Eigen's own words and through my elaborations.

The book's format mirrors Eigen's work chapter-by-chapter, focusing on a selection of his important ideas. Seminar member comments have been included after most commentaries along with my responses. The work as a whole explores themes whose origins are found across psychoanalysis, philosophy, literature, mysticism, and religious thought. Rather than a comprehensive or systematic exegesis of Eigen's work, these commentaries have a goal of expanding nodal aspects of his two books, while accompanying the reader through each chapter. The work stands alone, but is furthered by having Eigen's two books alongside for reference.

In this volume I have chosen to concentrate on *The Psychotic Core* and *Emotional Storm* because they address universal human concerns of madness and the enormous challenges of our emotional life, both of which continue to haunt *homo sapiens* to the present day. As a human group, we have yet to find ways of working profitably with emotional life and our psychotic selves, leaving humanity increasingly on the edge of oblivion and self-annihilation. Psychic reality can be full of music and wonder, but it also includes self-destructive tendencies that put us all at risk. My hope is that a fuller understanding and embrace of our human complexity might make us less afraid of ourselves and each other.

DOI: 10.4324/9781003257554-1

These commentaries grew out of my weekly seminar lectures on more than a dozen Eigen books. In those seminars our group immersed itself in his work each Sunday morning, one chapter per week. With each new book and seminar, interest in Eigen's work grew among both professional colleagues and the interested public.

It is difficult to convey the depth of appreciation group members expressed for what studying Eigen's work brings. Enriched by unpacking and associating to his ideas, Eigen's poetic style becomes enhanced in group settings, and intricacies of his thought gain clarity. As a result, psychotherapists and analysts from different orientations often felt their own therapy work deepen in important ways. *They* deepened from contact with Eigen's work. Others were moved by his ability to speak to their insides, giving voice to emotional sensitivities and longings for psyche's depth. My talks focused on providing amplification and context for Eigen's dense complexity. Among other things, group members learned or relearned the value of patience, negative capability, and creative waiting in their personal lives as well as with therapy clients. There is also something ineffable that cannot be spoken, something experienced beyond language that comes through his particular "voice." The power of Eigen's psyche to speak to our insides through written word and group dialogue evokes a form of soul creation.

Eigen's body of work offers no therapeutic system, no technique or template, and no "solutions" to psychological problems. Why, then, has it stimulated psychoanalytic thinking and depth psychology across myriad walks of life? I suspect this has something to do with giving priority to experiential life and complex realities of our emotional palette. In contemporary societies worldwide, these realms are increasingly subject to displacement, distraction, and disavowal in the service of evacuating or avoiding unpleasant feelings. Tolerance for and exploration of emotional life has become an endangered species.

Eigen's work takes us on a different path. He opens channels that help grow capacities for furthering inner experience, thereby quickening aliveness and life's reach. His work immerses us in geographies and strata of affective life, human sensitivities, and everyday emotional struggles, rather than shying away, glossing over, or pretending difficult stuff doesn't exist. Direct contact with inner life and guided struggle can become highways for personal development, and my commentaries try to emulate these while adding brushstrokes of my own.

In the pages that follow, I offer no academic critique of Eigen's work, but instead try to amplify and add to themes Eigen has already woven into colorful tapestries, ones that sing music of psyche. At times you can hear jazz-like riffs and rhythms in his words. His mind works associatively, with a rigor of radical acceptance and openness—a respect and passionate interest for wherever psyche is wont to go. He circumambulates with a curious mind and large heart. A mind that has learned how to grow itself through practice and hardship, attending to nuance, digesting impacts, and incorporating insights that flow from courage to experience psychic life more fully. In doing so, we might all find more tolerance *and* joy for what life brings, even in its sad, hurtful, traumatic moments.

Eigen observes and engages emotional life without judgment, turning his keen kaleidoscope to view psyche in different poses and postures, highlighting full spectra of harmonies and dissonance. He gives us mirrors into the fullness of what it means to live and grow emotionally as a human being. Through his lens our "psychic body" becomes as interesting and important to maintain as the physical body we carry around and rely upon. Why, then, do we not attend to processes and creations of psyche, mind, and spirit with similar care, daily exercise, and muscle-building? After all, our experiential awareness encompasses both body and mind, both physical and ineffable aspects of life. Quality of attention to psyche and inner life is part of what these commentaries circle around, with insight and understanding arising as natural offspring.

Eigen shows us different kinds of psyche-music, from spoken word and poetry to quiet intimations and felt awareness. There are qualities of silence too … whisperings from deep inside, and at times we catch a whiff of music with no name, no sound. Our physical body can never be separated from this choir. It contains its own musical rhythms, and for many, bodily awareness remains a primary conduit for feeling life. But in the pages ahead, it will be psyche that is in focus—our emotional life in the driver's seat with body-life right alongside, riding shotgun.

What kind of psychotherapy or psychoanalysis can result from careful attention to psyche's music? Are there unknown, unheard chords and melodies in our psychological lives waiting to be encountered, uncovered, created, whatever our mental "health"? Let me expand the metaphor a bit, to describe what I have found over the years.

First, we know that much work goes into training—either to become a psychotherapist or musician. We begin by learning the basics: intense study, practice, and supervised experience. We also learn about *our own* basics by becoming a patient and learning to *be* patient. A lot goes into learning our personal and historical notes and scales, as we simultaneously explore therapy models from schools that resonate with personal patterns of inner music. We get to know our therapeutic selves slowly, through careful listening and practice of elementary "scales" for several years. During this process we become conversant with our own "instrument," a little at a time. After some years we find this learning never stops—just as psyche's music never stops, nor do musical instruments and their subtleties. All involve forms of spirit that proceed toward *unknown* development. Unpredictable growth is part of life's ongoing mystery.

Depth psychotherapy neither stands still nor stops developing. Clinicians continue to discover more about psychical and emotional worlds even after many decades. This is partly why it's called a *practice*. We practice with ourselves while practicing with others. After growing enough confidence with basic scales and learning, we begin taking risks by listening to unconscious promptings, and spontaneously responding to those from our patients. With care, respect, and alliance, two psyches in a therapeutic couple might begin opening to different kinds of mutual music, a duet without notes on the page and with no predetermined direction or goal. This becomes similar to jazz improvisation, where one gets to participate in a musically unfolding process of surprise and discovery. It does not mean that dissonance, staccato, or off-key notes go away. No, these remain a necessary part of psyche's continuum of emotional music. Yet the atmosphere created by how we respond with our unspoken attitudes becomes key. Such attitudes and their intonations provide resonant support that allows patients to discover and create life-music of their own that feels right for them. This kind of depth psychotherapy must not be called "wild" because it maintains a therapeutic frame and container with structural limits and boundaries. As such, it can become a safe and "well-ventilated" space for opening to what is unknown and unpredictable, in dialogue with inner voices both loud and barely audible. Harmonious and discordant emotional music embedded in our sensory feeling universe, when given freedom to play and speak, allows us to hear our unheard selves better.

Application of technique in Eigen's therapy world would be a misnomer, but there are qualities of approach that can be highlighted. We can point to a handful of factors that are foundational to psychotherapy work. Among these are patience, waiting, and care-filled attention; sincerity of attitude and response rather than artifice or over-reliance on technique; sustaining diffuse yet concentrated foci; a devotion to feeling life that includes implicit good will and spacious acceptance, with a willingness to surrender to emotional impacts; and a matured tolerance for processing mutual woundedness when it occurs. These qualitative factors are important resources that give flesh to the therapeutic frame, whether or not emphasis is placed on transference and countertransference interpretation, evolving a co-constructed third, or simply spontaneous response and exchange.

When these qualities are accompanied by open curiosity for all that arises within sessions, we create a different kind of therapy than following prescribed sets of rules to arrive at predetermined destinations. It is more about letting our soul and unconscious speak and be heard, as well as offering good company for their further development. But this is not a therapy that fits everyone, and Eigen remains ever ecumenical by affirming that many therapy approaches can be helpful, including highly structured ones, depending on what is most generative for the individual patient.

Depth psychotherapy requires a certain kind of faith. Not belief in a particular theory or orientation, so much as faith in what can grow from regular relational contact over time, supported by sincere engagement, mutual goodwill, and unconscious rapport. In addition, there is another form of faith at work. Not a faith system or belief structure. Instead, this faith is akin to how Bion and Eigen speak about it: an attitude, approach, and receptive stance toward self and others that offers no surety or guarantee—a faith grounded in openness to the unknown with curiosity and respect for what arises, rather than holding on to expectation or agenda. This faith is not about remaining emotionally safe and secure, yet safety and security can paradoxically grow more durable from practicing with it.

Engagement in such a process offers a less common kind of emotional security for those who seek or need it. Not the fleeting "security" that comes from chronic defensive maneuvering, but a stronger, more realistic sense that grows from engaging the risky business of contacting oneself more deeply over time. This can generate a virtuous circle—as when developing courage and increased tolerance for experiencing oneself allows for receptivity to more of life's aliveness.

What kind of security is it that comes from contact and practice with our emotional worlds and unknowns of inner life? And who would seek this out? Often it is those who find themselves held fast by emotional suffering. Those who feel little choice but to summon courage and take the plunge into psychotherapy or analysis to discover deeper, fuller truths about their life, who they are, and what their pain is trying to express. Eigen says it this way:

> It is the security one gets from trying with all one's being to make contact with oneself, with another, with emotional reality. There is hunger for reality, for truth about life, oneself, others. A certain security comes from following that hunger, coming through the upset, living with the turbulence. Truth is highly charged, explosive, and if used wrongly, can wreck life. But without it, the soul is dead …
>
> (2004, p. 7)

In the commentaries that follow, I ask the reader to embark on a journey of discovery with me into those very realms we most often wish to avoid. We might even frame this as an adventure, a detective story, or mystery thriller … and why not? Books that highlight madness and storms of emotion can seem frightening and unnecessary during an era already burdened with more of these than we care to know. Yet the territory covered in this book could not be further from the kind of pandering to traumatic sensationalism we see and hear in the news each day. Instead, we are guided by Eigen with a firm hand and soft touch through deep and tumultuous waters. Can you imagine dark storms of psyche and psychosis informed by a poetic sensibility and creative imagination? Or psychical rhythms in emotional life structured by musical ones? Or wishes and idealizations as offspring of infinity? You might even be surprised to find parts of yourself in these pages.

We are complex beings, psychically and emotionally. Getting to know ourselves better from the inside can provide a firmer foundation for what occurs on the outside. Less fear of ourselves and others would be a welcome companion these days, and in the pages ahead I wish to echo Eigen from his original 1986 Preface of *The Psychotic Core*:

> This book is a bearing witness, a probing. Its value lies in whether it helps us become a little less afraid of ourselves in ways that are not destructive, enriching the quality of our experiencing capacity.
>
> (1986, p. viii)

Part One

Commentaries on
The Psychotic Core

The Core of Psychosis

I want to thank you for joining me on this journey through Michael Eigen's work. *The Psychotic Core* was Eigen's very first book, published in 1986 when he was 50 years old. At the time I am writing this, Eigen is more than 85 years old and has published about 30 books. *The Psychotic Core* is novel in its approach to psychosis because Eigen tries to do two things simultaneously. He expresses and conveys madness from both inside and outside the mind, both experientially and conceptually. His inside view uses expressive language often found in literature and poetry to convey felt meaning. At the same time, Eigen gives outside perspective with enough distance and overview to provide a kind of scaffolding from which to observe, understand, and make sense of madness. It is phenomenological in the best sense, using both subjective and objective methods of approach to the subject.

This double approach is a theme with many variations, and *doubleness* itself is a theme we will meet many times throughout these 12 commentaries. There are many kinds of *doubles*. I am not talking about simple rigid binaries, but instead relations between binaries, or ways they interact. This is an important difference. One example from inside a psychotic experience might be the doubleness of simultaneously feeling one's mind to be frozen yet spinning out of control. A kind of frenetic paralysis. Another double might be the reversal of turning the world upside down or inside out, as when someone feels their thoughts to be more real and substantial than the physical world, while the outer material world seems ghost-like and unreal. We will investigate different kinds of doubles and their relationships as we go along. Doubleness has a long history, reminding me of the philosopher Spinoza who said something like: no matter how thin you slice it, there are always two sides. Today in our post-modern world, we might say more than two sides; there are lots of sides and points of view. Multiple relations between and among "twoness" remain foundational, even as they are often obscured by extremes like rigid dualisms and binaries. As I hope to make clear, both our physical and psychical lives exist within various matrixes of doubleness that appear mostly hidden in plain sight.

DOI: 10.4324/9781003257554-3

In psychoanalytic writing we find pervasive forms of doubleness: Freud's conscious and unconscious realms, Melanie Klein's introjection and projection, and Wilfred Bion's + and—suffixes given to a number of different capacities. Eigen highlights moments of felt experience side-by-side with conceptual perspective. Both are important. Neither one by itself can provide what the other brings out. Experiential moments and conceptual perspective are different orders of reality, different domains or registers, yet they also interact and intertwine. Experiencing our experience is one side of the coin, and codifying or representing experience with image, symbol, or word lies on the other side. By putting these two sides together, they become a conjunction, and by trying to think in terms of doubles we find a fertile way to enter this book.

What is a conjunction? A conjunction is simply two things that go together—like day and night, or awake and asleep. Conjunctions are always found next to each other, and they can also have movement back and forth. A 24-hour cycle is one example. In Eigen's writing there are lived-moments of felt experience alongside of conceptual understanding, and these two sides also engage in a back-and-forth, an exchange or dialectic. When things work well, this back and forth becomes generative; that is, we can grow with exchange between experiences and our representations of them, between evocation and understanding, emotion and thought, where each side feeds the other to develop new or further moments of experience and representation.

One of the main goals of this book is to try to normalize psychosis. It may sound crazy, ironic, or funny to try to normalize something like psychosis, since we often think of madness as the height of abnormality. But psychotic qualities and dynamics are with us in "normal" ordinary life. Psychotic operations are more common than we think, and we see them every day in the news. Simple examples include misperception, distortion, projection, exaggeration, incoherence, and grandiosity. When I was in training on psychiatric wards in the 1970s and '80s, psychosis was mostly limited to whether someone showed signs of hallucinations and delusions. Those were definitive diagnostic indicators, and although still important, we will see that madness is both more subtle and complex.

We read in the first pages of *The Psychotic Core* that Freud started out looking at early-life narcissism as a way to understand not just psychosis, but also what came to be known as *character* or *personality disorders*. He did this by looking at the ego as its own first love and ideal. Borderline and narcissistic character formations share some subtle and not so subtle characteristics with more florid psychotic disorders. One of the original meanings of the word *borderline* was someone who did not fit easily into either neurotic or psychotic categories, but showed features of both. They were "borderline psychotic" or on the border between neurotic and psychotic organizations. Freud keyed on the term *megalomania* as one feature of psychosis, and C.G. Jung used terms like *psychic inflation* or *ego inflation*. Today we often hear the term *grandiosity*, another variation.

Showing aspects of madness in us ordinary folk can be helpful in lowering our fear response, but I also want to broaden our sense of what psychosis is all about, including which aspects might be pathological and which are not. Is it odd to consider that some psychotic aspects are not pathological? We don't have to look very far for examples. For instance, our dreams at night have psychotic elements but are not pathological. Freud thought dreams themselves are psychotic events. And we now know from neuroscience that we *need* to dream at night. It is essential for our mental health to have adequate sleep and dreaming. The irony is that if we do *not* sleep and dream enough, we quickly begin to deteriorate and can go crazy. If you've ever been forced to stay awake for more than a day or two, you know what I mean. Here's another common example: falling in love is a form of psychosis. Why? Because it is accompanied by a loss of boundaries and extreme idealization or overvaluation of the love object or person. And yet what a wonderful psychosis love and infatuation can be … at least until our idealized projections start to wear off! Another psychotic dynamic is at work in the psychology of power, charisma, seduction, and control, as when a loss of self occurs through submission to, or identification with a charismatic leader, guru, or rock star. Indeed, giving oneself over or surrendering with uncritical belief to anyone's charismatic personality is a psychotic instance.

In this book, I will also try to do two things at once, by reducing and expanding the subject matter of psychosis. Reducing madness by exploring Eigen's categories and conceptual dynamics—but expanding our perspective about the variability of psychosis and common characteristics that different forms of madness can take. To get a sense of this variability, here's Eigen's description from his preface:

> In the chapters that follow, we will see in psychotic individuals holocaustal rages, insidious self-poisoning, ghastly vacuousness, the abuse of cleverness, a poignant inability to keep pace with one's heightened sensitivity, the giving of oneself over to spirits and things, crippling shyness, hellish torment and self-deadening, the loss and rebirth of the self in fantastically rich and impoverished scenarios …
>
> (2018g, p. viii)

Have you ever read such a varied account of madness, all in one sentence? Eigen continues:

> My hope is that this book will help us to relax our gaze. The horrific has its own beauty, its own ecstasy, and we ought not walk around it as if it were not there, no more than we should become one with it. This book is a bearing witness, a probing. Its value lies in whether it helps us become

a little less afraid of ourselves in ways that are not destructive, enriching the quality of our experiencing capacity.

(p. viii)

In everyday life, we have a great many references to craziness. This is another sign of its pervasiveness and influence. There are many vernacular expressions about madness that permeate societies all over the world, and here are a few of them:

Insanity, lunacy, nuttiness, senselessness, flakiness, irrationality, psychopathy, sociopathy, losing one's mind, being delusional, deranged, crazy ... wackiness, zaniness, mania ... going bonkers, being off one's rocker, soft in the head, out of touch with reality

I'm sure you can think of others.

Throughout history, insanity has been feared, misunderstood, condemned, prosecuted, and persecuted. At the same time, certain forms of madness have had positive roles and uses in different cultures. Consider figures such as court jesters, oracular sages, seers, shamans, tricksters, fools, mystics, dreamers, and fortune tellers. And let's not forget forms of creative genius found in many unstable if not insane artists, musicians, writers, poets, and composers. In fact, much cultural value and artistic achievement could be said to come from "creative madness."

This is a complex subject because madness is not simply one thing. Another kind of double: psychosis can be linked with creativity as well as delusions. It has more than one side to it, more than one truth. Much depends on the form it takes and how it is used, or misused, and in some cases how madness uses us. Much depends on how psychotic operations function, both in one's life and the cultural milieu.

One way to enter the multiple nature of psychosis is by attending to two things at once, along with various relations between them. Constant conjunctions (after the philosopher David Hume and psychoanalyst Wilfred Bion) exhibit different relationships. It is best to view them using "binocular vision." For example, we might observe whether two things relate more by fusing together or repelling each other. Is there symbiotic enrichment or parasitic dependency? To view pairs and binaries according to the *kinds of relationship they exhibit* is different than pointing to simple dualisms or opposites. The idea is that the kind of relationship between the two matters as much as labeling the things themselves. To get a fuller view, we must include a particular context and how they appear to function with one another.

Let's look at what is common to everyone: our mental and physical self, psyche and soma. We humans are a living conjunction. Or consider breathing: in-breath and out-breath, another conjunction. Or your heart beating rhythmically, systole and diastole. Eigen gives us clues to his pursuit of doubleness in the book's preface, saying he is going to "... trace our double sense of self-other and mental-physical self through what I call the 'kernel of psychosis'" (2018g, p. vi).

Let's consider the mental and the physical sides of our being. Do we ever find them completely separated? How about breathing in and out, or the contraction and expansion of heart muscle? Do these ever occur apart from one another? These examples give you an idea of constant conjunctions. Another more mundane example would be the light switch on your wall. Is there ever a light switch that is only on and not off? It wouldn't be a switch, would it? A switch implies switching from one to another. On and off go together, like breathing, or heartbeat, or tides in the ocean. Note that in these latter examples there is a rhythm between the two. Rhythm and flow along with their absence become important in this book. We commonly call their absence stuckness, frozenness, or rigidity. Emotional flow or its absence are important signals for our psychological well-being.

Here's another kind of doubleness. Does a baby exist without another person? That's a rhetorical question. Some of you will remember D.W. Winnicott's famous saying "There is no such thing as a baby ..." (Winnicott, 1964, pp. 85–92), meaning no such thing as a baby alone and separate, without a mothering one. A baby cannot survive without a mothering person—another example of two conjoined as one. Baby and caretaker are fused together, occupy the same orbit, and are conjoined in physical, psychical, emotional, sensorial, intuitive space. Separate beings, yes, but also together as a form of oneness. Separate and together as one, simultaneously, like mind and body.

An interesting twist on the double nature of our being is their different relationship to time. The body, as we know, has a time limit. Our physical being has an expiration date, an unknown but finite span. But products from our mind or psyche appear to have no such limit. That's an odd difference. Our bodies are finite material beings, but our imagination and psyche are not.

Psyche, mind, and spirit ... these cannot be palpated. They are invisible to our eyes and the touch of flesh. Yet through the ages they've provided boundless forms of imaginative artistic expression, products that can last indefinitely. It is here we encounter Eigen the mystic with a first glimpse of our mysterious psyche. Psyche and creative imagination are boundless and infinite, both in their scope and throughout time. Our psyche and imagination are primordial, grounded in mystery. We don't really know what they are or how they arise. How can we say that mind, psyche, and spirit are infinite? Because works of art and music, literature and philosophy, along with spiritual traditions from thousands of years ago still speak to us today just as poignantly as when they were first created. Our physical material body may be finite, but products of mind and psyche arise from, or are grounded in, something infinite, timeless, and mysterious.

Eigen gives us another clue to how our minds are infinite. He asks: "... what kind of being raises wounds to an infinite power? What sort of person incessantly overestimates and underestimates himself as part of a lifelong drama?" (2018g, p. vii). The clue is our mind's ability to exaggerate ... and not just exaggerate, but psyche's ability and tendency to reach for the absolute, the *n*th degree, beyond hyperbole to something that feels "total." We are good at infinitizing, whether through wish or dream, imagination or idealization. This is a profound tendency to consider because such a capacity suggests that our mind is part of a fabric *woven from infinity*.

When I first caught on to this distinction between finite physicality and infinite psyche, it was mind-blowing. What brought it home for me was a story I heard about book burnings. Book burnings have occurred at different times to repress ideas. As this story goes, there was a bonfire of books happening with a large circle of people around it. Some were seriously intent on the destruction, happy to be destroying books thought to be evil—an attempt to deny, repress, or split off whatever was felt as threatening. Others around the fire were quietly weeping at the travesty of loss. But there was one person who was smiling, not because she thought this burning of books was a good idea, no ... but because she knew that what was inside those books could never truly disappear. The thoughts and ideas in them could not be completely extinguished because psyche, through effort of human consciousness, had already given birth to them. Even if they went underground for many years due to suppression from burning did not matter in the long run. The ideas themselves are immortal even if the physical books that held them were currently banned and disappearing. I sometimes wonder if this was partly what was meant by the saying "the pen is mightier than the sword." My translation: psychical reality can outlast and endure all kinds of physical punishment, war, even attempts at extinction ... yet survive.

Eigen starts this book with Freud and Jung, showing contrasts and similarities. Freud started out wedded to neurology and science but was fascinated by religion (which he called illusion). Jung also started from medicine but with interests in psychosis, religion, and matters of spirit.

We read in the first few pages that Freud was quite influenced by Fechner and Fleiss, both of whom grappled with their own psychosis. Freud questioned whether psychotic patients could be worked with in analysis, whereas Jung worked in an asylum and those with whom he could form an alliance. Eigen, in his therapy practice of over 50 years, has worked profitably in psychotherapy with many psychotic patients.

Another way to normalize madness is by looking at Freud's tripartite structure of the mind: the ego, id, and superego—all of which can have psychotic aspects.

For example, the *ego* originally arises out of a hallucinatory matrix and must develop anti-hallucinatory properties. The early ego is out of contact with the outside world and is given to wish-fulfilling operations. In other words, the ego must learn to distinguish what is real from what is not. Eigen says that for Freud, a kind of madness of the ego marks its foundation and evolution, but this is balanced by and competes with the ego's ties to the real world (2018g, p. 10). In his letters to Jung, Freud called the ego a clown (p. 10). Eigen says the ego is both a dangerous and a precious clown, attached to truth, but also to compromise and delusion. The ego itself is not just one thing. How it functions or is used in a given situation changes, depending on context, motivation, and purpose.

The *id* is characterized by Freud as a seething caldron of drives and impulses. The id lacks logic, is timeless and full of contradictions, and has disregard for boundaries, exhibiting reversals and distortions. The id could be said to be a poster child for psychotic tendencies, with its primitive drives seeking and demanding satisfaction.

The *superego* can be psychotic too. Instead of acting as our conscience, a guardian against id impulses and inappropriate discharge, the superego can spin out of control and become tyrannical, even persecutory, with its unrelenting perfectionistic demands on personality. In ordinary life, the superego exerts excessive pressure on expectations and ideals, just as the id pressures for discharge, pleasure seeking, and immediate gratification.

We see that all three of Freud's psychic structures show a propensity for psychotic operations, or have psychotic aspects, depending on how they function or are used in a given situation. This brings us full circle to another double embedded in our constitution: we seem to be woven from a fabric of both sane and insane qualities. We partly hallucinate and partly remain grounded in reality; we are made from a psychic palette of many colors and flavors.

Comments and Responses

What follows are a selection of comments from seminar participants along with the author's responses.

Comment 1: Freud and Jung got in touch with their unconscious and psychotic parts in different ways. I'm also wondering about the unconscious … the unconscious and psychosis. Does psychosis live in the unconscious? And how does the ego relate to that?

Response 1: Any part of the psyche can be psychotic depending on how it functions or is used. But we don't really know what the unconscious is or what psyche is. They are unknowns, mysteries. We can point to how they function in different ways at different times. That's part of what this book is about. The unconscious can be a source of rich support, or ominous and horrific, with much in between. Psyche and psychotherapy ultimately rest on foundations we know little about. We piece together our clients' psychoses in terms of symptoms, temperament, early trauma, family functioning, genetics, and so on. But how it currently functions in a person's life is also important. Distortions and fantasies are often built to compensate for felt injury.

Comment 2: I feel a little confused. According to what criteria can we decide that it's a psychosis? Because it seems to me that Eigen normalized the psychotic elements. So according to what can I judge it to be psychosis? In Freud, I know better because he was attached to social norms and also he believed in true and false.

Response 2: This book describes what Eigen calls psychotic "operations" or dynamics rather than psychosis as true or false, all or nothing. I'm going to highlight Eigen's views on some types of psychotic operations forming a wide spectrum ... from floridly psychotic to everyday examples. We will be looking at each of the chapter categories along with clinical cases that shed light on different aspects of what psychosis can be or mean.

Hallucination, Idealization, and Wish-Fulfillment

In the first commentary, we talked about pairings—doubles, opposites, or binaries that come together to form conjunctions. Using "binocular vision," relationships between two things can become two-way streets. In more common language, we speak about the value of seeking and holding more than one point of view in order to get a fuller picture. We do this in our clinical work. We try to see a person's issues from more than one point of view. We walk around the slices of life people bring, look at them from multiple angles and different vantage points (e.g., historical, emotional, cognitive, transferential). How to hold two or more things simultaneously is a challenge, and how to bring two frames or perspectives together and show their relations is not easy. In the mid-twentieth century Gregory Bateson offered systems theory, showing structural relations between pairs. He was also part of the group that came up with the double-bind theory of mixed messages. But structural relations alone do not tell us about how something functions or its purpose, or how it is used in a given situation. When we investigate things like function, purpose, context, and use, we begin to flesh out particular psychological moments.

We also discussed examples of two-within-one, like babies with a mothering one. We considered conscious and unconscious processes as conjoined, mind and body as both separate and together, forming us as one being. Today we'll explore inner and outer reality as not only conjoined but also separate ... distinguishable yet interwoven. The survival of early human groups depended on perceiving their environment accurately, adapting and adjusting to changing conditions, often moment by moment. Yet our early ancestors also held supernatural and animistic ideas about what they saw and felt. Inner beliefs and outer conditions were both important.

Here, we'll explore how our minds hallucinate and misperceive inner and outer realities. Such distortions are normally labeled illusion, error, or falsehood. Yet recently we have been living in a surreal world of alternate realities, with people in high places putting forth something called "alternative facts." We know that science excels at accurately sizing up the physical

DOI: 10.4324/9781003257554-4

world, and with its methods we can test our perceptions, do reality checks, set up experiments. That's what science does. However, with our private minds and feelings we have only ourselves and each other to check with. This raises problems. What happens when misperceptions of the world or one another get skewed, distorted by what we bring to the encounter? What if our viewing lens and predispositions are off the mark or influenced by early trauma, biased by fears? After all, accurate sensing and perceiving is not a given—we normally learn by trial and error. In psychotic moments, the mind has trouble learning; it has difficulty stepping back, testing and questioning. Actually, all of us have this difficulty to some degree. It takes extra effort to question what is presented to us. Normally, if I do not understand something you say, I might ask you: Did I hear correctly? Did you say X ... or Y? We can check in with ourselves and each other, amend and correct if need be. But how does a psychotic mind check in with itself or others, how does it assess accurately, when the mind and equipment doing the testing and checking is the very thing in question?

To call attention to this dilemma, Eigen writes:

> Few phenomena lead to a more precise appreciation of just what is achieved in "good enough" personality functioning than the shock of what can happen when madness appears. In psychosis, the raw materials of personality, such as the sense of self–other and materiality–immateriality, undergo startling transformations or deformations. Mental processes can speed up or slow down to such an extent that being an adequately coherent person is no longer possible. The psychotic individual may be mutely rigid, explode, then turn to putty. Clarity of ideas may oscillate with gnomic utterances. Such tendencies play a role in the mood swings of ordinary life, but in psychosis, they have a menacing finality that threatens to abandon the individual forever in shifting currents of disintegration and horror. The way individuals are ripped apart by psychotic processes brings home the realization that the emergence of a viable sense of self and other must be counted as one of the most creative achievements of humankind.
>
> (2018g, p. 29)

Being mostly sane is a creative achievement! Yet even if we think of ourselves as mostly sane, we also accept as real some things that could be called fictions. For instance, most of us accept the fiction that we have an inner "space" for mental contents like thoughts and ideas. We take for granted the inner space of our minds as well as the space we call external. There is a tacit acceptance of these different realms or "containers." One of them holds the inner reality of our thoughts and feelings, and the other is filled with nature, people, and events of history. We tend to believe that our thoughts, feelings, and motivations are "inside" us, part of inner space, but some psychotic minds do not or cannot believe this. They are challenged to know the difference between inner and outer. Ambivalence might show itself as oscillation between meaningless fiction and "hallucinatory certainty," while not being able to build anything upon either. The psychotic mind can even convince itself that everything is fiction. But if our mind is felt as fictional, if it feels dramatically false or unreal, then subjectivity itself becomes suspect. It gets discounted and becomes chronically filled with loopholes. Eigen says the psychotic subject takes advantage of, or is tortured by, loopholes of subjectivity. When inner mind-space becomes a fiction, it cannot serve as a foundation for anything to build upon since inner reality can collapse or be discounted at any moment, through will or whim.

In one of Eigen's examples, the ability to distinguish between inside mind and outside world becomes vague or disappears altogether. One can no longer tell whether thoughts are one's own, or if thoughts are being inserted by strangers. Eigen tells us that for the psychotic mind, the possibility of having a world with an effective sense of inside, outside, and in between is short-circuited. Even weirder is that inside and outside can be reversed. For example, I might believe that my private thoughts are causing bad things to happen to people out in the world. Alternately, I might be convinced that private thoughts of others are dangerous, attacking me or poisoning my insides.

Those are extreme distortions, but in everyday life the tendency to distort happens more than we think. Distortion is actually pretty common even among us normal neurotics. For instance, we sometimes tweak or bend what is more or less true in the direction of our liking. We might make things a little better or worse than they really are—that's common, isn't it? Like when someone exaggerates their job resumé to look good. We also make ourselves believe that things are a lot worse than they are, as when we tell ourselves, "I'll never be good enough to get that job." We adopt different attitudes and expectations depending on our temperament, situation, and sense of self. But then, with another short step, we can also make things seem or feel *infinitely* better or worse than they are, with statements like "The world is about to end," or "Utopia is just around the corner."

Our minds have the power to amplify and diminish, to puff up and deflate beyond what is realistic, and we can exaggerate in either direction all the way to positive and negative extremes, like heavenly bliss or hellish torment. Psychotic moments happen when we *absolutize* or *totalize* our perceptions and beliefs about the world, turning these into dense convictions that become closed off and impenetrable. For instance, "My god is the *only* true god," or "I *always* vote my party line," or "We'll *never ever* get through this pandemic." The capacity for absolute thinking shows up in many ways. Just now I used the words *only ... never ever ...* and *always*. Those are absolutizing words that convey totalistic thinking. It is good to be wary of totalities that are inflexible or rigid. As Eigen writes: "[It is] no accident 'total' is the root for 'totalitarian'" (2005, p. 85).

Of course, we all make distinctions and comparisons every day when we say something is better or worse than something else. But in psychosis such judgments get pushed to extremes and can even become felt realities. To go to extremes in any direction is part of what our creative imagination can do, and also part of what psychosis can do. Our imagination is multifaceted and can be used in all kinds of ways, with hallucinations having their own spectrum of compelling power. Eigen writes that hallucinations grip us with convincing magnetism because of their grandeur. Hallucinations feel larger than life, more real than ordinary, and thus express megalomania. There are many links and connections between megalomania and idealization, wishfulness and hallucination, depending on context and how they function.

I sometimes think of wish-fulfillment, hallucination, and idealization as siblings. They often work together to ward off psychic and emotional pain. The drive to escape from emotional pain and suffering is basic. In Freud's writing, Eigen tells us that wish-fulfilling operations are a form of hallucination that babies use to cope, for instance, when in the midst of parental absence or physical hunger. If one's tummy is growling and no one is present for a feeding, a baby might hallucinate being fed or soothed. This leads to questions about where hallucinations come from and why they often take idealized forms. But substituting imaginative hallucination for reality is not only a reaction to emotional discomfort. Far from it ... artists of many kinds use imaginative power very creatively in their work. So where might notions of the "ideal" come from?

In ancient Greece, Plato thought that objects appearing in waking life are really just replicas or shadow representations of an ideal reality, but not ideal reality itself. The Ideal Forms reside in another realm, a heavenly realm beyond reach of our senses. More recently, Freud and Jung offered different views on possible origins of ideal or beatific moments. Freud speculated that a sense of the ideal comes from early blissful merging, the baby at the breast. Jung's archetypes and individual personality types are thought to have a say in what is ideal and what isn't.

Of course, in everyday life we idealize a lot: a certain car or career, a star athlete, political hero, spiritual guru. Nearly anything can be idealized, including transference in psychotherapy. But where or how does idealization itself get its start?

One way to approach this is to think of idealization as partly hallucinatory. When the infant feels a caretaker's absence, they get conjured up in the baby's mind for comfort, perhaps while also holding a teddy bear or soft blanket. When adults become very hungry, they are prone to imagine favorite foods that will satisfy the moment. These are simple examples of wish-fulfilling operations that rely on forms of hallucination, conjuring up a reality that is not present by using our imagination.

In thinking about origins of idealization, Eigen offers a critique of Freud:

> Freud began by arguing that the overall and most basic function of hallucination is to reduce psychic disturbance and, in effect, to achieve a painless state. It accomplishes this by making the subject believe he is satisfied when, in fact, he is not. That is, pain is hallucinated as absent and pleasure hallucinated as present. But before one realizes it, one is speaking about bliss, well-being, a sense of perfection, not simply pleasure or pain. A minimum (absolute painlessness) becomes a maximum (a beatific moment), as if the null-point and infinite fullness were equated.
>
> (2018g, p. 49)

> … ideal experience is exploited, but not credited in its own right. It is always treated in terms of "something else" (womb, breast, epiphenomenon of a drive or defense, etc.) … Ideal feelings can inform many objects of experience and so cannot be accounted for by any one of them. … The propensity to experience ideal moments is irreducible and constitutive, not simply derivative (although, like any other primitive given, it can be used in many ways).
>
> (p. 50)

Simply put, we are beings prone to idealizing.

Apart from psychotic and creative uses, how do imaginative ideals commonly function? This brings us to another double. Our ideals can be used as a spur or a thorn. Idealizing can provide inspiration or become a recipe for emotional pain. On one side we need our ideals—some live for beatific moments because they feed us, motivate us, help us stretch and reach. But when ideals spin out of control and become commanding or absolute, they become tyrannical thorns that persecute by demanding perfection. We set ourselves up with high expectations only to feel let down and demoralized. Our cultural zeitgeist feeds into this. We imagine (wish, hallucinate) an ideal self, an ideal life, an ideal body, an ideal partner, and an ideal bank account. Ideals can become a self-tyranny in the form of exaggerated expectations and wishes for perfection. The double-edged sword: enriched by ideals, wishes, and imaginative longings, but also hurt by them when excessive and persecutory.

Eigen describes an important difference between psychotic content and the overall function or purpose of a psychotic breakdown. Although there is often significant meaning in hallucinatory and delusional content pointing to soul injury and trauma, it is also important to assess how a given psychosis functions. Eigen asks us to consider whether a given psychosis might be serving more of a *defensive or reparative* purpose or function.

Psychosis can be a defense against too much aliveness, too much psychic flooding and overwhelm, too much splintering and fragmentation, or some combination. As defensive, it is a desperate attempt to ward off and try to control realities that intrude and impinge. Psychosis in this mode partly functions as an escape from psychic and emotional life, at times leading to self-deadening or self-nulling. One can literally lose one's mind. To use older language, a progressive *decathexis* of ego can occur. Along a continuum of protective cocoon to psychical self-extinction, one risks becoming trapped in empty isolation with little chance of outside engagement or nourishment.

Eigen sees examples of these extremes in some psychotic people he meets on the street. Either bizarre ranting to ward off other people and internal voices, or deadness and hollowness from "life sucked-out or stamped out by forces of circumstance."

However, there are different kinds of psychotic breakdowns. Some arise as reparative attempts, as when development of the personality has gone awry early on, and repair or regeneration in the service of a stable life is sought. For such people, Eigen writes about the prospect of coming through psychosis in a fuller way, with learning and growth of self. This is a prolonged process of putting oneself back together from the bottom up, and there are no guarantees. He writes:

> ... not all afflicted persons appreciate or benefit from their psychosis. Some are permanently broken. Others may not even realize they are ill, but drift dully along at a low level of existence that barely approaches human. Many carry their illness like a stranger, or a burden they do not really feel is part of themselves. ... The therapeutic task is to help the individual take his illness seriously and turn it into a challenge. It is a task that may not meet with success. ... Much preliminary work is usually necessary before the real struggle can begin. However, a psychotic individual should have the right to discover whether or not his illness can become a true journey of the self. Even partial success leads to a quality of experiencing one might have missed if one simply tried to control, get rid of, or otherwise short-circuit what one is up against. I do not want to idealize the horror and waste of mental illness, but I do wish to stress that it *may* open up a psychic dimension of decisive significance.
>
> (2018g, pp. 20–1)

In sum, our capacity to hallucinate is fundamental. It is a part of our makeup from the beginning and throughout life. We are hallucinatory, imaginative, wishful beings, but how such capacities function and are used in any given situation varies tremendously.

It is a radical statement to say that hallucinating is a part of how we operate throughout life, yet Eastern lineages tell us the world we think we see and know is really just illusion, or *maya*. Buddhist traditions also say ordinary reality is "relative" and illusory. In Western psychology it is fundamental that we often project or overlay reality with our unconscious lens and preferences.

Much of what our mind does is make up what we think to be true and real, legitimate or not. The ability to differentiate between fact, opinion, and illusion remains problematic to this day.

How then, might we arrive at reality itself, the thing itself, the *really* real? There is no answer outside a given context or concrete example. Generalizing in the abstract gets us nowhere. Eigen's view seems to be that anything and everything can be real or unreal depending on the particular context in which it arises and how it functions. Hallucinations might express hidden truths of wounding and wishful desire, just as they can serve as hostile defenses to confuse and push others away. At their best, creative hallucination adds to culture by producing art, music, literature, and wisdom.

Eigen writes that hallucinations appear to come from a common source in that

> they are part of a broad and deep imaginative capacity that helps make human life possible ... perhaps the basic invariant is that the hallucinatory mode of being is constitutive for human life. It is no mere secondary offshoot of wounding (although it may function that way) nor is it an epiphenomenon of physical processes, but rather a primary, determinative category of the human psyche. Like any human capacity, it acts in diverse ways.
>
> (2018g, p. 78)

Comments and Responses

Comment 1: I'm reminded of the importance of Eigen linking psychosis and psychotic process with trauma. He writes on page 47 (2018g), hallucinations "are meant to restore the world of objects lost or destroyed," and I thought it was beautiful how he wrote that.

Comment 2: In the last sentence of that paragraph Eigen says, "Wounded wishes find a home in hallucinations."

Response: Thanks for adding those...

Hallucination, Megalomania, and Emotional Pain

Reading *The Psychotic Core* is challenging. There is a lot to absorb, and the ideas presented alternate between being densely packed and associative. Eigen's writing style may be more associative than most, but this is one of his more systematic books. Some have a hard time with Eigen's work because he has no overarching theory or system and no specific model for doing psychotherapy. Even so, there are hints and clues throughout his large body of work that, when taken together, offer something of a coherent vision for working with the life of mind and psychical reality. Primary importance centers around emotional life—what furthers it and what obstructs it; even the question of whether and how we are able to contact ourselves and experience our feeling life. Eigen affirms that emotional life is difficult and we're mostly infants at dealing with it. He addresses our feeling life as an intimate partner, one that we each have different antennae for, different forms of contact with, and different capacities for engaging.

Affectively, we're each put together a little differently, while also having sameness and commonality. The poet, the scientist, the businessperson, and spiritual leader speak their own "languages," often appearing to have little in common. This makes it seem as though the human race is composed of more than one species. For those who do clinical work, you have likely come across patients with such minimal sensitivity resonance that it feels nearly impossible to work together. Sometimes persistence and sticking it out is worth the effort and the relationship becomes productive. Working with what is difficult in relationships is part of the therapy field. But if the chemistry is clearly off and feels unworkable, either person can transition out, say adieu, and that's not such a bad thing. It's common sense that we cannot work with everyone, just as everyone cannot work with us. Perhaps thinking we can or should be able to work with everyone is an unrealistic wish. Idealizing oneself as a "perfect therapist" is an example of what Freud called *megalomania*. Better to be realistic about who we are and what we can do, as this fosters humility.

Experiencing our emotional life is not a given. Some don't bother with it at all. For others, feelings are an overwhelming presence and tough to handle.

DOI: 10.4324/9781003257554-5

Often, our availability to feel our feelings or experience our experience varies. Experiencing anything in life presents us with challenges to our capacity for receptivity and engagement. How much can we take in? How much can we process? There are good reasons we humans have trouble with emotional life; being open to experiencing life's fullness is often more than we can handle.

> The impact of reality is far greater than our ability to process it. We can't take too much reality. Our equipment simply is not up to it. If we are lucky, persistent, patient, hungry enough for the real, our equipment grows into the job, building more capacity to work with what is. Nevertheless, we are always behind the impact of the moment, at best able to process crumbs broken off from the whole. But those crumbs can be rich indeed!
>
> (Eigen, 2004, p. 8)

Whether we speak of the impact of inner or outer reality, they are often more than we can fully attend to, let alone absorb. Going slow and being kind to ourselves during this study of psychosis is important because we can only break off a few crumbs at a time, and Eigen's crumbs can be plenty. He is often literary, poetic, and metaphorical in his writing. Sometimes I tell people who have trouble following him, "Just let it wash over you," or "Read him like you would poetry." There are many ways to dive into Eigen's abundance and come back up for air with something useful, if only a paragraph per week.

By engaging in this study of psychosis, we're actually probing and practicing having contact with psychical pain. Those of you who do clinical work know that increased capacity for contact involves increased ability to undergo the suffering that others bring, touching injuries that lie within ourselves. Thus, it is very important for therapists to spend time doing their own therapy work.

D. W. Winnicott speaks of a difference between psychological health and illness in a surprising way in his book *Human Nature* (1988/2015). "Probably the greatest suffering in the human world is the suffering of the normal or healthy or mature person"(Winnicott, 1988, p. 80). Why does Winnicott say this? Eigen tells us in another book it's because *suffering is actually part of health*. If we are alive, we cannot avoid emotional pain and suffering. The more we grow our psyche, and the more we engage with others, the more we expose ourselves to emotional suffering. Eigen says we make ourselves smaller in order to avoid pain. Less psyche means less exposure to pain. "A corollary to the idea that one curtails psyche in order to avoid suffering is: the more one cares, the more open to suffering one becomes. One truncates caring to downplay pain ..." (2018c, p. 31).

The idea of making psyche smaller for defensive purposes fits with what Eigen says about defensive uses of psychotic operations to ward off painful intrusions from inner or outer sources. Even so, Winnicott and Eigen offer encouragement about what happens when we sit with people who are in emotional pain. Whether we're aware of it or not, we grow emotional capacity and increase our psychical muscles by doing so.

In the next commentary, we'll meet Eigen's first two case examples: Carl and Frank. As a prelude, I want to contrast two realities—our actual moment-by-moment experiencing on one side and synaptic firings of the brain on the other. We could use different words for this distinction, like mind and matter, imagination and neurology, or awareness and flesh. It is a division on par with Eigen's terms *materiality* and *immateriality*. Our brain is material, and our experiences are immaterial. Our brains are measurable, but our private inner experiences are not. This distinction mirrors one of the oldest divisions in philosophy between matter and spirit. As we continue, we'll eventually find these two realities more and more mixed together and interwoven, even as they are often thought of as separate. Eigen puts it this way:

> It is becoming more common today to think that brain and experience are not simply two terms split off from or reducible to one another, but rather that they may be viewed as entering into a mutually constitutive relationship. Each sets requirements that dictate the structural possibilities of the other. Our understanding of the mutual influence of brain and experience is in its infancy.
>
> (2018g, p. 22)

One of the ways Eigen speaks to us is through metaphor. Poets and writers use metaphor all the time, and some believe science itself partly originates from an "as if" or metaphorical use of reality. But it's far from metaphorical to stub one's toe or cut a finger. Physical injury is real and measurable. Emotional pain is just as real but not objectively measurable. Metaphor helps point to aspects of feeling life, and we sometimes use images from the physical world to express emotional experiences. For example, we say "He was a bull in a china shop," or "Their expressions were as cold as ice." Material and immaterial realities woven together.

The psychological universe Eigen addresses is vast. One metaphor for studying his work might be like buying a sweater that is too large. We might need to grow into such a sweater. But if the sweater is way too big, we could get lost in it. And if it is too small, then we might feel constricted because it is too tight. But when a sweater is just a little bit bigger, we have room to grow into it, and I feel that by stretching ourselves in this book, we're trying on a kind of Michael Eigen sweater hoping to grow into it. At times the "fit" might feel off—too wide, too loose, not systematic enough. I recommend taking this book a little at a time and going at your own pace. Or as Eigen sometimes says: "dose it out."

There are many ways to think about what is "real" in psychological life. Philosophers will gladly tell you in abstract conceptual terms what they think is real. But for many of us, what is real is anchored in experience itself, our subjective sense as most immediate, the closest thing to us. This does not mean absolutely anything can be real just because we feel it, think it, or hear it. The psychotic mind is often convinced what it hears or sees is real. No, we remain obliged to test our perceptions and assumptions, often ferreting out what is grounded in some form of consensual reality. But even this has a caveat, as tightly knit groups can provide echo chambers of unreality, with cults being an extreme example.

There are many approaches to questions of realness. In clinical terms, Winnicott wrote about *not feeling real* as connected to early trauma and false-self structures. Winnicott worked with patients who could appear quite successful by societal standards, but who did not live in their own shoes. They were not able to feel enough contact with an inner essence or personal core, so as to foster spontaneous aliveness as a source of continuing development and growth.

Hallucinations themselves can be real or unreal, used in different ways and for different purposes. Eigen reminds us that this is true for any of our human capacities. We learned in the previous commentary that hallucination can be used as a wish-fulfilling operation to avoid or deny pain and discomfort. Hallucination can also be used narcissistically to glorify or gratify our self-image. Yet we also hallucinate when we dream at night, and when we engage in creative reverie or artistic imagination. Creative hallucinations are capable of generating symbolic, musical, and aesthetic meaning of all kinds.

Bion says hallucination can sometimes be used to negate mind and meaning, attacking the right of meaning to exist by breaking and erasing links. This becomes a negative or anti-hallucination in the service of mind annihilation, a "deathification" process that converts being into nonbeing, where links and connections are ripped apart and snuffed out. Over time this leads to a hollowing of psyche. It may sound awful, but similar moments of shutting down and shutting off happen to all of us when we feel overwhelmed. Much like infants, we fade out for self-protection, go unconscious or blank, and disconnect.

There are so many different functions and potential uses of hallucination. The diversity of views we read here add complexity to ancient clear-cut divisions between sanity and madness. One hundred years ago any form of hallucination was thought to be a hallmark of craziness. It's refreshing to read functions of hallucination having different uses and purposes, especially positive and creative ones, not just pathological.

Eigen explores some of Freud's and Jung's views in these pages. Both thought that megalomania was foundational in psychosis. Freud believed he could account for megalomania in terms of sexual and aggressive drives and the infantile psyche. Jung believed a patient's god-like feelings were not accounted for by such drives alone and that Freud's view was limited. Instead, Jung felt that grandiose states were partly drawn from an underlying collective substratum of psychic life, a kind of phylogenetic unconscious. From this premise Jung built his theory of archetypes, in which age-old forms and structures play a role in organizing our experiences. Jung believed that hallucinatory experience grew out mythic or religious dimensions that had strong valence. By contrast, Freud felt that religion was error or illusion, an opiate based on regressive infantile longings. These differences became a pivot point around which those two pioneers broke away from one another. Freud wanted to account for psychopathology through forms of libido gone haywire, but Jung thought this too narrow and brought in expanded elements, including alchemies of spirit and instinct, symbols and drives mixing in various ways. "Jung detailed the oscillations in psychosis between inflation and deflation, since megalomania and the severest self-depreciation always go together" (2018g, p. 54). That's another double we often see in clinical work—the over and undersides we call grandiosity and deflation. Both are common moments of self-experience. Some days we feel woefully inadequate and rather dumb, whereas other days we might be too sure or full of ourselves. Perhaps it is only when such extremes oscillate rapidly, fuse, or become chronically hardened and at war that we can say pathology is present.

If Freud and Jung claim megalomania is something fundamental, then none of us are immune. I see this as a wake-up call and something to monitor. In one way or another, forms of grandiosity are part of everyone's mentality. We all have areas where we feel absolutely sure and certain, or believe we know more than we do. This "more" is part of how we're built. Our mind is always out ahead of itself. Take the child learning to walk as an example. Delighted by the power of their new upright position and body locomotion, the child wants to go beyond walking … to running! Pushing past their ability, they fall down more than once, but through trial and error become better, steadier. Could we extend this example and say that *any* wish or impulse, any reaching beyond ourselves is a mild form of megalomania? And yet, how else could we ever grow if not by going beyond ourselves, failing, and trying again? The drive to go beyond ourselves is also part of who we are.

Some view megalomania *only* as reactive, a defense against narcissistic injury or neglect, i.e., we puff ourselves up to compensate for feeling low or ashamed. But Freud and Jung say no, megalomania is a primitive given, part of our basic equipment, and it would not disappear in a perfect world that was somehow absent of injury or neglect. Eigen writes that the vision of such a perfect world without insult or injury would not be an antidote for megalomania, but instead another expression of it (2018g, p. 58). The question of how we use our capacities taps us on the shoulder at every turn. We begin to see how closely tied together wishes for perfection, idealization, and megalomania turn out to be. How they function together in a given situation makes all the difference.

What we do or don't do with our emotional pain is an ongoing challenge for all of humankind. Avoidance of painful stimuli is universal throughout nature. At the level of pure sensation, even single-cell organisms recoil from irritable stimuli. Touch a sea anemone and it pulls back. Feel an itch and we scratch it. If the sun is too bright, we put on sunglasses. These are natural reactions to try to avoid distress or modulate it.

But humans are not single cell creatures. Psychical and emotional qualities of heart, soul, gut, and mind create a human universe of great complexity across many levels. Our lower brain and limbic system are interwoven with a frontal cortex and much more. Our feelings of guilt, love, conscience, and joy are not palpable, not entities to be physically located and measured—they are invisible experiences influencing our lives just as much as physical metabolism. Indeed, the physical and psychical sides of life affect one another in deeply reciprocal ways.

We do many things to avoid, deny, and dismiss painful feelings, and all the defenses we enlist or walls we erect *not to* feel, can make things worse. If we repress difficult feelings, Freud tells us we're subject to a boomerang effect—the return of the repressed. If we dissociate, split off, or compartmentalize what feels wrong, we lose contact and connection with ourselves. If we become inflated and convinced superior knowledge or status will protect us, we are vulnerable to narcissistic injury or acting out when things go wrong or emotions boil over. And if we take a wrong turn with Jung's collective unconscious and fuse our ego with archetypes, we may end up like Icarus: flying too close to the sun with psychical wings made of wax, melting and perishing from the heat and pull of gravity.

An important question is how to meet emotional pain and psychical disturbance without causing further injury? If they are inevitable parts of life, what do we owe them, and ourselves? Avoidance, somatization, repression, and denial are not helpful coping mechanisms in the long run, although at certain moments they allow us to survive. Some practitioners see the fate and trajectory of psychical pain as the alpha and omega of psychotherapy, the core of our work.

Eigen (1998) sometimes paraphrases D.T. Suzuki who says that even if one were able to reach a state of mental peace, perfection, or "nirvana," disturbances in life would not magically cease or disappear. Instead, our mental attitude toward them would have changed.

At another extreme, psychosis can devolve into a self-deadening process: a progression toward nonbeing, a disappearance into nonexistence. Promiscuous use of opiate drugs is one example from our time, but psychotic self-deadening can annihilate psychic life without any drugs. This form of quiescence and emptiness reflects something quite different from Freud's return to psychic equilibrium, Winnicott's quiet restful states, or Buddhism's life-affirming "emptiness."

Doing away with emotional pain is never final. Our sensitivities, dreads, and anxieties might be soothed or even banished for a time in light of good feelings, but wait a day and disturbance returns. It is part of the agony of life that we can never succeed in extinguishing emotional suffering. Nor can we prosper and grow from excessive indulgence or wallowing in it. A balance must be struck, and in the realm of emotion life this will always be a fluid balance. Eigen provides watchwords, helpful touchstones for practicing with our feeling life. Two of these are *tolerance* and *partnering*, both important capacities we will return to more than once.

Comments and Responses

Comment 1: I just want to make a quick response to Eigen's critique of Jung.
  Because I think you and Eigen make some good points about the importance of differentiation in the context of wholeness.
After two years of analysis with a Jungian analyst myself, I saw I totally mis-
  understood the word *wholeness* when I first came into the work. Because
  I think I was seeing it as a kind of assimilation into the ego. You know,
  "I'm going to collect these parts of myself that have been abandoned into
  my conscious or unconscious," but that's not it at all. It is more a process
  of making room at the table, so to speak, for all of these other voices that
  I don't normally get a chance to talk to ... and offer a chance to let them
  have their say.
Response 1: Differentiation and wholeness together, helping one another.
  That's a wonderful example of Eigen's "distinction-union," and
  Winnicott's "psychical democracy," thank you.

Commentary #4

Phenomenology, Evasion, and the Primacy of Experience

Why does Eigen mention *phenomenology* when it comes to psychosis, and what kind of "evasion" is he talking about on page 79 (2018g)? Eigen tells us there are various uses of the word *phenomenology* that have different lineages. Some seek to describe how consciousness may be structured in order for awareness to arise. Others involve attention to experience itself, using gestalt theory and philosophical investigation. What they share in common is a quest to return "back to the things themselves." But what are these things themselves? The linguistic meaning of the word *phenomenology* is simply the science of phenomena, our everyday moment-by-moment experience. In its various uses, phenomenology can mean many things. Partly, it was an attempt to turn away from more distant, conceptual, abstract notions of human awareness and human experiencing—something of a rebellion against explanations or descriptions of experience from a safe distance. Instead, it is a return to what is immediate and compelling in our concrete sensuous lived-experience, an attempt to transcend the subject–object split.

One such view tries to describe experiences *as they present themselves,* even if fragmentary ... and fragmentary is often how we find our attention and awareness to be. One example of the difference between staying close to experience versus conceptualizing it can be found in clinical writing that tries to force conceptual terms into something more immediate and felt, by using the phrase "experience near." I find this to be an odd locution. Almost as if we paradoxically need to point out and emphasize from a distance the importance of feeling life. There's an irony to the phrase "experience near" because it sometimes signals how faraway we are. But perhaps we need reminders to bring us back to basic felt impact. One reason I admire Eigen's writing so much is the way feelings come through his words.

Eigen speaks of the *primacy of experience* in our lives, and in this, his first book, we begin to feel some tones and textures with his colorful language. For example, Eigen contrasts Freud and Jung on how they approach destructive and creative forces associated with unconscious depths, highlighting Freud's many "filters" (Freud's list of defenses) for handling these strong forces with

DOI: 10.4324/9781003257554-6

rubber gloves, or kid gloves … in effect saying that Freud was, in one sense, more insulated from direct contact with emotional forces than Jung, who risked through immersion. Eigen goes on to say of Freud's approach that the unconscious must be "a very explosive pea to require so many mattresses" (2018g, p. 86), a reference to the children's story about a princess who was bruised overnight by one single pea underneath many thick mattresses.

If we elevate "primacy of experience" we encounter psyche through many different channels and conduits: emotion, attitude, felt senses, intuition, judgment, self-reflection, bodily experience, and so on. We sense ourselves in multiple ways. We also experience other people with what Eigen calls our *psychic taste buds*. Eigen means these psychical-emotional taste buds quite literally. We actually taste each other psychically. So-called first impressions are but one example, and only a beginning. The more contact we have, the more we take in from one another.

If, as mammals, we sniff and smell one another's pheromones in silent ways, then it makes sense we also smell and taste each other's psyche. Qualities of personality, attitude, and disposition come through. We have psychical antennae—a set of sensitive nonverbal receptors that comprise our psychic taste buds, and these manifest at different levels of awareness: as resonance or its lack, feeling tone and attitude, facial expression and body language. Some of these nonverbal conveyances we don't even have names for, and taken together they comprise what used to be called a person's "vibes," short for *vibrations*.

But what exactly these psychic taste buds might be in scientific terms is hard to pin down, and trying to do so might be beside the point. Perhaps trying to use abstract causal models to "explain" psyche are one part of the evasion Eigen is pointing to. Descriptive models freeze psyche, constricting fullness and fluidity. Feeling life is open to possibilities that causal models cannot capture. Such "explanations" for psychical processes take us away from our immediate sensing, adding layers of distance and abstraction. Psyche is by nature fluid, moving, alive, and multidimensional. Causal notions tend to be linear, static, and unidimensional.

Eigen wants to stay at the level of *impact* from experience itself. He says the way he writes presupposes "having a taste for subjectivity." We come closer to this with metaphor. Like when we say two psyches resonate like friendly tuning forks, or repel each other like the wrong side of magnets. We feel such words and images differently than academic or scientific descriptions offering maps of our psychological brain. On the other hand, physical processes are often represented emotionally, as when we say someone is "starved" for attention or feeling "smothered" from too much.

What happens when the lived sense of our experience becomes too abstracted? One danger is the significance and impact of felt meaning becomes degraded to the point where the cartographer's map takes precedence over the actual territory. We need both sides of course: lived moments and conceptual maps, immediacy and understanding. We must weigh the value and cost of each, and psychotic phenomena bring this issue into focus.

For instance, some medical models of the mind do not need to know, or even care to know, what the significance of psychotic symptoms might be. Such a stance ignores meaning, the symbolic history of emotional trauma, one's current situation and its potential trajectory. To get at such things we need to ask what a given set of psychotic thoughts and hallucinations might be expressing, as well as what the person's symptoms might be hiding, leaving out, or covering over.

At one end of a continuum is the view that hallucinations are nothing more than meaningless byproducts of physical processes: a view that nothing can be gained by examining them. Is this an evasion, a defensive use of science? I once asked a brain scientist how he thought of the phenomena of dreaming, and what purpose dreams might serve. His answer was that dreams are simply nighttime noise, a kind of neuronal excretion of daytime residue that our brain and nervous system perform while we sleep. His medical training reinforced the idea that dreams have no personal meaning, only a nervous system function to clear out the rubbish, the random leftover minutiae of the day. This made me wonder about his own dreams and whether they held any meaning for him. It brought home how differently we can view dreams, a nighttime occurrence we all have in common.

Throughout history dreams have played powerful roles, sometimes leading to life-changing events, even war. Dreams can offer epic journeys, grand visions, and be future prognosticators. Following Jung, dreams can function at times as wise and emphatic mirrors, providing contrasts and exaggerations to waking life as well as compensatory messages. Dreams are like messages in a bottle from who knows where.

Not every dream is profound and meaningful. Often dreams are fragmentary and never reach completion. They leave us hanging. Isn't this part of their mystery? Bion thought most dreams are aborted—stopped before full conclusion is reached. Eigen seems more generous when he says dreams *can* signify aborted processes, but they can also function as probes or "running starts." Mystery is part of their function. Mystery as structuring growth and development, helping us stretch.

Privileging only the physical side of our being, we might never inquire into the meaning or purpose of hallucinations and delusions. But from a psychological perspective we need to ask how these things function in a person's life. Are they forerunners of a more radical breakdown coming, and if so what kind? Does the situation seem acute, situational, or more chronic? And what is the person's attitude toward their situation? Do they acknowledge something is wrong or deny anything is wrong? Are they more concerned, curious, or worried about their mind (a positive sign), or are they oblivious, unconcerned, and indifferent—suggesting a poorer prognosis? Could their experience signal a necessary breakdown to make room for the possibility of repair? Are the symptoms a cry for help, attempting to find safety for a needed breakdown, in order to rebuild a sense of self on firmer ground?

One can endlessly interpret obscure hallucinatory and delusional content, without a clear sense of whether psychotic symptoms are more in the service of defense or repair. Content and function are never independent of one another. For instance, psychotic obscurity can be defensive, sometimes intentionally meant to throw others off by remaining aloof and mysterious, or to maintain a hidden sense of superiority.

Eigen says it is crucial for the clinician to be clear about what their orientation is and, in particular, what is meant by "having a self." What does it mean to be a person or self? Are we just a bunch of chemicals and neuronal synapses needing to be treated with other chemicals? What does it mean to be or have a wounded self, a traumatized self? Wounded selves often lie beneath psychotic symptoms. Much has been written about fragility from early trauma leading to breakdown later in life.

> One of the most common ways to avoid the challenge hallucinatory experience raises is to view it as an unfortunate by-product or desperate result of an injured sense of self. If the wounded self is helped, the need to hallucinate will diminish and disappear of its own accord, or be confined to more normal functions like dreaming or loving or creative work.
>
> (Eigen, 2018g, p. 80)

Eigen says this approach is only a small step better than regarding hallucinations as physical byproducts of the brain, because questions of meaning, function, and purpose are never addressed.

Sciences of the physical body use categories and methods that do not properly address how psyche, soul, and spirit actually move, dance, hide, grow, and evolve. Science insists on causal explanations—this leads to that—but psyche does not function in such a linear way. How can one first get to know the "what" of any particular psychosis, let alone the "how" and "why," if the "what" remains vague or keeps shifting? As Eigen writes, "We are very far from knowing what 'what' is. Descriptions are interpretive approaches open to further shifts of meaning. They create possibilities of vision and are as inexhaustible as the capacity to experience anew" (2018g, p. 80).

Just as the common housefly has many outward-facing eyes, Eigen says we humans have many inward-facing eyes. If science or psychoanalysis believes it can quickly get to the how and why beneath the what, we must wonder if evasion is at work. To think we can arrive at some kind of causal explanation is facile and "… gives the impression of dealing with known or fixed entities when, as a clinical method, (psychoanalysis) exists at the interface of shifting realities" (2018g, p. 80).

Psychotic symptoms can also be defensive resistance to joining consensual reality. This can take the form of stubborn refusal, a hostile and aloof stance born of fear, or when delusions of omniscience play a role. There are many varieties of psychosis as well as all kinds of mixtures in individuals. Eigen wishes to respect this fact by seeing individual differences within sameness.

For instance, he highlights recurring structural patterns of hallucinations that tend not to vary. "They are all involved with problems concerning self-other, in-out, psychic reality, meaning-meaninglessness, and mind-body" (2018g, p. 78). These domains represent scaffolding or "containers" for hallucinations to be filled in with individualized content.

Why are hallucinations so compelling and larger than life? There is an extravagance to hallucinations that includes our being able to see and hear what is not sensuously present. Eigen tells us that when this capacity works properly (as in creative imagination), it brings a freedom from literalness that gives rise to great achievements of culture. Beethoven heard things not available to others. The painter Kandinsky saw imaginary color and movement that he was able to bring to life on canvas. But in psychosis, image-making and imaginative capacities run amok and go wild. Images that might function symbolically are taken literally and vice-versa. The abstract can become concretely, seemingly real, and then reverse. Symbols and images can come *alive* as if they are inspirited beings, while magnetic dramas of self and cosmos take place idiosyncratically and in a consensual vacuum.

Any mental property can occur with hallucinatory vividness. Image, sensation, percept, thought, word, symbol—any of these can be "numinously cathected" (to combine a bit of Freud and Jung). They become imbued with significance in extravagant ways. Hallucinations magnify, infinitize, and distort. Eigen says that unlike the mystic who has won freedom from attachment to images and particulars, the psychotic becomes caught and chained by images and held fast to them, often with obsessive qualities (2018g, p. 84).

Terms like inflation, grandiosity, and megalomania can be used interchangeably at times. They all convey expansiveness and over-estimation, while what remains hidden from view are undersides like self-depreciation, unworthiness, contraction, confusion, and feeling damaged. We refer to some of these polarities with common labels like superiority and inferiority, top-dog and underdog, over- and underrepresented sides of ourselves that manifest in myriad ways. Clinical examples might include the person who complains of low self-esteem but hides a secret sense of superiority and entitlement. Or the boastful know-it-all who feels invisible shame and inferiority and is compelled to compensate for show.

Sketches of Two Case Studies

In his first two case presentations, Eigen's clinical examples include both mental and physical aspects. He emphasizes the contrast between body and spirit. Frank's psychosis was mostly connected with his distorted body image and its productions, whereas Carl lived in a transcendent realm of spirit, fighting horrifically with God and the devil. Frank sticks close to home base, obsessing over his body functions. Carl goes off, or out of his body, to see imagined realms of heaven and hell in faces ... mostly hellish devils.

> The confusions that most readily became manifest in Frank's case tended to be on a body ego level. That is, his hallucinatory imagery was predominantly involved with physical objects: penis, feces, mouth, stomach, and so on ... the kind of well-being he yearned for felt more like material substance than of the spirit ...
>
> (2018g, pp. 95–6)

> Carl, by contrast, did not seem to know he had a penis or anus, or that feces mattered. His drama was lived out in almost purely transcendental terms. ... The explicit terms of his hallucinations were trans-corporeal: God and the devil are pure spirits battling for his immortal soul. Eternal life or death was at stake.
>
> (p. 96)

> Carl's god and devil function as others or horrific self-objects or mad aspects of the self. The link is annihilation, loss, dread, "almost," "not quite," the eternally immanent—the mirage of final catastrophe. Who, if anyone has made this threat? Do such horrific threats at least offer the solace that someone was there enough to be threatening? Surely, someone in Carl's life must have been tantalizingly menacing or, at least, domineering ...
>
> (p. 99)

Carl's hallucinations of God and devil indicate an unraveling process has begun. First, frightening images and voices intruded and demanded to be taken seriously, soon becoming an ultimate focus and concern. Immaterial images and voices grabbed Carl's attention, but by working with them over time, they "... revealed themselves to be great globs and sources of energy to be broken down and reworked. They showed themselves as raw materials and transforming presences" (p. 99). Eigen hints at one of the many variations on themes of rebirth and repair, here alluding to Carl's sequence of breakdown and potential reformation.

What can we say about Eigen's "treatment plan" for such cases of psychoses? What is his process? At base, it is not to avoid or downplay, not to soothe or quickly medicate, nor to doubt or dismiss ... but instead to take time and observe closely. He slowly and in dose-related fashion solicits the content and dynamics functioning in each person's psychotic material. He begins to see mixtures of gods and devils that have formed the hallucinatory obsessions plaguing both men. Eigen says that to face distortions between and within the foundational presences of our being can begin a journey with the potential for transformation. Can Carl or Frank do this? Do they have the inner stamina and resources? Does Eigen? We'll find out more when we meet them again in the commentaries ahead.

What about those of us labeled "normal neurotics"? Where do we find our hallucinatory anxiety represented as part of our psychical insides? Historically, one place these live is in mythology, often hidden among cultural artifacts we all share. I'm not sure if Eigen is addressing Carl or the reader when he says, "One must look into Pandora's box, at Medusa, Eurydice, Amor, the naked Father, the face of God ..." (2018g, p. 99). Perhaps Eigen is daring both Carl and us to become more familiar with our own inner plagues? A challenging thought upon which to end this commentary.

Comments and Responses

Comment 1: I was very affected by reading this chapter, and I found that I started to understand more about psychosis as connected to the very base of our being, as something very primary. What I don't see is why this kind of state, the hallucinating state, causes so much suffering? What is it that makes the suffering? I have a patient who is schizophrenic, and she is now balanced with some medication. But there is nearly no real content. Every time I ask her how she is, she says, "I'm fine." There is like an emptiness ... I don't know her for a very long time, by the way. But now, she started to bring in dreams. I am very touched by it—that there are dreams that she brings to me, and she is telling me. It's like something is coming into being, becoming more alive, in a way. I can understand she is very much afraid of any possible attack, a new attack of psychosis. She is fearful. But what is it that makes the suffering in hallucination?

Response 1: What is it that makes the suffering? Something has gone terribly wrong somehow. We could call it injury or wounding, trauma, neglect, misattunement, poor attachment, a rupture in the continuity of being, maddening toxic nourishment. There are so many possibilities and combinations. But suffering is there because hallucinations are signaling a need to resist reality considerations using extravagance, megalomania, deadening, and so on. Sometimes hallucinations are flooding, horrific, and terrifying, and sometimes hollow. All of which convey suffering. With your patient, I am impressed she brings you dreams. She is telling you by proxy about her dream of herself and what is going on in her mind from the unconscious side. That's very helpful. Bringing in her dreams may be a good prognosticator. Some aliveness is there, but it is coming through her dreams; she is perhaps too frightened to tell you about her waking life, perhaps it feels too empty and she is fearful, but her dreams might tell you where her sparks of life and her injuries may be hiding.

Mindlessness

I want to amplify a point that the reader missed from our last commentary discussion. Namely, that reliance on our different models and maps of psychotherapy is foundational. We cannot do without them. They represent our science and understanding, orienting us to specific frameworks. The plethora of models tells us something important about human diversity. But in equal measure we need immersion in moment-by-moment experiential impact and use of our intuitive senses as guides. These two domains work together, back and forth. At their best, *in vivo* experience and conceptual understanding are reciprocal partners that add to one another.

Models and techniques of psychotherapy can take on various roles during one's career. Perhaps a musical analogy will help.

Learning to become a therapist or analyst is a little like learning to play a musical instrument, except that as a therapist, the instrument is ourselves. We grow from our training, using models that resonate. We also learn about *ourselves as an instrument* in our own therapy or analysis, and while working with patients in various training settings. By analogy, we learn a new musical instrument by taking lessons, first becoming familiar with the physical instrument along with musical notation and theory. Learning to play is then about practicing. We practice the notes and scales; we practice the basics over and over again until we know them well. At some point we might start to improvise a little. This is not possible when first learning. But at some point, our learning and ability, comfort and confidence come together such that we add our own spontaneous music to what we've learned and practiced. Doing therapy has been like this for me, and after about 35 years I'm happy to say I'm still learning and practicing. I find I listen and respond differently to people than I did even a few years ago. As psychotherapists, we never stop "becoming." We are always in the process of development.

In an intensive long-term psychotherapy, we often experience unconscious-to-unconscious communication occurring. This is hard to talk about because it's not an objective thing, and it's not a predictable or technical thing. Our

DOI: 10.4324/9781003257554-7

intuition plays a role. We also make mistakes and get the signals wrong. No one learns without errors. Missteps do not invalidate intuition and sensing. As we learn to be receptive and permeable to our own deeper layers, this capacity mirrors something within our patients and resonance has an opportunity to deepen.

C.G. Jung commented somewhere about explicit and implicit knowing that relates to the process of psychotherapy. To paraphrase: learn the best you can, study everything you can, and know as much as you're able. Then, when you sit with your patient, let it all go ... forget everything and just be present. I take this to mean that all you've learned is still back there in your mind. It's part of you and you can trust it to be available when needed. Getting caught up in fitting theory to the person during sessions risks missing the immediacy of the moment.

When listening to patients I sometimes ask myself: of all possible responses I could offer, what might this person be able to receive and use right now? It's not something fully thought out or calculated. My sense in the moment concerns what might further something in my client. Will it open up or shut down the flow of exchange? From another side, silence is not necessarily a bad thing. Much goes on during silences.

There are many kinds and qualities of silence, many ways of being mindless or empty, and many kinds of "nothings." Silence might have nothing or everything to do with a patient's so-called resistance. Silences or gaps can also signify a thought-seed or new perspective has been planted ... and is being quietly absorbed.

A colleague once joked about all the recent workshop brochures with *mindfulness* in the title. He asked if it wouldn't be better to have more workshops on mind*lessness*—how to create more psychic space and breathing room. Another colleague was tired of attending workshops where people talk only about what is known, or what they know. He finds it more interesting to talk about what we don't know, including the limits of what's knowable. Part of our complexity is that both a full mind and an empty mind can be used in many different ways. Full and empty are meaningless outside of their context and use. Clinically, one can be too full of knowing and cause harm from lack of attunement, just as one can forego technique or agenda yet still be helpful.

Fullness and emptiness wear coats of different colors, like siblings with distinct personalities. In this chapter Leila becomes full of inner chaos when she finds Eigen's therapy door locked. The unexpected produces shock: she mentally spins out while also becoming frozen, paralyzed ... then blank. Lenny's blankness is a much different state of not-being-there, approximating the unresponsive zero point of oblivion, whereas Leila has lots going on inside that she expresses at different times.

Trying to talk about mental states is a difficult task, and Eigen says it is never more problematic than when we ask how the mind can be mindless.

I started compiling a list of words that convey mindlessness. Some examples: oblivion, the zero or null point; caesura, gap, blackout; denial, dissociation, splitting, fragmentation; dying out or dropping out of existence, self-deadening processes. There's also numbing out, spacing out, blank stares, vacuousness, hypnoid or trance states. Psychical entropy or "winding down" has been allied with Freud's death instinct—a decathexis of ego or self. Dissolution, melting down, and self-obliteration; annihilating emptiness, self-vanishing, paralysis, frozenness, fading out, feeling underwater, being gone …

One feature all these may have in common, depending on person and context, is an attempt to try to avoid or defeat pain, escape from psychic and emotional suffering.

However, there are also spiritual lineages that make use of pain and disturbance as starting points for practicing. But at extremes of suffering, one may try to extinguish oneself psychically, or even biologically, if pain becomes too great. At lesser intensities of psychic disturbance, we all employ defenses and thank goodness we have them. They provide doorways of partial escape and distraction, helping to offset life's travail.

In psychosis, withdrawal of energy and loss of interest in outside objects can be accompanied by more or less investment of energy or cathexis toward ego or self. Mixtures of megalomania and de-cathexis are observed. The outside world is shunned and avoided because it's seen as causing pain, but how does one ever successfully escape from one's *inside* world? As long as we are alive, we are vulnerable to suffering.

Case examples in this chapter show different forms of mindlessness addressing the question of psychic pain.

In the case of Lenny, we are given a term from André Green (1996, p. 203) called "blank psychosis," a state with no sign of psychic aliveness. A blankness that is described not as a weakness of integration or hypnoid state of dissociation, but a vacancy or emptiness of mind and personality. Lenny did not seem to be defending against anything, nor was he demonically possessed, clinging, demanding, or delusional. Eigen says there was no stubborn willfulness from Lenny. "Even an autistic child who whirls and squeals and will not or cannot speak is possessive and controlling" (2018g, pp. 107–8). Not so with Lenny, whose blankness made him invulnerable, like a thick coat around him that psychic contents could not get through.

By contrast, Leila would get wound up and disoriented by anything unexpected. Her mind accelerated and spun into catastrophes of fear, abandonment, and numbness when she found Eigen's office door locked. Two different portrayals of mindlessness:

> Lenny's slowing down and Leila's speeding up reflect two paths that invite us to oblivion. They are the underside of mastery, the vast, numbing paralysis that awaits us when pain passes a certain boundary.

(2018g, p. 109)

and

> The individual who bitterly complains about losing his I-feeling and who is pained by a sense of numbness (e.g., Leila), is not the same as the individual whose I-feeling and affective density were never strong enough to be missed (e.g., Lenny). In the latter instance, one hopes to stimulate a sufficient self-feeling the individual will find worth struggling for.
>
> (p. 113)

Another way to view full and empty aspects of self is to compare Bion's and Winnicott's ideas on our starting point as infants. Eigen as a young man was fortunate to spend a little time with both Bion and Winnicott, and he felt supported by each of them. You can read more about these encounters in Eigen's books titled *Faith* (2014) and *Flames From the Unconscious* (2018d).

Winnicott and Bion show a sharp contrast in their approach to the beginnings of psychic life. To paraphrase Eigen and oversimplify, Winnicott begins with goodness, and Bion begins with catastrophe. Winnicott comes across as more the optimist, and Bion more the pessimist. Winnicott has a view that we come into the world with basic or primordial goodness, a positive whole life feeling, whereas for Bion the birth process itself is damaging. Simply being born challenges us with effects that can be explosive, dissociative, and traumatic—all before we are fully "conscious."

At our earliest point in life Bion underlines *catastrophe* as an ingredient. He compares physical birth to the explosive birth of the universe. Astrophysicists indicate the universe began with a big bang, an explosion. Babies usually (but not always) begin life with a scream, a cry, or wail. Is this a cry for loss of the womb? Is it shock from breathing our first gulp of air? Is it the transition from being a watery creature to suddenly becoming a land and air creature? Throughout history, birth has been seen as traumatic for both the one being born and the one giving birth.

Birthing new ideas can also be explosive, revolutionary, and traumatic—much like Copernicus, Darwin, and Freud, each of whom changed humanity's view of who we are and where we've come from (Bagai, 2021, p. 93).

Why does Bion start from catastrophe? Perhaps one need only look at the man's history to get a sense of this. Bion was wounded by early attachment and abandonment issues. He experienced wrenching, abrupt cultural dislocation as a small child. As a young tank commander in World War I, Bion wrote that he died psychically, both on the battlefield and from shame afterward. His history gives a sense of the formative importance of catastrophe, threaded throughout life, yet interwoven with his love of nature, poetry, and art. For Bion, catastrophe and chronic dread are basic, and for some people these can become a kind of glue that cements personality together. Think about all the violent, frightening, catastrophic movies many people love so much. Could it be that we seek trauma by proxy as a way of defending against our own? A vicarious projective identification used both to distance and entertain?

Winnicott's view of starting points comes from a different direction. Winnicott grew up in a family of the Wesleyan faith, a quieter, more pacifistic belief system than some. Whereas Freud thought psychic life was an active process, Winnicott viewed passive quiet states as equally important to active states. Winnicott's concern was babies having a secure sense of continuity at the beginning of life, a trust that grows from a sense of "going on being" without major disruption or trauma. That there is good enough continuity of being allows the personality to develop and consolidate without undue interruption. The self has breathing room to find, discover, and create itself. Daily disruptions are, of course, inevitable, and perfect care and attunement are impossible ideals, but most caretakers are "good enough" such that traumatic disruption is kept to a minimum. Under such conditions, when bad stuff does occur, it usually gets corrected soon enough, and the baby's sense of continuity returns. Trust thereby increases, and confidence in one's capacity to come through temporary upheaval grows. However, it's not just the outside world that can cause traumatic moments. Invisible impingements from inside the infant can also feel like an attack on continuity of being.

> A sudden rush of blood through his head or intense pangs of hunger can disrupt and overwhelm his sense of continuity. The infant may scream out of fury and panic in the face of such uncontrollable upheavals. ... A state of stuporous mindlessness replaces the sense of ongoing being. The supportive intervention of the other brings the infant back to life and restores his sense of continuity.
>
> (Eigen, 2018g, p. 122)

Eigen connects Winnicott and Bion a little bit by saying that a sense of catastrophe may well be an embedded part of us, but catastrophe itself is not necessarily primary (2018g, p. 121). The first catastrophe may involve loss of positive life-giving things, such as loss of secure attachments, rather than an early sense of primordial dread.

We are partly made of mindful somethings and mindless nothings, and both full-mind and empty-mind can express themselves quite differently.

A thought experiment: we take it for granted there are lots and lots of "somethings" in the world, too many to count. In Taoism this is the world of 10,000 things. These objects are palpable and measurable, but how do we measure a nothing? How do we quantify emptiness? What can we do with the absence of something, an empty nothing? Bion felt this empty nothing could be terrifying, like an eternity of silence in outer space without echo ... or a yawning void of abyss ... or falling through darkness forever. Reversing our perspective, there are also lovely, supportive, quiet nothings. There is generative soothing emptiness. Deep sleep is one example of a lovely nothing. Deep dreamless sleep provides full waking lives with restoration from generative emptiness.

Eigen says it is an odd quality of catastrophe that it can refer to both something and nothing. But nothingness and mindlessness do not have to be catastrophic. There are almost as many positive qualities to empty moments as there are good feelings. States of cozy solitude exemplify comfortable moments of nothing, quietly enjoying one's own company—being rather than doing. Getting lost looking out the window is one example, reverie is another.

Even reverie and meditative emptiness can be full of thoughts coming and going, just as one can quiet the mind with deep regular breathing and trigger a relaxation response. This can be a very useful nothing. There's also a gap of "nothing" between inhale and exhale. The still moment between out-breath and in-breath is a rhythmic pause, a little like quiet moments of dawn and dusk.

There are, of course, stuporous, hazy, dissociative nothings as well as pitch-black vacuum-packed nothings. But emptiness is not, a priori, a menacing or persecutory nothing, unless perhaps trauma has made it so. The poet Keats wrote about *negative capability*, a state where one does not feel compelled to fill in everything by "irritably reaching after fact and reason," but instead tolerates waiting in the unknown moment (1818/2002, pp. 41–2). Marion Milner (1987) went further and portrayed emptiness as being full and abundant, even pregnant. A pregnant emptiness is a lovely hope-filled nothing, like the creative emptiness of the poet's blank page or artist's white canvas. There are empty states of mind while taking a bath or shower, or doing the dishes. So many kinds of pleasant mindless moments.

Going deeper, Winnicott and Eigen speak of an extremely supportive "nothing" that we have more or less contact with—what Winnicott called an *incommunicado core*—a quiet source of support deep in the center of our being. Some might feel this as a life spark, a heart smile, or God-sense. It is a boundless source of support we may not even know we have. It is a core resource that holds and supports the depths of what Winnicott calls our primary aloneness.

Eigen calls this incommunicado core a "boundless unknown support," and Winnicott traces it to a time *before* clear self-other awareness, when we were maximally dependent on another person who we did not know was present. You can get a little sense of this by imagining a young child engaged in solitary play while a parent sits quietly in the room, providing a background supportive atmosphere. The feeling of safety and comfort from a loving presence is close at hand, but a presence that does not intrude or disrupt the child's serious business of imaginative play.

Eigen and Bion come together in the idea that one way to meet catastrophe is through something they call *faith*. But this faith is not the same as belief. The faith they are pointing to is radically open, an attitude or approach of surrendered absorption to the moment at hand. We are having a crisis of faith right now with the COVID-19 pandemic. What kind of faith can remain open and receptive in the midst of such catastrophe? Eigen calls faith pure receptivity, a kind of alive waiting in not knowing, remaining curious.

How might we use this faith that Bion and Eigen speak of? As you might guess, there is not one answer, function, or use. In the therapy room, faith becomes an open attitude of receptivity, something beyond Freud's evenly hovering attention. Eigen calls it a pure receptivity or psychic nakedness ... an alert readiness, an alive waiting. He says, "[Bion] calls *Faith* the psychoanalytic attitude, which includes the discipline of being without memory, desire, expectation, or understanding" (2018e, p. 21). This approximates a state of being without agenda or knowledge, purposefully raw and receptive to whatever comes from the patient or via intuition and reverie. Bion used this form of faith to engage in psychotherapeutic work.

But not so fast. Such a state is impossible to achieve. Nobody can remain for long without memory, desire, expectation, and understanding. Even so, trying to achieve or ultimately arrive at such a state is not the issue. The main thing is fostering an inclination and discipline toward the attitude, stance, or approach this kind of faith points to.

With practice, we can remain open even when uncomfortable ... alert to evolution of unknown horizons. Eigen says this is something like learning the gesture of repeatedly starting from scratch. We might need to anaesthetize or numb ourselves at times, but unlike psychotic mindlessness we come back. Instead of remaining frozen in oblivion or sealed off in catastrophic inevitability, we can look again. We have freedom for different thoughts and perspectives. We benefit from waiting to see how things develop and reform, rather than acting on impulse. Flexibility is valued for its own sake, whereas obsessive fixation and rigidity often function as markers of psychotic operations.

Boundaries

This commentary delves into the chapter titled "Boundaries," and there are several ways one might approach these pages. One of the overarching questions concerns what kind of "self" we are or have. What do we mean by an ego or self when we speak of boundaries, and what are the possibilities? Here, Eigen continues to explore aspects of our dual nature.

We have a physical body self, and we have a mind self, or psychical self. These two parts of us are not simply connected but thoroughly intertwined. Our physical body self is a visible, palpable, finite, material self that walks around in the physical world. It has physical needs like eating and sleeping. We also have a psychical self, an invisible mental self that thinks and feels, imagines and dreams, reflects and wonders. It may seem a little strange or artificial to talk about the self in these ways, since body and mind usually work together seamlessly. But in psychosis the two can become confused with one another. For linguistic convenience, let's say we experience our bodies through a body-ego feeling, and we experience our minds through a mental I-feeling. Eigen's chapter explores mixtures of body self and mind self, with special questions about our mind or mental I-feeling. His chapter also explores boundaries concerning self and other from the beginning of life.

Our body is physical, measurable, and finite but our mental self can distort and hallucinate our body self. Anorexia is one example. Eigen says what most of us know—that our I-feeling normally waxes and wanes a little. But a psychotic person can take their mental experience to extremes. Their I-feeling can shrink until it disappears or expand to feel larger than the cosmos. How is it that our minds can do this? It's amazing to think our mental self can expand to include all of existence, or feel at one with it. Communing with the ocean or watching the night sky gives a taste of this. Our mind can also contract and shrink to the point of vanishing. Bodies do not have such elasticity, but minds do.

You and I experience these same expansions and contractions, but in less chronically distorted ways. For example,

DOI: 10.4324/9781003257554-8

> In states of absent-mindedness or creative absorption, [our I-feeling] may
> fade for a moment. It may grow keener when caught in conflict. In the
> case of prolonged psychic stress, it can become numb and die out. In
> physical illness, I-feeling may contract to exclude the body. In health on
> a sunny day after a swim, it may include not only the body, but the entire
> universe as well.
>
> (Eigen, 2018g, p. 143)

In Eigen's chapter, we meet an early and relatively unknown analyst who
worked with psychotic individuals. His name was Paul Federn, and Federn
used similar terms to describe this division of the self. He spoke of a body-ego
feeling and mental-ego feeling. He viewed our awareness as variably located
or focused in our body. This is different from focusing conscious awareness
on thoughts, feelings, and ideas, which leaves the body less in focus. Marion
Milner combined these two in interesting ways when she wrote about "big
toe" Zen, where one concentrates awareness on one's big toe from the inside
(1987, p. 259). Freud's (1962) starting point was that our ego or self "is first
and foremost a *body* ego." Eigen tells us this declaration of *body-ego as primary* became a fundamental tenet throughout virtually all psychoanalytic
thinking. Keep in mind also that for Freud, ego, libido and body are primarily seen as active, or active agents. Libido can be directed toward self
(as in primary narcissism) as well as discharge of drives. In Freud's view,
libido actively aims to procure satisfaction through drive-discharge to return
to equilibrium. We might consider Freud's active view of I-feelings alongside Winnicott's notion of quiet or passive states of being, ones that are not
overtly active yet remain open and aware. A lot of activity goes on in quiet
passive states. Passive states tend to focus awareness on inner perception,
and Winnicott was one who valued and underlined the importance of quiet,
nonactive states.

Eigen begins by guessing what babies inwardly experience and go through.
He says babies are partly understandable and partly not. Some of the time
babies act similar to other creatures, as though they are born into a structur-
ally coherent world that fits them. But at other times the infant does not act as
if they inhabit the same world we do. The baby's distress and pleasure are not
always things we can understand or connect with outside events.

> Momentous upheavals seem to come out of nowhere … reactions are
> unmodulated and unbounded. Perhaps [the infant] sees something
> nightmarish. Or perhaps a sensation … for which he lacks a frame of
> reference overwhelms him … At such moments, we glimpse a world in
> which feelings and visions are magnified beyond all sense of proportion.
> Affective images and sensations, infinite and gripping, spread across the
> universe. Perhaps the infant then lives in a world that approximates what
> we later call hallucination. The coordination of everyday perception

with fantastical experience is one of our fundamental developmental tasks.

(Eigen, 2018g, p. 140)

This echoes his first chapter. We start off as hallucinatory beings, and the ego must develop anti-hallucinatory capacities to grow into reality considerations.

In one way, Eigen is comparing the baby's magnified blissful and wrathful states with his patient Carl's psychotic exaggerations. We are told there is competition between Carl's perceptual accuracy and his psychotic hallucinations—an interplay between what's real, what's playfully imagined, and what gets hallucinated with overtones of terror. Everyday perception in hallucinatory psychosis does not disappear (psychotic people don't walk into trees). Instead, everyday perception provides a framework that supports hallucinatory dramas—it functions as a staging area or launching pad for hallucinatory boundlessness, and this boundless tendency can also threaten to sweep ordinary perception away. How does Carl begin to rein in his distortions?

We learn that Carl begins to clear a little in the hospital, but objects retain a hallucinatory glow. Then, points of interest (like the sharp lines of the nurse's face and her physical activity) begin to take on a more playful aspect. Instead of seeing nurse Sharp only as a sinister devil, Carl could now see her as a stimulating and comforting presence as well as an energizing mountain. Eigen says,

> For the moment, perception and hallucination achieved an uneasy but workable alliance. Although their boundaries blurred, they reinforced rather than tore each other apart. Carl was able to breathe a little easier. His interest in another human being was aroused. The experience of the human as a valid dimension showed signs of taking hold.
>
> (2018g, p. 141)

Coordinating materiality and immateriality can be very difficult in psychosis. Carl alternates between feeling he has no body and feeling his body is the only thing that counts. Leila reported seeing her body from above, and she was repulsed by the idea of re-entering her skin. In Frank's world, spirit seemed to vanish altogether in a fecalized material universe.

Remember the old puzzle about which comes first, chicken or egg? Eigen challenges us to reconsider this in relation to body and spirit. What if our ego is not originally a body-ego, as Freud thought? Federn observed in his work with psychotics that body-ego feeling was frequently lost *before* mental-ego feeling was lost. A depersonalization of the body came before mental functioning went awry. We see this in those who disregard basic hygiene and body care. Eigen then mentions that after sleep, mental-ego feeling often awakens before body-ego feeling. We awaken mentally first, often at the tail end of dreaming. And sometimes, if we move too quickly out of sleep, the dream state awareness of our mental-ego can vanish. From such phenomena Federn concluded that "[m]ental ego feeling ... is the first to be experienced by the child; ego feeling related to the body and to perceptions conveyed through the body comes only gradually" (Federn, 1952, p. 442). Eigen elaborates: "Federn reasons that if the I contracts and expands to include or exclude the body, it cannot simply be derived from body states" (2018g, p. 143). Thus, in infancy, we might say that our mental I-feeling gradually comes to encompass the body. From this point of view:

> It takes time and development to discover I must be where my body is. The I-feeling, as such, has a certain primacy ...
>   This primary I-feeling is supposed to exist before a sense of spatial boundaries develops, and so can be anywhere and everywhere. Primordial I-feeling drenches the entire cosmos. Everything is invested or imbued with I-feeling. Original I-feeling is infinite.
>
> (p. 144)

This turns Freud's view upside down. Psyche, spirit, and soul come first and have primacy over the physical body. Accordingly, if our mental-ego feeling is imbued with infinity, we must find a way to fit into our smaller, finite body self. Over time, we are forced to rein in our boundless I-feeling in accordance with body boundaries.

Eigen says, "One must contract to fit the body one is part of. One can only be where one's body is, although it feels otherwise. A smaller I, more successful in material terms, becomes dominant. But a nostalgia for boundlessness lingers" (2018g, p. 144).

Eigen reminds us that for certain individuals our double sense of boundlessness and limits is too much to handle and can be a source of unbearable pain.

> In Federn's terms, we must learn to give up our original, larger I for our smaller I in order to survive. ... We may have to know how to shrink ourselves to get along, but we must also know how to stretch, to let our self out for air. ... We live through the tension between our larger and our smaller I.
>
> (2018g, p. 145)

> Freud tended to study the conflictual basis of depersonalization of an ego already attached to the body. Federn raised the possibility of the ego's refusal to enter the body in the first place. In both accounts, the problem of pain is central.
>
> (p. 146)

Eigen critiques conventional methods for dealing with psychosis. He says these tend to emphasize correcting deficiencies in reality testing as the most essential thing. Often this leads to the practical issue of how to adapt the larger I to the smaller I as quickly as possible, or shutting out the larger I altogether. But if we take Federn's view seriously, we must strive to build creative tolerance for our dual sense of boundlessness *and* limits ... both our cosmic and practical I-feelings.

> One task is to allow the larger and small I to "adapt" to one another, to give each its due. Each has a story to tell, a life to live, and much to contribute.
>
> (Eigen, 2018g, p. 146)

> Our experience would not be what it is without a double sense of materiality-immateriality. It is part of what gives our experience its resonance, depth, and elusiveness. ... Our mysterious I-feeling spreads through earth and heaven. For Freud it comes from the body, for Federn it moves toward the body. Where is its point of origin? We grow and fade in the mystery of doubleness.
>
> (p. 147)

Our Ambiguous Starting Point

Eigen evaluates prevalent theories about our starting point as a separate self. How exactly do we begin life apart from our origins? Are we in union, or are we separate—are we one or two? Are we autistic yet distinct with some awareness, or autistic and inside an unconscious bubble of sameness? How do we emerge from oneness or sameness to become distinct if there is no distinction to begin with? Responses to this dilemma are offered, but become strained to take account of subject–object separation and merger. Winnicott tries to get underneath the issue with transitional experiencing, a place in between self and other that encompasses both and tries to undercut subject–object dualism. A parallel example is the paradox of creation and discovery. The baby finds or discovers something (e.g., the breast, toy, face) and, upon discovering it, feels creative power, at least in early omnipotent phases. Finding and creating go together. Transitional objects carry the meaning of both what is and is not the parent, and what is and is not the self. Like the child clinging to a teddy bear or blanket—the experience is part parental comfort and part ownership of one's own self-soothing capacity. An identification that is also a separation. It is not simply "both-and" inclusiveness but a paradoxical intermixing, or dual sharing.

Previously we tried to account for ourselves as whole human beings composed of two things: mind and body. Now we'll explore our self as a separate being who was once wholly merged with another. In doing so, we'll consider both our oneness and twoness, our simultaneous merging and separation, our union and distinction. We are both a mind and body, and we are a self who originated within another person. Are we one, are we two? Both one and two? Such thoughts point to mysteries that are ultimately paradoxical and unsolvable, but perhaps we can play with them a little.

The Permeable Self and the Concept of Undifferentiation

> The mystery of doubleness is nowhere more intensely encountered than in our sense of self and other. We feel both connected with, yet separate from ourselves and others. In mystical communion (co-union), the self feels wholly in union, yet distinct at the same time. At deep levels of our being, we feel part of others and others part of us, yet we also maintain areas of difference. We may swing back and forth, now emphasizing the dimension of union, now that of difference, whereas the two belong together and make each other possible. Distinction-union appears to be a constitutive structure of our beings. Take either away, and the self would disappear.
>
> (Eigen, 2018g, p. 147)

To my mind, this is a profound recalibration of what it means to be a self. It also sheds light on psychotic struggle.

> The psychotic individual seems to approach zero or infinity by trying to separate union-distinction. The psychotic self may approximate moments of absolute fusion and/or isolation. In either case, the psychological structure breaks down or becomes grotesquely distorted. The individual lives in a swamp or vacuum. The self becomes sponge-like and spineless, or brittle and rigid. More often the self goes both ways at once and is confused by its mixture of nettle and putty. It is scant comfort to realize that the bizarre fragments of psychotic reality are deformations of universal structures.
>
> (p. 148)

Eigen feels many theorists do not make a good case for oneness, union, or undifferentiation as a starting point of self, at least not without acknowledging some differentiation or distinction as also present from the beginning.

All positions that start with undifferentiation have similar problems. If there is no difference between self and other, then self and other cannot yet have arisen. Before self-other awareness is the blankness of nothingness or just being. ... All forms of self-other awareness involve some kind of differentiation ...

Strictly speaking, to exist and be undifferentiated is not possible. Anything that is, must, in some way, be differentiated. Otherwise, it could not be noted, addressed, or engaged.

(2018g, p. 150)

One can use this reasoning with those who claim enlightenment experiences that produce states of absolute oneness, where self disappears. The question becomes: Who is present to notice this oneness is happening? Without some distinction or separate awareness, how would it be registered? Would it be like saying "I must have been asleep because I can't remember being awake?" That would be an undifferentiated sameness. But with just a little bit of distinction or separation, we might say: "I was in this amazing place of at-onement, with quiet relaxed fullness permeating every pore of my being, and just enough awareness to notice my immersion in it."

Ideals and our idealizing capacity are connected to our natural ability for stretching, exaggerating, and magnifying things, touching areas akin to the grandeur of hallucination. At times we even "idealize" in opposing directions. We could label catastrophe a "negative idealization," or distortion in a negative key. Heaven, bliss, and ideals of "purity" are positive idealizations, magnifications of satisfaction or goodness.

Where does this capacity to idealize, absolutize, or infinitize come from? What might be its origin?

It is an odd property of psychoanalytic thought to confuse the capacity to create ideal feelings with the objects idealized. For example, the existence of ideal states are attributed to the infant-mother relationship (womb, breast, maternal functioning, etc.). However, if the mother as mother is gradually discriminated from early ideal states, the critical implication is that the creation of ideal states precedes the perception of mother *qua* mother or, at least, cannot be derived from her.

The question as to why energy or intunement should give rise to a sense of the infinite is not asked. It is taken for granted that this sense is a part of human experiencing. Yet it is precisely its existence that is inexplicable. Why we should be creatures capable of encountering boundlessness is a mystery. Our capacity to do so must be grappled with in its own right ...

Something that approaches everyday perception vies with, complements, and intertwines with ideal reality. ... The psychotic stumbles on this complexity and is pummeled by it. He is drawn to and pulled apart by the extremes of our nature. ... In distorted fashion, he lays bare raw materials with which we must come to grips. The extremes of psychosis—hallucinatory struggle in an intensified reality, mindless vacuousness, relentless activity, vegetativeness, whirling abstractions, entombment in concreteness—present us with indications of what in our makeup we must take into account if we are to be a viable life form. It is too easy for unity to become obliterating fusion or separation to become autistic-paranoid isolation. Both tendencies operate in varying balance and intensity throughout a multidimensional spectrum. For the human self to succeed, adequate ways of relating to the processes that constitute us must be found.

(Eigen, 2018g, pp. 161–3)

Comments and Responses

Comment 1: My curiosity is about the "I-feeling." With the body it's pretty clear, like when my foot hurts. But in terms of location ... the mind's I-feeling ... You know, where is that in terms of location? Is that pre-existent, or is that something that is created? Where's the location of the mind's I-feeling?

Response 1: It could be anywhere. That's fascinating, isn't it? Some people think our mental I-feeling is up here [pointing] in the head or brain. Some people want to reduce my mental "I" to physical sensation. But our mental I-feeling is private and invisible ... it can't be "located" the way our body parts or skin sensations can. Where is yours located? Where is your I-feeling ...?

It's fluid, isn't it? There are many kinds of psychical and experiential states felt to be in different areas ... not just in one place. Some people feel feelings that have no location at all. How is it possible that we can feel or sense something without location? This is part of the mystery of psychic life ...

Hate, Fear, and Aggression

An odd paradox: the more I study this book on madness, the saner and more grounded I feel. I hope this might be true for you as well. In this commentary we take up the first part of the chapter on hate. Hate, like rage and fear, is a primal, powerful emotion. Eigen begins the chapter writing about fear and hate being mixtures, hyphenating them as hate–fear, or fear–hate. They often go together. So many of our emotional states are mixtures whether we recognize it or not. It is not contradictory to feel two different or even opposing emotions at the same time. In the realm of feeling life there may be conflictual mixtures, but there are no contradictions. Whether toward parent or partner, I can feel irritation and love simultaneously. They don't cancel each other out; both are felt as real. Contradiction is useful in formal logic and science up to a point. Either/or thinking and logic help science discern distinctions among phenomena accurately, but psychological and emotional reality are different. If we observe extremes of either/or, black and white thinking, they are usually related to defensive needs and show up as distortions and rigidity, qualities often observed in so-called character disorders.

In this chapter, Eigen starts by giving us a glimpse of his patient Ron and the congealed, hardened emotions he observes in Ron's physical body and demeanor. Eigen sees Ron's emotions as stuck in his physicality. He then contrasts Ron's situation with more fluid emotional states that babies go through, saying that babies are in a more continuous flow of many different feeling states that have not had time to "solidify." Most infants' sensory and emotional life is in constant flux rather than rigid or stuck. Infants' needs are totally dependent on a caregiver's proper attention and fulfillment. Emotionally, babies go through many storms of feeling that change from hour to hour and moment to moment. Eigen's point is that, unless there is a chronic pattern of poor caretaking or devastating trauma, babies usually ride through swings of feeling without getting stuck in any one of them.

So often it is lack of flexibility and rigidity in our emotional life that causes problems. The inability to allow different feelings to offset, modulate, or modify one another is one sign that pathology may be operating.

DOI: 10.4324/9781003257554-9

Eigen discusses different ways that hate can arise, both hate toward self and hate toward others. One way is when feelings of deficiency or insufficiency arise that evoke hateful feelings. In the last chapter, one of Bion's psychotic patients was described as suffering from a lack, or failure, or refusal to conform to rules of discourse and clear language. This was in the section on "Catastrophe and Doodling in Sound." Eigen says he cannot tell whether Bion's patient was exhibiting destructive hate or a sense of his own deficiency, but that destructive hate and a sense of deficiency often go together:

> In psychosis (but not only in psychosis), a profound sense of deficiency may generate hate-filled processes and vice-versa. It is precisely the individual's felt inability to participate in ordinary human interaction that drives him to set up alternate realities in which he reigns supreme and is victimized. From a seemingly inviolable position, he can attack threatening reality and spin it out of existence. He is left with a kingship of a non-existent kingdom in which he, too, disappears.
>
> (2018g, p. 118)

Another source of hate is the link with thwarted love, unrequited love, or feeling rejected in love. We've all heard news stories about someone being assaulted or murdered because they were spurned or rejected in a love relationship. Statistics tell us that more people are murdered by someone they know than by someone they don't know. Even in small doses, feeling rejected is very hurtful. One person might express vengeful feelings when they're hurt, *externalizing* blame as a defensive reaction, believing the other is at fault. Another person might *internalize* the hurt and withdraw, feeling unworthy or flawed, believing "I must be no good or unlovable," and so on.

There are many ways love can go wrong, and many ways hate can be destructive. Incapacity or unwillingness to work with various kinds of psychic and emotional pain is prominent in psychosis. Even for those who are better able to work with emotional reality, everyone's way of defending against or metabolizing pain differs. But no one escapes from the task of processing emotional pain in one way or another, even if this means deadening psychic life to escape from ourselves. At the same time, we all need to rest from ourselves and take breaks from emotional life. That's different than using chronic escape mechanisms that isolate or remove us from reality. When we're not able to work with difficult emotions, their negative energy can become lodged in our physical body, as with Ben and Smith in this chapter. We'll also see this dramatized in the next chapter when we learn more about Eigen's patient Ron.

We read that both hate and love are demanding and aggressive. Love filled with desire is not a passive thing. Love can be aggressive, demanding, possessive. Some authors tie hate to the death drive but Eigen has a different view. Hate is filled with energy, albeit negative energy. Surges of hate are sparked with hot aliveness but can be corrosive too, behaving like acid when hateful feelings come to be recirculated internally. We could speak of many qualities and flavors of hate: loud, aggressive vulgar hate and brooding silent hate; simmering angry hate and hot explosive hate; calculated ice-cold hate and impulsive vengeful hate.

Forms of hate can be directed both inward and outward. We know that chronic hate and anger turned inward can lead to depression and somatic concerns. Hate turned outward, especially by those who hold positions of power, can injure and destroy whole societies. In the US and elsewhere, we are currently witnessing a surge of anger and hate toward a range of externalized dislikes and "wrongs." Odd as it may seem, hate can also be enlivening and powerful, and at times expressions of hate can enable people to experience themselves more fully. Once again, there is no "one size fits all," no emotion that has only one way of being used or expressed. Emotional expression and its uses and meaning are always context dependent, and the psychotherapy office is a setting where we pay close attention to the different forms feeling life can take.

Eigen says we are beings who are rich in love, anger, hate, and fear. But the death instinct or death drive is something different, something else, and should not be loosely tied to hate in its destructive form. The death drive is not simply love gone wrong or a rest from sentience, but rather a collapse of the possibility of emotional aliveness. The death drive is the undoing of life, an entropy, a winding down, a conservative force. It is something we can see each year, by analogy, in the natural world as decay sets in after the autumn season—a fading out of growth and life. In psychoanalysis Freud viewed this death drive as a tendency to return to a time before birth, a time before all birth … a quiescence. And Bion went further, calling the death drive a force of anti-life, as well as anti-rage, anti-knowing, and anti-faith. For Bion the death drive undoes or unravels or destroys whatever is available. In contrast, Winnicott didn't have much use for a death instinct or death drive. He thought the life drive by itself could account for aggressive and destructive forces. The life drive is greedy.

Eigen uses a contemporary example:

> Today, our economic system is fused with the taste of power and feeds on its own ambition. Henry Kissinger called power an aphrodisiac. A kind of life drive gone wild. For the sake of gain, it destroys—poisons air and water and land and psyche. The life drive, once productive, once in service of survival, has itself become a menace, a threat to life. There is enormous resistance or incapacity or unwillingness to take in and work with what we are doing—denial of the violence inherent in our sense of life. Addiction to gain, dominance and power promotes more addiction to gain, dominance and power … and an inability to let in and counteract the negative effects of this spiral contributes to its momentum.
>
> (2018f, p. 78)

Throughout history, we've seen that fear and hate have been ingredients in a wide array of human ills, conflicts, and dysfunction, from interpersonal and cultural wars to cold wars and world wars. Many people wish to do away with hateful emotions, along with forms of evil and madness. But as we've seen, it's more about how these powerful forces come to be used than the emotions themselves. Any strong emotion can show itself in different ways. Love can be used to control, coerce, and manipulate. Love can be possessive and suffocating, and love can also express a most beautiful, amazing emotional connection. Similarly, hate is not just a bad thing. Hate can signal legitimate protest, conjuring rebellious energy and life force to initiate change and development. Could we say that Gandhi or Martin Luther King Jr. or Nelson Mandela transmuted their hatred toward oppressors skillfully? In Hannah Green's book, *I Never Promised You a Rose Garden* (1964) she writes that violent hospitalized patients had a better chance of recovery than compliant ones. I saw examples of this when I worked in locked psychiatric wards decades ago. It turned out that those patients who were passive, unconcerned, and uninterested in their own psychotic symptoms had a much poorer prognosis than those who were frightened, angered, and disturbed by what was happening to them and who actively fought against their internal and external confusions and distortions.

How to use any strong emotion in co-creative and nondestructive ways remains an ongoing evolutionary challenge. Hate and anger can be empowering when directed against injustices, and they can also be corrosive and destructive when used poorly. But however used, hate, fear, and aggression contain aliveness and deserve to be handled with care and respect in their own right. Eigen often references William Blake who said something like "the devil is pure energy, and energy is eternal delight." It's how the devil's energy gets channeled and used that marks the difference. Our era has seen both the creation and use of sinister weapons as well as music from the Rolling Stones as enlivening expressions of devilish energy.

Returning to the origins of hate dynamics and the baby, we read how babies grow through experiencing multiple tensions in relationship to caregivers before words are available. The mother or caregiver is by nature divided between care of the infant and self-care. The baby by nature is demanding, but cannot by itself produce the care and attention it needs. There is self-sacrifice and self-assertion for both baby and caretaker. The baby makes her way in an atmosphere in which she feels both wanted and unwanted, but cannot yet know that others have needs too, and the baby must come to grips with this tension. Eigen says that in so many ways, our earliest desires run up against and/or fit in with the desires of others, and the very quality of our desires is affected by this interplay.

For example, one important development is when the baby's teeth start to grow. Teeth can be aggressive. Teeth are the baby's very first weapon. We rip things apart with our teeth. We grind up food and even bite our cheek and tongue at times. Teeth are sharp and dangerous. Before the baby has teeth, nursing at the breast cannot really hurt the mother. But with the coming of teeth, the infant can physically hurt the mother during nursing. "Even if his initial use of teeth is a spontaneous and joyful exercise, he soon learns its complex consequences" (2018g, p. 172). The baby who bites must learn to use restraint or risk losing the breast. "The baby is caught between his wish to bite and his need to hold back" (p. 172). Conflicts between self-expression and inhibition begin to form. How does the baby maintain a balance between self-assertion and inhibition when thrown into such an ambivalent situation? To use one's teeth, whether in pleasurable or aggressive ways, might bring punishment or worse. But not to freely use one's teeth sets the stage for anxiety, guilt, and inhibition.

This brings us to Melanie Klein's important work and her early hate dramas organized around the infant's reactions to dependency. In Klein's view, the infant envies the caretaker's creative and nourishing power, as well as the caretaker's superior size and ability (Eigen, 2018g, p. 177). The infant feels less than, but also dependent on this greater god-like person. This inequality precipitates anxiety and depression. Along the way, combinations of anger and hate, projection and introjection, guilt and reparation, envy and gratitude are exercised. Eigen summarizes by saying that Klein depicts an envious war between hostile and greedily loving powers. And in psychosis, these hostile powers, when introjected and deformed, can become like inner gods, grandiose and exaggerated, at war within the psychotic self. Eigen tells us psychotics often experience themselves as caught in an internal struggle between competing grandiose gods or demons. This competitive struggle involves both an internal megalomanic self *and* an internal megalomanic other, and both may be tainted with hate. One thinks of those who hear command hallucinations and the warring confusion as to whether it is the voice of God or the devil.

Alternately, some psychotic patients may try to escape and maintain good feeling by pretending that pain is always somewhere else or doesn't exist at all, using manic defenses. Emotional pain, catastrophe, and things that feel wrong or persecutory get pushed out of sight, and instead an idealized reality is used to substitute for real living. But this strategy leads to a life of evasion from self through deception. Eigen reminds us that *negative* affects and emotions are part of what makes life feel full and whole, if we can tolerate and learn to work with them. Yet capacities for tolerating and working with negative feelings are lacking in both the sane and insane.

Eigen ends his critique of Klein's destructive impulse, guilt, and reparation with a question about what's most basic. Is the answer to the problem of hate that we always need to be making up for who we are? Do Klein's ideas reinforce a vision of the self as basically bad, something that needs atoning for? Are we humans mostly monsters that must always be atoning through guilt and reparation? (Eigen, 2018g, p. 178). If Klein were around today, one wonders how she might view the prevalent absence of owning guilt feelings, and how blame has become so externalized, weaponized, and pervasive. Both trends seem to be increasing in tandem.

We've reviewed hate as involved in defensive and reactive modes. Hate as a defensive reaction to personal insufficiency or deficiency, and hate connected to envy and dependency needs. In his section on anal metaphors and mind–body splits, Eigen reminds us how much of our common hate language uses anal imagery. Swear words and phrases make generous use of shit, asshole, and spoiling processes linked to stain, garbage, and toxicity. Eigen says the young child may become confused about its own waste products and what they mean about oneself. The production of a bowel movement can be a heroic creative act for one being potty trained. It's an impressive accomplishment providing a sense of control and mastery, while also a smelly product from a hidden part of the body. On the other hand, one can come to identify oneself with shit: "I'm no good, I'm a shit, I'm a shitty person …" which, when colored by hate or despair can become "who cares, who gives a shit." On a global scale, megalomanic superiority links up with weaponry to "lay waste" to others in war. Murder and tantrums, both individual and societal, try to get rid of hated contaminants and dreaded spoiling elements. The asshole is seen as an ambiguous organizer and one of the devil's favorite hiding places (Eigen, 2018g, p. 181).

Winnicott has another view of hate, rage, and fury. He points to early aggression that is not mainly defensive or reactive. Its main function, he says, is *creative*. Creative fury or rage. Perhaps this is similar to William Blake, who viewed satanic energy as radiant energy, readying itself for particular use?

How a caretaker responds to the infant's early aggressive and destructive drives becomes quite important for development, and Winnicott's *use of object* addresses this and is taken up in the next commentary.

Comments and Responses

Comment 1: I'm not a therapist. I'm sorry if this sounds kind of dumb, but …
   In the situation where the mother responds with negativity to the baby's aliveness and produces a sense of guilt in the child … then, in the therapeutic alliance, I would think the goal of the therapist is to affirm the aggression? Like how does affirming aggression go about restoring … or taking away the guilt for being alive if at first the mother has done that consistently?

Response 1: It likely depends on how embedded the mother's guilt is, but first, for the therapist who is confronted with aggression: do not retaliate. That might seem obvious. You know, don't attack back. That's not going to do any good. That's just affirming we can attack each other. Another thing is, don't collapse and disappear … don't abandon. Don't collapse and convey, "I can't deal with your attack." We must meet the aggression somehow, and it's good if we can meet it with a certain quality of containment. That's not always easy to do, but can help. I'm glad you brought this up because it is still a challenge for all of humanity.

Commentary #8

Hate, Self-Hatred, and the Death Drive

Now we're going to focus on the second half of Eigen's chapter on hate. We ended the last commentary with questions and dilemmas about the relationship between hate and the death drive or death instinct, discussing how hate, aggression, and the death drive are multifaceted and can function in different ways. On a physical or biological level, the death drive unwinds or undoes the life drive. One simple analogy is found in nature: if the life drive is represented by spring and summer, we might say the death drive is represented by fall and winter. That's an example from the physical or material side of life.

But in emotional and psychological domains things are more complex. The death instinct or death drive is not the same as hate or aggression, although they may make use of it. Hate can be enlivening as a voice of protest. When turned against the self, hate can be destructive and deadening. The fact that the same emotional energy can have both self-affirming and self-destroying tendencies exemplifies the kind of beings we are and the complexities we must work with.

An important clinical question for writers like Winnicott and Eigen, and urgent for society at large, is how these negative drives or forces might be used less destructively, or even be put to beneficial use.

How to use any strong emotion in creative and nondestructive ways remains an ongoing challenge. Hate and anger can be empowering and motivating, promoting change when used productively. Hate and anger can also be corrosive and destructive when used poorly. Yet however they are used, hate and other hot emotions are a life force to be reckoned with, not simply bad or wrong in themselves.

The splitting of function and use, whether inside us or through social protest, is variable. In Portland, Oregon, during the summer of 2020, we had weeks of continuous nighttime protests. Different groups were demonstrating and protesting against racial and economic injustices. One group's protest was mostly carried out in peaceful, nondestructive ways, working for changes through government, corporate structures, and economic pressure. But there were also protests that sought revenge and retaliation, injuring people and

DOI: 10.4324/9781003257554-10

burning buildings that symbolized injustices. Such contrasts and extremes are one example of splitting and also show how aggressive energy can be used differently. When it comes to our different tendencies and capacities, their particular function and use in a given situation requires ongoing scrutiny.

Hate and destructive feelings can be split in their internal use as well—as a defense against inner pain, to keep others out, block intrusiveness, and create walls against too much permeability or loss of control. There can be hate for my own perceived badness, or bad parts of myself. Often hate is used in a battle against a hated self, a wish for destruction of what feels damaged or crippled. But even in such instances, destructive feelings also contain a vital spark, a desire for change, a wish to correct something, and are not solely about annihilation. One exception is when self-attack is in the service of extinction or self-erasure. This occurs in impulsive suicides and in slower processes of cumulative self-numbing and hollowing out of psychic life. Self-hate in this context is a form of death drive moving toward a maximum of inertia or entropy, a zero point of stimulation—psychic life extinguishing itself, which at times takes the physical body with it.

How might aggression be used positively in psychotherapy? This is a less common question. More often we think of negative instances—a patient or a therapist acting badly or being cruel. But there can be positive, even therapeutic aspects as well. When Eigen writes that the therapist also uses his or her "teeth" and has a good "bite," he means this as something growth producing, born out of goodwill and sincerity, by challenging the patient in potentially useful ways. In this context, the therapist's teeth might be offering a difficult perspective, something thought provoking, incisive, or experientially new— perhaps with an eye toward throwing dysfunctional patterns into doubt. At their best, such biting or incisive exchanges are devoted to the patient's well-being and not simply to relieve emotional tension or discomfort, unavoidable as these are at times. Instead, each partner in the therapeutic couple might be challenged to stretch, find, and exercise new psychical muscles, or experience areas of opening that have been foreclosed upon or blocked by developmental obstacles (in the patient) or theoretical and technical rigidities (in the therapist). Of course, such responses must be built on a foundation of mutual respect and care, with the therapist's sensitivity to the patient's inner resources and capacities uppermost in mind.

Let's return to the baby and caretaker with examples of different responses to aggression. Let's say the baby kicks the mother or caretaker with a spontaneous aggressive kick. What is the quality of the response? What is the atmospheric emotional response before words are available to the infant? Nonverbal feeling-toned responses convey important messages to infants. In one example, Eigen draws on Winnicott imagining two possible worlds (2018b, p. 60). In one world, a caretaker's response to the baby's kick was to avoid being hurt, but accompanied by spontaneous pleasure in the aliveness of the baby, feeling glad the baby was "alive and kicking." It was not felt as attack so much as a spontaneous life force. In a second imagined world, the caretaker drew back and took offense, felt the kick was hostile. The response was moralistic, conveying a sense that kicking is bad and wrong. The first response supported a quality of aliveness, an affirmation that aggression could be expressed and contained with benign limit setting. But the second response shut down the baby's aggressive aliveness with a punishing negative reaction. Such feelings are communicated without any words (2018b, p. 61). So often in therapy too, it's the tone and emotional atmosphere created by our responses that have impact. The quality of response conveys an atmosphere beyond any words used.

Destructive uses of hate in society are all too common, like hate expressed as violence toward others in the name of so-called truth, but under the guise of self-righteousness. An example prevalent today includes believing one is the sole carrier of truth, not subject to questioning, thereby shutting off and shutting down multiple perspectives—gripped by only one perspective based on megalomaniac self-certainty.

Psychotic processes have, as one of their common denominators, intensified megalomania, which is not simply one thing, but expresses itself in different ways. We all engage in exaggeration and hyperbole at times, but we usually don't get stuck there. There are moments when we think or feel something is total and absolute, but psychosis tends to become trapped in that state. Whether we call this rigidity, a hardening process, or inflexibility, somehow psychic fluidity is lost, and the capacity for psychic and emotional multiplicity is lost. It is no longer possible to offset or modify one viewpoint or emotional state by another, by trying on a different perspective.

On Self-hatred

Self-attack and self-hatred work in different ways as well. In psychosis we've learned there are often inner competing voices that fight with each other and feed off one another, so that cycles of self-attack keep spinning, hardening, and depleting the self. But there are also self-attacks that attempt to cleanse something wrong, aimed at potentially redoing or resetting oneself. Perhaps we could speak of self-attack being on a continuum, with self-discipline as one of the healthier, more productive forms, at least if one does not overuse self-discipline to tyrannize and persecute oneself with excessive expectations. Instead, more moderate uses of self-discipline can aid creativity, like attempting to grow new habits or abandon old ones.

The theme that runs through all case examples in this chapter is self-hate, and Eigen says that self-hatred is basic and pervasive in mental illness. Let's look at some of Eigen's clinical examples.

We see hardened patterns of dysfunction and disjunction in aspects of Ron's demeanor. One is the mismatch between his small, twisted physical frame combined with large, loud nonstop complaining. This made him seem clownish, like a caricature.

Patient Alison was stuck in a frozen cycle because she could not admit any bad feelings and defended against these by expending great energy holding onto only good feelings. Her efforts at maintaining control eventually exhausted her body and wore her down.

Patient Paul turned fetish objects into items he could control for isolated pleasure, after feeling out of control due to early life overstimulation from his sister, combined with his mother giving him enemas. Paul's early feelings of helplessness helped his needs for control to become uncompromising.

> A person who hates himself often does so for good reason. He feels there is something very wrong at the bottom of his being. He has taken a wrong developmental turn. He is not the self he wants to be, could be, or should be. His self-attack is most basically an attempt to right himself. Through self-attack, he hopes to tear away what is keeping him from being more truly and fully himself.
>
> (Eigen, 2018g, p. 208)

This dynamic comes closer to the case of Carrie, who screws up again and again with the hope that her God will not forsake her, but will come back to find her again after she has gone wrong and acted badly.

In the section on madness and multidimensionality (2018g, p. 210), Eigen keys in on the word "foreverness," the feeling and sense of forever as a type of boundlessness. He says a sense of foreverness traverses the spectrum of human experience. There is a part of our mind that believes we will live forever. Our conscious awareness cannot fathom its own permanent absence, even though we see it happen to others. Moments of beatific or dreadful experience can also feel eternal or forever. Freud says there is no such thing as death in the unconscious. Eigen writes that an acute sense of mortality and death can sharpen our sense of the eternal now, the preciousness of being alive and living. Then Eigen drops a thought bomb when he says, "In general, an idealizing feeling and the violence of life go hand in hand" (p. 211).

Why is an ideal *feeling* linked with violence in life? We come back to ideals as doubles, or multisided. We need our ideals—they are things to live up to and reach for—and we must also be very cautious when we find ideal feelings linked to self-certainty. Absolute thinking and feeling forecloses on other options. And there are negative valences to ideals and ideal feelings, not just positive ones.

Some recently overheard examples of negative idealizing and distortion:

The Covid virus signifies the end of civilization itself.

This is another totalization or absolutizing view because it is too sure of itself and has a tone of finality.

> We will need to be isolated from one another *forever* ... there is no going back.

The word *forever* is another signal that one is at an extreme, indicating distortion. The feeling in the moment can be real and seem absolutely true, but it does not take into account that conditions are always changing and that nothing is "forever." One hundred years ago it took some time, but conditions eventually did change and the so-called Spanish flu went away. It did not go on forever. Whenever we absolutize, our ideals partake of megalomania because they infinitize or totalize with an accompanying sense of self-certainty.

History is full of violent ideals, whether the crusades or utopian visions of Stalin, Hitler, and Pol Pot. Eigen amplifies this theme, citing religious ritual in its many variations: violence as part of creative destruction by Hindu gods or violence as part of God's will in the Old Testament. In Western religions, aggressive hate is sometimes called "holy wrath" or "pure hate." Eigen reminds us that on an elemental level, emotions like rage, fury, wrath, and hatred carry a feeling of numinous power—another megalomaniac example. But is it God or the devil who is applying these emotions, and with what kind of vision, with what quality of use? Many millions have died in the name of religion and ideology, which themselves often promise megalomaniac ideals.

> When we hate we think we are or ought to be God. When we are angry, we feel we are right about something. We hate when we feel it is too difficult, if not impossible, to redress a wrong. We are impotent gods. However, hate is not entirely without hope, or it would die out. Stupor or compliance might take its place. When we hate, we want our will to be done.
>
> Hatred simplifies. It splits the world into those who are with us and those who are against us. Even when our hatred is right, as it often is, it may lead to disaster because of the absolute, oversimplified terms it needs in order to thrive.
>
> (Eigen, 2018g, p. 211)

Ideals that are absolute or total become dangerous because they are intolerant of other perspectives, values, and orientations. At the individual level, this is part of what happens within the psychotic mind, with the added complication of ambivalence and oscillation among the mind's inner warring factions.

The psychotic mind holds narrow perspectives and little flexibility, especially when accompanied by a grandiose sense of certainty and need for control. A sense of control spurs one on because that is exactly what seems to be missing. Extremes of both obsessive narrowness and megalomaniac inflation were seen in Commentary #3 on Hallucination, where we witnessed rigidity and inflexibility in Frank's obsession with his body parts and Carl's attempts to wrestle with God and the devil as they fought for control. Frank was stuck in the physical, and Carl was mesmerized by the psychospiritual. If one feels too small and powerless, one usurps power by holding grandiose beliefs and self-certainty. Both involve distortion, but there is also terror at loss of control over one's mind as well as shame mixed with hate at feeling alien and outside common humanity.

At the end of the section on "The 'Unwanted' Patient," Eigen gives a descriptive overview of his patients Ellie, Pat, and Ron:

> The patients in these case histories generally externalized their problems and showed very little spontaneous interest in psychic processes. When the latter occurred it was usually obsessive and used to reinforce a self-hardening process. Such persons have been forced to undergo gross personality distortions patterned after inordinately destructive early object-relations. The egos of these patients have a marked incapacity to process aggressive feelings in wholesome ways. The self's hate is aimed, in part, against its needs and love wishes and leads to a reproachful attitude toward an apparently ungiving or overwhelming world. If the therapist fully opens himself to the attitudes of these patients, he will tend to feel injured or drained. The patients themselves have erected barriers to influence this by repelling those who venture near. At the same time, the intensity of their deepest needs compels them to attempt to draw the other into their orbit and merge. Hence the therapist, like the patient, is in danger of feeling pulled apart by the patient's conflicting tendencies.
>
> (2018g, pp. 201–2)

The clinical aim is to try to help the psychotic mind temper itself, to soften and modify extreme inner positions and feelings, as well as offset rigid distortions in order to gain more inner freedom.

Whether we are sane or insane, the issue is partly about coming to terms with our multidimensionality, which is embedded in the complexity of being human. "We may or may not learn better ways of meeting and handling ourselves, but we are not going to wish our multidimensional nature away" (Eigen, 2018g, p. 212).

Comments and Responses

Comment 1: Here in this chapter, Eigen is saying he is actually welcoming the hate; he looks for the hate as a sparkle of life. It touched me very deeply, this thought ... to look for the hate. Like saying, "There is the life sparkle" or "there we can find it." It was a new thought to me, and I am very thankful for this understanding.

Response 1: And I'm thankful you brought that thought to the front and center. Because to welcome hate seems counterintuitive in therapy, but it can actually be very productive. People often want to run the other way and resist or avoid hateful feelings. Or else indulge such feelings and project them onto others rather than looking inward. We don't want to deal with hate when we have trouble with our own feelings of hate, especially hidden self-hate.

Comment 2a: At the end of this chapter on shock of madness and multidimensionality, there is the sentence: "The death-rebirth archetype would not be possible without madness." I was like, "Okay, what does that mean?"

Response 2a: The extreme poles and intensities of archetypes can be maddening, or madness producing, and they can also be growth producing. But why would the death-rebirth archetype not be possible without madness? I think Eigen is bringing together madness with megalomania, here as extravagance ... e.g. "living forever." Any archetype necessarily partakes of or draws upon megalomania, or evokes it, because archetypes are laced with power of the numinous and feel larger than life.

Comment 2b: ... Or fear of death—that can make people kind of mad too ...

Response 2b: That's been known to happen [smiling].

Comment 2c: And if you can't go through the dying ... like in alchemy, there is a lot that you have to go through in the death process to come up again, like the Phoenix myth.

Response 2c: That ties-in, because there are all kinds of psychic death, right? Just like there are all kinds of hate and destruction. If mini psychic deaths can be handled well enough, we come back up again, and they lead to renewal and hopefully growth. Another example is Freud's regression in the service of the ego. Then there are "myths" that proceed in the opposite direction, like the Tower of Babel and the Garden of Eden, where things start out promising and end badly.

Comment 3: In my experience, if someone has had a near-death experience at birth, then it is very difficult to differentiate psychic death from literal death.

Response 3: Yes, a kind of "psychic equivalence" that feels like literal death. When we are injured and die emotionally, when we die psychically, that's fully half of our being human. The question Bion and Eigen ask is whether we can die psychically and emotionally and then be alright again? Can we develop that sequence? It's an important rhythm to get the hang of.

Epistemology and Reversal

In this commentary we're going to explore the chapter titled "Epistemology and Reversal." *Epistemology* is a big fancy word, but it's really just a branch of philosophy having to do with our theories of knowledge and how we know what we know. This seems particularly important today in light of things like "alternative facts." *Reversal* is less complex on the face of it, but reversal too has many ways of being used. Reversal commonly refers to switching back and forth, or changing direction, like when we put the car into reverse gear. In everyday life, breathing in and out is a reversal, and sleeping and waking is another. Regression is a form of reversal, but so is health coming out of illness. Why does Eigen put epistemology and reversal together? As we've noted, conjoining two things can also help us see relations between them, when we don't settle for simple binaries.

One idea is that knowledge of self and world is incomplete without the ability to reverse perspective. We need more than one perspective to be sure the scope of our perception and knowledge is not limited by narrowness or extremity of only one position or one view. Eigen focuses attention on both mind and body, not just mind. In addition, not only the individual self or psyche is of concern, but rather a self that includes and presupposes others. This leads to an ethics of self together with others in all our interwoven aspects. Part Two of the book will address such ethical concerns more fully.

If in the physical material world there are substances like water that can reverse from solid to liquid and liquid to gas, then back again, we might look to our emotional life for similar reversible dynamics. Our moods and feelings reverse; our likes and dislikes can reverse; even our perceptions of people we think we know well can reverse. The most common examples of percep-tual reversal are found in those classic optical illusion figure-ground drawings. One of these is an image of a flower vase or chalice from one perspective and two faces in profile from another. A reversible figure and ground highlights different perceptions and different realities.

Eigen gives an example of both epistemology and reversal in the very first paragraph of his chapter. He writes about what it means to be a naïve realist,

DOI: 10.4324/9781003257554-11

as when we take our immediate perceptions for granted as true and real. For example, let's say we are looking at the Pacific Ocean to the west in the late afternoon, facing the setting sun. What we observe is called a sunset. It's the time of day when the sun appears to be traveling down into the ocean beneath the horizon. But one does not have to be an astronomer to realize that from another perspective, the horizon of our spinning earth is actually rotating upward at great speed to meet and swallow up the so-called setting sun. So with reverse perspective another reality occurs, leading to a different kind of knowing. We don't call this event a "rising horizon"; we call it a setting sun. Our choice of perspective matters because it relativizes our thinking and knowledge. In our minds and imagination, we can sometimes reverse perspective at will. We can take an extra step or moment to consider what any given reversal might look like. We can go back and forth, similar to looking at the figure-ground drawing.

In everyday life, there are many examples of reversal. We use our memory and imagination to go back in time or into the future. Conjoined reversals show themselves across many aspects of psychoanalysis too, as with Freud's life and death instincts, Melanie Klein's projection and introjection, Alfred Adler's inferiority and superiority complexes, Jung's compensatory dynamics and a reversal he called *enantiodromia*.

Eigen writes, "The movement from destruction to stability is but one of a series of reversals at work in psychosis. ... Freud noted that reversal is an elementary operation of the mind, one of the earliest defenses, perhaps preceding defenses" (2018g, p. 216).

Freud felt that reversal was earlier than repression. In one way, reversal can be seen as connected to splitting, as when we compartmentalize and turn love into hate— deny one side and jump to the other. Recall reversal from Eigen's chapter on Hallucination (Commentaries #3 and #4), the baby hallucinating the presence of an absent breast, for example. We can reverse affect too—likes and dislikes, joy and sorrow—as well as create mixtures like "bittersweet." Eigen says the general ability of the mind to distinguish and unite is allied with an elemental capacity to reverse experiential perspectives.

In psychosis there is exploitation and distortion of this capacity for reversal in both our concrete physical bodily realm and our invisible, non-locatable psychospiritual realm. In effect, both the material and immaterial, visible and invisible sides of reality can cause the psychotic mind to have problems, evoking defenses against painful confusions and impingements, which compel construction of alternative realities that are attempts to escape, avoid, or deny psychic pain. At the extreme, one might even try to disappear into nothingness or believe they are more powerful than life itself.

Space, time, and self are all implicit in what Eigen calls the "fiction of inner space." Why? Because psyche is invisible, it is not touchable or locatable. It took me awhile to grasp what Eigen means by inner space or psychic space, because we take it so much for granted. We don't think about how the sense of inner space and outer life and their mixtures serve our sense of reality. For instance, there is a different quality of inner space when we feel overworked and on a strict deadline, versus our inner space when we awaken to the first morning of a long holiday. The former feels stuffed, densely occupied, and pressured, whereas at the start of a holiday we feel inwardly expansive and light, with more freedom. But what happens? The night before vacation is over, there's often a reversal back to more inner density.

Practically speaking, psychic health means operating in the world with a seamless sense of inside, outside, and in between—realms that are not stuck or frozen in any one of those positions. It also means psychic life is not moving so quickly or oscillating so rapidly that inside and outside blur together and collapse in confusion. Instead, most of us experience a more natural flow, with fluidity and flexibility between realms. For the psychotic mind, such distinctions as well as movement between them regularly get short-circuited or all jumbled up.

We see examples of these dynamics in two case studies at the beginning of this chapter. Jane had unconsciously mixed up air and food as unknowingly tied to her mother. For Jane, these material and immaterial dimensions of reality had become conflated. For Carl, objects took on obsessive concern in the context of his mental fantasies and projections, tied to a grandiose sense of omniscience and control. His trying to control the moon is not a very sane thing to do, but *playing* with the moon and its beauty is something different and can be quite wonderful. Carl was obsessive in his efforts to dictate and control; the lighter, more provisional feel of playfulness came only later. Winnicott felt the ability to play freely was one sign of a mentally healthy person.

Eigen tells us that the curious philosopher, like the child at play, holds assumptions and ideas provisionally rather than absolutely. But the psychotic subject may reject the provisional altogether by not holding assumptions about anything, instead seeing through everything as fake or false and not wanting to be burdened by any of it. Just as easily, at another extreme, hallucinatory certainty and megalomania can take over, leading to frozen places of delusion that ossify and refuse to develop or grow. Both of these extreme attitudes show a failure to allow alternate perspectives to arise and offset one another. The psychotic person's inner resources for tolerating psychic pain are either not available or poorly developed. At the outer edges, the psychotic mind gets stuck in the mud of delusional certainty, or else flies off loose and high into endless, anchorless space.

Eigen writes of another doubleness I find compelling. It is a doubleness concerning personal and impersonal aspects of life. He starts by fingering our I-feeling or self-feeling, and then contrasts this with something called the "anonymous I." He wants us to get a sense of both our own I-feeling as well as an anonymous part of us. But what is an *anonymous I*?

Generally speaking, it is part of a vast domain we might call "otherness" that includes but is not limited to the unconscious mind. Eigen points out examples from other authors (2018g, pp. 230–6). For instance, Freud's self as both a subjective center of experience, and a system of psychological functions. A kind of reversal between subjective and object points of view. Merleau-Ponty viewing the body as a center of subjectivity, but also noting an awareness of something other than our own will or control that keeps us in life. Freud's id was originally "it" in German, to underline the impersonal aspect of instinctual life. Fairbairn focuses on need and neediness as a form of otherness within us that demands our attention. Jung observed different aspects of the self as if they behaved like centers of subjectivity with their own discrete personalities. For Jung one of the major psychic dramas occurs between ego and the "otherness" of Self. In contemporary relational theory, some refer to otherness as "not me" states.

> Otherness is a principle within and between all psychic dimensions and is constitutive of subjectivity as such. The I on every level is touched by otherness—from its most intimate to its most objectified reaches. "I am I and I am another" echoes unendingly throughout the subject.
>
> (p. 238)

I am and am not my body … I am and am not my mind. Eigen is underlining forms of sameness and difference together. I and not-I together are basic ingredients for how we are built, and also how we grow and continue to be "born." Distinction-union, or sameness and difference, is everywhere part of us.

Let's consider the physical body as an approach to this question of otherness, or not-I. We know our body is a primary part of our being. For some, the body is everything and nothing feels closer. It is our physical reality, full of feeling and sensation, pleasure and pain. We breathe in and out, our heart beats; we digest food, circulate blood. We depend on our body for physical existence, yet strange as it may be to say, our body is not solely our own. There is an impersonal side we do not control. For example, our body can get sick. We can catch a cold or cut a finger, but with care the body returns to health. The otherness of our body does these things by itself. Likewise, we cannot demand or expect our body's energy to be consistent. Physical energy fluctuates higher and lower, faster and slower, often without our consent. Even with our best intentions and care, the body has a mind of its own, so to speak. It has its own rhythms, pulses, ups and downs, few of which we directly control. To what extent can we say that our body is totally our own? And if it is not ours, whose is it? Our body is other because it is partly independent, and we often marvel at its good functioning unless something goes wrong. It's an intimate conjunction—our body as very personal but also impersonal or nonpersonal. There is nothing closer than one's own fleshy feeling, and yet we become more distant or estranged from our body during severe illness.

What about the other side of our being? Is our mind, psyche, or consciousness an "other" to itself? We could apply the same thought experiment we did with body.

Generally speaking, our I-feeling is roughly correlated with our conscious awareness of self and world. It's the place our psyche inhabits, even if this is a placeless place or psychic space. Is our mind only an I-feeling, or is there more to our mind than that? Do we possess our I-feeling or does it possess us? Is there an I-feeling without a relationship to ourselves, without reflexivity? Isn't having an I-feeling part of what we mean by being self-reflective? When we relate to our self, who is doing the relating to whom? How many selves are part of us? Aren't we both an I-feeling as well as unknown to ourselves? It seems so, since if we were totally coincident with our self, if there were no distinctions but only a self-sameness without difference, we would never change or grow. It seems we need an anonymous I as part of our mind-feeling, otherwise it would be impossible to surprise ourselves. There would be no possibility of something new arising. Instead, we are a complex intertwined mix of both union and difference, separate and unified. The poet Rimbaud wrote, "I am another," and Walt Whitman said, "I am multitudes" (Eigen, 2018g, p. 228). We are both separate and together as dialogic beings, even when silent, even while asleep. Perhaps an anonymous I brings us our dreams?

How can sameness include difference? To paraphrase Eigen's use of Heidegger, identity itself requires a relational aspect; sameness implies the relation of "with" ... that is, sameness requires a mediation, a connection. Mediation within identity includes moments of distinction or difference, and Heidegger (1969) refers to this mediation as an abyss or a wellspring in which both humankind and *being* appropriate and deepen one another (2018g, p. 228).

Our I-feeling can also vanish when there is no separate awareness of self. Artists and writers speak of becoming so engaged in their work that their sense of self disappears in "focused *un*awareness," during creative flow. The ego or self gets eclipsed. In creative moments we lose awareness of self when it becomes solely a portal or conduit for what runs through it.

Even our perception of time tells us we are not a static sameness, as when we say, "I was different back then, compared to who I am now." We are both the same and different at any given moment. We are always going beyond ourselves and never quite catching up. Our conscious I-feeling leaps ahead to plan the future and looks back to consider the past. And unlike the psychotic subject, we take all this for granted.

The psychotic mind can create distortion as well as be victimized by it. But if we remain at the level of play, creative distortion can be fun, and exaggeration can be entertaining.

Eigen tells us that true reversibility involves the *play* of doubleness, which is lost in psychosis. The play of doubleness is fluid without being slippery, grounded without being stuck. Healthy forms of reversibility allow for rhythmic swinging back and forth—a reversibility that can hold its ground as well as move freely according to circumstance.

Some of Freud's reversible polarities included active-passive, sadism-masochism, voyeurism-exhibitionism. One of Jung's themes involved compensation for one-sided attitudes. Jung's emphasis on spirit and psyche could be thought of as compensatory to Freud's emphasis on instinct and drives. Bion gave examples of how psychospiritual and material reality can reverse: a psychotic subject may try to treat everything animate as inanimate, and vice versa (Eigen, 2018g, p. 244).

> Again, it is not the ability to reverse per se, but rather the network of attitudes that provides a context for such work that is crucial. Reversals are freeing and/or imprisoning, depending on a variety of conditions. An individual may spin out of existence when caught up in constant, high-speed reversals or come to a standstill if the reversal is too slow. In either case, as suggested in earlier chapters (1, 2, 3, and 5) self-world obliteration occurs. On the other hand, the subject's ability to persist in reversing experiences into their opposite can finally break through a sense of constriction and open new worlds.
>
> (p. 246)

Rapid swings of reversal, oscillations resulting in indecision are seen in Carl's case—an ambivalence on steroids. So too with some hospitalized patients I've worked with who could not make up their mind about anything. They went back and forth indecisively, as if in silent or not-so-silent war with themselves. A frozen spinning state of reversal that leaves one confused, exhausted, and unable to function.

Eigen writes psychologically about airiness and heaviness, spacious freedom and engulfment, the unanchored spirit world and the anchored material world.

Look again at Carl who appears quite ungrounded. He sees through solid objects and melts or dissolves them with his mind. He defies the physical universe, trying to exert power over the moon and bring it down from the sky, refusing to comply with dictates of material reality. But he also falls in love with trees and finds containment in the texture of tree bark. Carl uses the texture of bark to stay grounded. When Jane came to realize she was confusing food with air, she let go of heavy material substance to the extent that she could breathe air more easily again.

The presence of absence, acceptance of empty space, openness to the unknown without expectation, allowance for unknowing, foreclosing on the need for certainty that forecloses on itself, as well as holding lightly, provisionally, and waiting—these all have in common diminished needs for control along with curiosity for what arises next. The psychotic mind appears unable to tolerate such things.

Our needs and neediness also act as impersonal "others." They are forces that demand we meet them.

> Nothing is closer to the I than its neediness, yet nothing is more impersonal and obliterating. Need runs roughshod over the I, yet enlivens it. It can flood and drown the I, but the latter is flat and dull without it. ... The I is personal-impersonal through and through.
>
> (Eigen, 2018g, p. 233)

Comments and Responses

Comment 1: I was intrigued by this, on page 210 where Eigen (2018g) says: "Many patients benefit by having their self-hate respected." That feels like a kind of reversal too, and really fascinating. Because in general, the therapist's response might be to try to soothe that person or say, "You don't *really* hate yourself to the degree you think." I think to respect someone's self-hate is similar to Eigen *leaning into* hate, as opposed to resisting against it or only seeing self-hate as negative. I've been much more conscious with my clients to be able to respect what they're feeling— where they're actually at.

Response 1: Over the years I've gravitated more and more toward staying with my patients wherever they're at, trying to receive whatever they're feeling and not try to change it. That's part of co-union and being with. It doesn't mean one cannot also offer growth challenges and different ways of viewing things. Something fruitful happens when we can become resonant with what the patient brings in, especially when painful. And when we don't or can't do that, it might be a signal about our own resistance or anxiety.

Commentary #10

Schreber and Rena

In this chapter Eigen details two case examples of psychosis. The first is Daniel Paul Schreber, a famous case Freud wrote about. The second is a woman named Rena, one of Eigen's patients. Each of these clinical studies is filtered through Eigen's core components or "psychotic operations." Rena's case includes some session notes, and both she and Schreber are put side by side to show areas of similarity and contrast in their psychotic landscape.

To be clear, there is no getting to the bottom of things with these two case studies. There is no absolute or correct or final perspective from which to view and describe them. We will neither cover everything nor solve the problem of Rena's and Schreber's psychoses, but instead survey the field of their dynamics to find areas of emphasis worth noting, looking for whether and where we might find growth possibilities in their personalities.

To begin, here's a little overview to summarize some of the similarities and differences between Schreber and Rena. I refer the reader to the section in this chapter titled the "Kernel of Psychosis" (2018g, p. 282). There, Eigen writes:

> It is difficult and perhaps unfair to compare Schreber and Rena, but it is a useful exercise. Both are concerned with what it means to be embodied, the difficulties of being one sex or the other, and the role of embodied being in transcendent vision. One difference is that Rena came to know that she was concerned with constituting a viable relationship to body experience. Therapy was a frame of reference that let her consciously use her psychosis to constitute a fuller sense of self. Schreber, too, got to a larger sense of self. However, a basic split between everyday life and his cosmic vision remained.
>
> Rena was born at a time when there are therapists at home in conversing with madness. Schreber's doctors never ceased to view his productions as alien, however fascinating. Schreber learned to circumscribe his vision and keep it neatly packeted. It was his private affair. On a deep level, it united him with humankind and the cosmos. But on the plane of daily living, it made him freakish and he had to guard against its intrusion. In

DOI: 10.4324/9781003257554-12

the end, this split did not work. He succumbed and ended his days in an institution.

Rena could allow her "inner life" to pass through another subject. Her thoughts and feelings intermixed with mine for better or worse. A gap remained between us, a distance she often experienced as mean. But in her case, the distance was felt acutely because intimacy was also possible. In time, a more difficult, but psychically sophisticated appreciation grew of just how profoundly intertwined distance and intimacy can be. For her, the cosmic reality and the everyday reality became ever more closely connected ...

In part, Schreber's sense of freakishness was centered on his becoming a woman, whereas Rena's involved her masculinity. The image of being a freak was Rena's rather than Schreber's. She could live out her sense of freakishness and be a penis person with me and her friends. In the end, Schreber could be a savior for no one. Each had to seek salvation through becoming the other sex. But Rena could find a cultural and therapeutic ideology that took her imagery metaphorically. Schreber never ceased taking his imagery literally. No one showed him how to do it otherwise. He lived out his femininity with people who did not fully appreciate it and ultimately it could not support him.

(pp. 282–3)

I want to draw attention to the difference between metaphorical thinking and literal or concrete thinking. It is a crucial distinction. Even today, metaphorical thinking remains undervalued as an important capacity. *Metaphorical thinking* is partly an ability to link or connect two things into an "as if" reality, even though they do not logically go together. When we say that someone has a heart of gold or nerves of steel, we don't mean these literally; we mean them figuratively or metaphorically.

Here in the United States, *literal* interpretations of religious texts and the US constitution are often the most conservative ones, allied with fundamentalist views of different kinds. There are also scientists who object to metaphor, who only give value to what is concrete, precise, and "factual." In the so-called hard sciences this is useful because the reality in question is measurable, observable, and repeatable. But this is not possible with human emotions, values, or meaning. Our minds and psyches do not lend themselves to the same methods of inquiry as physical reality. Moreover, if science wants to investigate consciousness, it must do so *using* consciousness, resulting in an unavoidable circle.

With metaphor, one might think of Eigen referencing Bion's notion of "being murdered into life." Although we feel the impact of this statement, we also need a metaphorical lens to make sense of it. Clearly it is not literal murder he is talking about. Concrete physical murder is absolute and final, and like "the end of the world," it is something that literally happens only once. But in a metaphorical sense, emotional and psychic murder are real in their own way. When such injuries happen repeatedly there is damage to well-being when not part of a rhythm of growth. Psychological and emotional murder occur with different names and labels—like when we feel shamed by an authority figure, or rejected and shunned by someone we love, or are not seen accurately by parents or important others. Both Rena and Schreber suffered from forms of psychological and emotional murder, leading them into psychotic terrain.

In both these clinical cases, we find opposites split apart, rigidly bifurcated, and fighting with each other. At times these forces are violently opposed or confused, leading to reversals. Today we might label Schreber manic-depressive or bipolar, although Eigen does not rely on such labels to describe the course and content of Schreber's illness.

Both Schreber and Rena displayed alternating genders and sexual preferences, along with wishes for gender transformation, whether literal or metaphorical. It is interesting to speculate whether Schreber or Rena would become transsexually identified today and feel more in sync with our era.

Schreber and Rena did display common bipolar symptoms: they exhibited extreme swings of mood, sexual and religious imagery and preoccupation, excitability and nervousness ... and to a greater extent for Schreber, grandiosity. One wonders if he also exhibited pressured speech and went without sleep during his manic phases. Eigen imagines him as "always busy," and says of Rena that her restless rotation of imagery kept her confused, but alive. In our contemporary materialist culture, where physical reality is given preference, we use a diagnostic system whose roots are based on a medical model, rather than a fuller range of interpersonal and emotional dynamics. The medical model is most concerned with describing behavioral "symptom clusters" that chemical treatments are used to address. Yet this is only one part of the picture, and we may miss what an individual psyche is trying to tell us. By addressing only behavior and brain chemistry from the physical side of life, we find ourselves very far from the kind of synthetic and humane understanding in case presentations from Freud, or the extended care and unique attention to transformations of personality that Eigen offers with his patient Rena.

Schreber, of course, did not have psychotherapy or psychoanalysis in his day, nor anyone versed in understanding psychotic processes to help mediate, or offer context and explanation, for what he was going through. Fortunately, Rena did have this with Eigen, and they worked together for about seven years. For Rena, the split between her cosmic visions of psychotic confusion and her everyday reality could eventually link evermore closely together, partly from working with a therapist who could hold both realities, but also one who would challenge her thinking as the moment might call for.

Having someone to rely on as a therapeutic container and agent in the midst of confusion and agitation makes a big difference, and we see a profound contrast between the care Schreber received from his first doctor, Dr. Flechsig, and his second doctor, Dr. Weber. It seems as though Dr. Weber's fondness and respect for Schreber, shown by inviting him to family dinners and being interested in his ideas, provided an atmosphere that was therapeutic—one that was benign, supportive, and inclusive. Today, of course, we would not invite our patients from the hospital home for dinner, as that would run afoul of our ethical codes and practice standards.

But in Schreber's time, sympathetic communion helped him feel wanted and valued—something he did not feel from his own father. Schreber began to write his memoirs during his second breakdown, and we read he fought with Dr. Weber legally to be released from the asylum. Both of these aspects, writing and fighting, can be therapeutic in their own way. Writing was a way of documenting and objectifying what Schreber was going through by putting it to paper. Arguing with Dr. Weber and the courts for his legal freedom was a way of asserting and testing the soundness of his own mind. Eigen hints that this latter aspect could be a variant of Winnicott's "use of object" formulation, where one's anger and fighting spirit are accepted and contained well enough to facilitate forms of growth. How many times in our own therapeutic work have we seen positive results when, with good enough containment, anger is allowed expression, acceptance, and acknowledgement by both parties, rather than being acted out, exploited, or repressed.

These two complex patients were caught between different extremes. Eigen tells us that both Rena and Schreber struggled with embodied and disembodied experience, sexuality and aggression, separation and merger, order and chaos, internal bombardment and fragmentation, as well as states that felt more benign and controllable, if not integrative; and sometimes... even ecstatic. Rena was said to use excitement defensively at times, but this also allowed her a feeling of aliveness. Such double-sided examples remind us to be cautious when seeing anything one-dimensionally, or from only one perspective.

It is tempting to delve into aspects of Rena's and Schreber's uses of hallucination, mindlessness, boundary issues, hate, epistemology and reversal, but we cannot do justice to them all. However, Eigen does this within his section headings, providing detailed descriptions. We will only touch on a couple of these for their interesting dynamics. One such dynamic involves Rena's progress discovering her body in new ways with Rolfing, while also feeling freakish and, in her words, "like a penis person."

One of the things Freud has been castigated for, and perhaps castrated for, as feminism has thankfully taken root and continues to blossom, is his concept of penis envy. I'd like to say a word about this, not only as someone who happens to have male anatomy, but also as one who grew up feeling like a small skinny boy with a girl's name.

One can view the penis controversy as a metaphor for power relations in general, not simply concrete physical anatomy. It is all too easy to fuse and confuse the literal with the metaphorical. But just as the Oedipal conflict is not literally about killing one's father or mother, and instead about ways of superseding or going beyond one's parents while negotiating guilt and triangles, so too we might think of active agency and personal empowerment as metaphorically expressing something "phallic." In an analogous way, I see breast envy and birth envy as expressing generative and life-giving abundance—what one might call an "ovarian" model and dynamic. Here we confront a different kind of doubleness, where metaphor gets based on literal and psychical gets based on what's concrete and physical. But rather than splitting into polarized realities and fighting over literalness, here's a complex example with Rena.

Eigen wanted to help Rena experience her own sense of active might and power, and as she began to do so over time, we are told that Rena paradoxically became more open, softer, and more tolerant of her own annihilation anxiety. Eigen offers an extended assessment of this complexity in light of Rena's situation vis à vis male ideology and culture (see 2018g, pp. 285–6).

Schreber was also wounded at the hands of an abusive father, one who had social status and esteem, but who treated his son very badly. Partly from this trauma, Schreber felt himself in battles with God. He felt himself the center of a hostile universe in which all the efforts of demonic forces and others were directed against him. However, believing one is the chosen target of a hostile universe is just as grandiose as believing one must be savior of the entire world. There is megalomania in both paranoia and narcissism. The turning point between Schreber's world of hostility and greater harmony came during a gap, a pause or caesura, during which Schreber died out or blacked out and, in a sense, was reborn. When he resurfaced and came to, Eigen says that Schreber was still megalomaniac, but now in a positive key rather than a hostile one. There is speculation as to why this change of valence occurred, including Schreber's change of doctor. It appears that the shift from hating to loving delusions came during his second breakdown, when Schreber's doctor changed from Flechsig to Weber. Importantly, Dr. Weber was someone who liked Schreber, respected him, and took a genuine interest in him. This may have allowed a different framework and atmosphere to develop whereby Schreber could experience his psychosis in more positive, harmonious, even ecstatic ways, rather than as negative, hostile, or frightening.

Dr. Weber, unlike Dr. Flechsig, was felt to be a stable, positive mediator, one who today we might call a "good object." Weber took an active interest in Schreber and helped him through a period of recovery. But Schreber's fixed delusions, even though positive, continued to be grandiose, leaving him vulnerable to another relapse after his wife became hospitalized. Today we might think in terms of attachment issues marking the difference, as Schreber seemed to decompensate with his loss of secure attachments, but for a time he was helped by both his wife's and Dr. Weber's caring influence. Both Schreber's writing and his relational bonds were therapeutic, but insufficient to produce a lasting sense of stability. With psychotic processes, Eigen tells us that primordial, originary, cosmic experiences of psyche must be worked through with a real flesh and blood person, one who not only supports and contains, but also provides realistic barriers and challenges to one's delusional confusions.

One important contrast between Schreber and Rena has to do with a difference in their rhythmic aspect of falling apart and coming back together. Schreber underwent one major reversal that we might call a death and rebirth sequence. But Rena had the good fortune of experiencing *many* of these sequences in her therapy. In Eigen's therapeutic worldview, psychical death and rebirth is not a one-time occurrence but an ongoing rhythm of emotional life. We die inside ourselves when we are psychically injured, emotionally murdered, or shamed, and yet with help and understanding from a friend or psychotherapy, we also recover. We can learn to survive ourselves and others and come through, and this rhythm of destruction and re-creation is a model for building resilience and increased capacity. Dying and coming back does not have to be as dramatic as Schreber's. We routinely "die" each night when we surrender to sleep and unconsciousness, and then we "come back" when we wake in the morning with a sense of renewal. Likewise in our physical body, cells are dying and being born continuously, an ongoing rhythm of micro death and rebirth. It is similar with the travail of emotional life if we can learn to tolerate the rhythms.

Eigen highlights this rhythmic difference between Schreber and Rena.

> A major difference between Schreber's and Rena's paths was that Schreber's vision did not allow for falling apart as an ongoing condition of change. He and the world fell apart, died, and came together. ... However, rebirth was taken as a final state, an achievement that, in principle, could and must be absolute. In therapy, Rena learned that falling apart was a constant part of growth processes. The life of the self thrives on falling apart over and over again. Rena took falling apart as a necessary part of her path and not something to be transcended, bypassed, or overcome once and for all.
>
> (2018g, pp. 299–300)

Having come through this chapter, we have a sense of what Bion may have meant by his notion of being "murdered into life."

Comments and Responses

Comment 1: I wanted to comment on destruction and re-creation, death and rebirth. Our political situation now is being destroyed in the US, and we are going through some catastrophic change, as Bion would refer to it. Hopefully we'll get to the other side, and we can re-create a different society, or a different democracy.

Response 1: That's my hope and wish too. At the moment it does feel like a death. Thank you for bringing this up. Many people feel ongoing trauma around the world. Not just psychically and emotionally, but on so many levels—politically, spiritually, interpersonally, and in daily life. The polarization and splitting feels awful and seems to be increasing. Eigen and Aner Govrin engaged in a video conversation a couple of months ago (in April 2020) about ways we might get through this pandemic together. Eigen responds to many of the issues we're struggling with. You can find it on YouTube here: www.youtube.com/watch?v=vRkaj3A4Egk

The Psychotic Self

In this commentary we are considering the chapter titled "The Psychotic Self." Eigen begins by reminding us of a difficult truth: psychosis is a fact of human life. As scary as psychosis may seem, aspects of it are both closer to us than we imagine, but not as frightening as we might believe.

Just the idea of madness is unsettling, something the average person resists knowing or makes jokes about. But looking at the world today, we see lots of madness on both large and small scales. We can easily pick out categories, elements, or "operations" from Eigen's book and apply them to the daily news. For instance, we see hate and fear-based biases, lack of respect for boundaries, mindlessness as a means of escaping emotional pain, hallucinatory wishes for idealized solutions, and all sorts of minimizing and exaggerating—to an extreme of even fabricating what is true or real. There's increasing *intolerance* for diversity of viewpoints or simply listening to one another. Such attitudes are the opposite of those found in psychotherapy, where we lean in to listen carefully (with full care) to the entire spectrum of a person's mind, heart, and soul.

Let's remember that each of us is never very far from experiencing a transient psychotic episode. All it takes is three or four degrees of fever, and we can become delirious. If we go without sleep for just a day or two, we begin to feel a sense of unreality, fragmentation, and disequilibrium. If we happen to get a little food poisoning or the wrong drug, we can experience hallucinations and paranoia.

Although we're never very far from psychotic experience, to some extent we're also protected. We're protected by our ability to test reality around us, check ourselves, question our perceptions, take a second look, and weigh alternatives. We also get protection from the nighttime rest our minds receive from sleep and dreaming.

The phrase "balanced judgment" is itself a sign of sanity. It means being open to comparing alternatives and using discernment, rather than prejudging and presupposing.

DOI: 10.4324/9781003257554-13

I like Eigen's term psychotic "operations" because it is less all-encompassing and absolute. It discerns dynamics and elements of madness rather than lumping everything together. Operations depict our ways of perceiving and misperceiving, distorting and exaggerating reality. As we've seen, something as commonplace as idealizing can be inspiring yet also create distortions and exaggerations similar to delusion. We've learned from past chapters and commentaries about connections between wish, idealization, hallucination, and delusion. But I also want to underline dreaming as a positive instance of hallucination. Dreams may be psychotic, but they are important for psyche's ability to process feeling life. Dreams can mirror our mad selves as well as search for antidotes, and there are many ways dreams and reality converge and comment on one another. Optimally, dreaming and reality take each other forward—a back and forth or dialectic of dreaming and daily experience that offer mutual nourishment from conscious and unconscious exchange.

In the first part of his chapter, Eigen divides the psychotic self into a *corrupt body self* and a *corrupt mental self*. He also brings together *omnipotence* and *omniscience* as parallel psychotic delusions that express power wishes, offering clinical examples using omnipotence with physical bodies and omniscience with invisible minds.

We could substitute the word *corrupt* with other words, like *warped*, *skewed*, or *twisted*, but more simply it's about exaggerated distortions as hallmarks of psychotic thinking. In today's digital world we speak of corrupted files, discs, and downloads. Another meaning of corruption is associated with power, greed, and unethical behavior.

Omniscience and *omnipotence* reveal themselves as psychotic distortions. We have Carl's dreams of the fat man and mafia boss as forms of physical excess, representations of omnipotent greed and power. We also have the character of Dr. Omnis, an omniscient know-it-all who learns the importance of tolerating both emotional pain and the pain of not knowing as essential capacities for psychic growth. We read first about how Carl relates to the fat man and mafia boss and the uses he makes of these dream figures in therapy. We watch their transformations and Carl's ability to gain distance and perspective. We also read of Eigen's supervision using dreams from Dr. Omnis's patients.

Corrupt body self figures are often caught up in dramas revolving around a delusion of or a wish for omnipotence. Corruption of the mental self hinges more on a sense of omniscience. Omniscience refers to limitless mental power, whereas omnipotence refers to limitless physical power. Colloquial speech distinguishes between the know-it-all and the bully, between brains and brawn. Many fables suggest that the self must face dual tendencies in extreme forms, as expressed by such figures as the Magus-Magician and stupid, fearsome monsters. The Old Testament God condenses omniscience and omnipotence in ways that at times make

Him seem like a big baby. Omniscience and omnipotence can be seen, in part, as two aspects of infantile narcissism, one emphasizing mental, the other physical reality. In psychosis, the spread of either can be horrifying, but the work of omniscience is finally more dreadful.

(2018g, p. 320)

By "spread" Eigen means proliferation of distortion, but why is omniscience more dreadful? On an individual level, a physical bully can dominate only so long as no one else is stronger. Physicality has its limits, and sooner or later belief in one's omnipotent superiority can be toppled and fail. However, belief that one is all-knowing is more difficult to see or correct because thoughts and beliefs are invisible. Omniscience insulates itself by not attending to experiences that might falsify it. Current examples include the many "echo chambers" of social media.

It is difficult to overestimate the role omniscience plays in deadening one's capacity to experience. If one knows what is going to happen ahead of time, one does not have to experience it. The individual scarcely realizes he is inured in omniscience. In effect, he lives from omniscience without knowing it ... the details he experiences, which might make a difference, are glossed over. ... Everything is evaluated in terms of his omniscient frame of reference.

(Eigen, 2018g, p. 320)

In more normal situations, our experiencing and accrued knowledge work together, they correct and modify one another, and their ability to offset one another can be nourishing. But when we lack such attitudes, or believe we already know and are certain of everything, then it's easy to become smug and indifferent to other views, and this makes for a certain obliviousness. When these aspects combine with positions of power, omniscience becomes dangerous:

... an omniscience-inflated subject fills himself with a sense of infinite privilege and foists his personality on others instead of suffering limits in the struggle to know. Exacting privilege through assertion of omniscience seems to be a peculiarly human mode of achieving power. It is a subtle form of madness that is widespread and it takes on arrestingly florid forms in overt psychosis.

(2018g, p. 321)

We see such attitudes today, whether in corporate and finance sectors, or in heads of state around the world.

In psychotherapy there is always a balance between what we know and what we don't, between knowing and not knowing. Eigen gives an extended clinical example in his supervision of Dr. Omnis, whose overuse of pretending to know caused harm to himself and others. Dr. Omnis needed his omniscience to keep his sense of self intact, but this broke down by negatively affecting his personal life as well as the lives of his patients. Dr. Omnis became aware that his need to cover up his patients' wounds was related to his need to blunt his own pain. Luckily, he sought supervision to sort out why such things were happening.

Eigen treats us to a few anecdotes related to Dr. Omnis's patients' dreams that highlight how those patients viewed him. For instance, the playful seal could solve problems that the wise old owl could not, and a female patient dreamt that a blind woman could now see. Having to know everything had made the person blind and, correlatively, not having to know everything allowed her to see. These dream snapshots underline how unconscious communication between patient and therapist can sometimes reverberate and intertwine. A more extended analysis of Ms. Ferva's dream about the mouse, pond, and snakes offers a wonderful example of initial collusion between patient and therapist—here related to the triumph of the mouse, at least until prompted by Eigen to consider other alternatives. Because dreams are multiply determined and have more than one possible meaning, Ms. Ferva's mouse and snake dream was beneficially reworked by Eigen to offer other views.

For example, it turns out the dream mouse was not as powerful as believed by Ms. Ferva, in spite of the mouse having a fleeting sense of triumph in making the snakes disappear. The snakes themselves were not simply or only a representation of something evil. Eigen proposes that their numbers might signify intensity, and the snake image might reflect unconscious wisdom. We are reminded once again that our little ego does not and should not dominate or preempt unconscious offerings. Perhaps most important is the lesson that when our ego dismisses, demeans, tries to control, or has a hostile attitude toward unconscious life, hostility can reverse itself and turn to poisoning one's conscious attitude.

Attitudinal relations between conscious and unconscious realms remind me of the late James Grotstein who, as Eigen recalls, opined that the id needs protection from the ego (2016, p. 97). More generally, the unconscious needs protection from the conscious ego. Why? Freud felt the id needed to be reined in and channeled by the ego. Grotstein's idea is that our conscious ego tends to dominate psychic life by thinking it knows best (2000, 2007). With such an attitude, lesser value and respect are given to unconscious promptings and their potential wisdom. I say "potential" wisdom because not everything coming from the depths is necessarily wise. Capacities for conscious discernment and judgment are important. Like the dialectic between experiencing and knowing, exchanges between conscious and unconscious realms can, when working well, help further development and growth. By contrast, an aggressive "usurping" by either conscious or unconscious domains can lead to a one-sidedness that spells disaster. "A symbiotic relation between different capacities is different from a pillaging model: interweaving rather than plunder ..."(Eigen, 2016, p. 99).

Dr. Omnis brings up a dilemma we face in clinical practice. How do we use knowledge side by side with spaciousness of the unknown to help our clients, and what's a proper balance between knowing and not knowing? Perhaps it goes without saying that this will be different with each client and contextually dependent in the moment. Too much "knowing" from the therapist can feel suffocating, just as too little can feel abandoning.

We saw one variation on this theme at the end of the last chapter, when Rena learned by trial and error over seven years that always running toward the light, with its associated excitement and sexuality, did not do away with dark feelings. Her dark womb of depression and feelings of suffocation were difficult to work with even when they could be brought to consciousness and explored for growth prospects. Patients grow trust from feeling support and safety in order to risk examining unknown or distasteful parts of the self.

Dr. Omnis's avoidance of his and his patients' emotional pain meant that he needed to grow more capacity for accepting and tolerating a fuller range of negative feelings. But when we first meet him, Dr. Omnis's pretensions of knowing had caused harm. Eigen underlines how our sense of "knowing" is such an implicit part of our experience that knowledge itself can become a refuge and anesthetic. Omniscience can even become its own content, infinitized, and take on an invisible life if its own.

> Knowing and not knowing are so finely interwoven that together they constitute an essential characteristic of our capacity to experience ...
>
> It is a paradoxical and essential characteristic of our beings that knowing and unknowing can be imbued with a sense of infinity. Almost any important area of experience can be infinitized ...
>
> The sense of convergence of knowing and unknowing, together with a sense of infinity, is possible, in part, because experiencing as such is intangible and ineffable. We cannot locate a thought as we do the brain. However much we associate emotions and centers of consciousness with the body, or read a soul in a face or a gesture, something invisible remains. This may be summarized in the adage that consciousness sees and hears, but cannot be seen or heard, at least the way spatially localizable events can. The basic invisibility of experiencing contributes to a sense of boundlessness that tinges our existence.
>
> (2018g, pp. 328–9)

Unintegration

Most people are familiar with terms like *disintegration* and *integration*. We find these in psychopathology and mental health books as well as in common vernacular. Integration is sometimes thought to be a gold standard for good psychic functioning. However, we should be careful not to infinitize the goodness of integration without also looking at how it is used. First off, integration is never a final state or absolute resting place. It is similar to the ideal of wholeness or completeness, which, if we're lucky, can be a momentary blissful experience before life throws more in front of us that needs assimilating. All gestalts or "wholes" can be viewed as in process and fluid. They are qualified and incomplete with regard to future moments, and usually open to more development, if omniscience doesn't dominate. Moments of feeling whole or complete are valuable in themselves, and they are also waystations or rest stops along the road of experiential life.

Winnicott speaks of disintegration as a form of breakdown, a kind of splintering or fragmentation in which the center does not hold. By contrast, integration is a coming together, a unity. One root of the word *integral* is being whole or complete in itself.

We have integration as a coming together and disintegration as a falling to pieces. On one end of the spectrum integration is a union of wholeness, and at the other end a splitting into fragments. But there's another realm in between these two polarities of union and distinction, wholeness and fragmentation, and Winnicott calls this other state or realm or process "unintegration." Unintegration is "middle ground" so to speak, because it is neither of the two extremes but draws something from each. Eigen writes: "Unintegration refers to the chaos of experiencing before it congeals into psychic formations that can be used defensively" (2018g, p. 334). But defensive use of any tendency or capacity is only one possibility.

Unintegration is also called *creative formlessness* by Eigen, and creative play is another term Winnicott uses. In fact, Winnicott (1953) says that formlessness, play, and a state of unintegration are part of a nexus of related experiences that reinforce and enrich each other. To amplify Eigen's examples, we might think of reverie, purposeless musings, and daydreaming... or just sitting quietly for a time, observing one's thoughts and feelings. Perhaps contemplative prayer is one form of unintegration. Part of what these have in common is space for not knowing, a relaxation of ego control, openness to what arises, with no predetermining what might come next. Eigen says that "In a state of unintegration, one does not know or think one knows what will happen next. One is not closed off from oneself" (2018g, p. 335).

In our nighttime dreams we give up ego control to another kind of mind or intelligence. During sleep, the ego cannot manipulate psychic life at will, although abilities for lucid dreaming can help in some situations. For example, we might try to rework a past trauma or recurring nightmare by lucidly dreaming a different sequence or ending.

But there is also something underneath dreaming that gives rise to dreams. What could it be, this "something beneath dreaming" that gives rise to dream life? We don't know ... Perhaps a fertile form of otherness? Pregnant void? In another book Eigen writes:

> We sleep not only to dream, but to allow contact with places dreaming cannot reach, that reach toward dreaming ... sleep enables experience outside the reach of waking and dreaming to move towards dreaming's reach ...
>
> Shall we call this a wordless, imageless unconscious, a portal through which our lives are fed impalpably and ineffably by experience that accesses us in dreamless sleep? As though god or nature or evolution has safeguarded something from our use of it, a special form of contact that we cannot ruin with our controlling narratives, or our lust for power, or our fears ... which gains access to us when our ordinary focus and selective attention, even the foci of our dreams, are out of play ...
>
> (2014, p. 2)

Winnicott connects the aliveness of dreaming with unintegration and opposes both to the rote rehearsal of chronic fantasies. In his vision, unintegration leads to dreaming, which works over, enriches, and stimulates vital emotional experiences. Through unintegration, the personality gains a chance to reset or reform itself. In genuine rest and emptiness, images arise that reflect the state of self and redirect the latter's movement. Insofar as a person is addicted to stale, compensatory fantasies, he tends to cut himself off from deeper and more spontaneous urges to reshuffle himself. For most of us, fantasying may be inevitable. Fantasies mark our wounds and hopes. But insofar as they cover the same ground and do not lead anywhere, they function as mirages, even if they finally come true.

Not so the capacity to dream. Dreaming rubs our noses in the realities we hope to escape in fantasy. ... They force us to focus on what we would rather push aside. They teach us that the very fabric of the self includes what antagonizes us. Our dreams give the lie to our pretensions to be in control, no matter what.

(2018g, pp. 335–6)

Comments and Responses

Comment 1: I think it is in *Playing and Reality*—Winnicott gives a case study of a woman with whom he had a three-hour session, and in the end, he says something like: We had three hours to use and to waste. And it made me cry. That's Winnicott giving an example of just letting be. You know, letting "unintegration" happen. We had three hours to use and to waste—which is what they did. They did use them, but they couldn't use them if they couldn't also feel "we can waste them."

Comment 2: I just want to mention a piece from page 333, which really spoke to me about the role of the therapist in terms of play. It's the second paragraph:

> Winnicott stresses the need for the analyst to be receptive. He must lend to the patient an alive and perceptive presence, an atmosphere implicitly rich with psychic nutrients. He, too, must be able to play, to allow spontaneous oscillations between form and formlessness. So often it is the analyst's attitude or mood that determines whether or not a drop into formlessness is possible. A crucial element in creating a facilitating atmosphere is that the analyst not make believe he is omniscient.
>
> (Eigen, 2018g, p. 333)

Comment 3: I've been thinking about omniscience and omnipotence as ways of control. And then I thought about the word *surrender*. There is something about surrender that happens in therapy. Like when someone brings in parts of themselves that are helpless, or not knowing, and how scary that feels. But there is a capacity, I think, that does grow in that process of being able to talk about these aspects of the self that feel so shameful. And, I think, we do live in a culture that really promotes "knowing" and *not* being helpless. You know, not being efficient with time, not being productive … I'm really grateful for this chapter because it gives an antidote to the madness our culture creates around dependence and helpless feelings.

Unintegration, Madness, Suicide, and Epilogue

We've set a good foundation for grasping the many ways psychosis and psychotic operations can show themselves in both illness and health. Eigen's book offers a wide embrace and penetrating understanding of this difficult area humanity grapples with, both individually and collectively.

Part of his wide embrace is found at the beginning of the section titled "Unintegration, Madness, and Suicide" (2018g, p. 336). Eigen uses different words to point toward something unknown and perhaps unknowable, an unknown X that supports our very being. In psychical reality it goes by many names and labels, none of which completely do it justice. "... a feeling permeates us that something goes on beyond what is graspable and that we are its results. The notion of causality, whether magical, theological, poetic, or scientific, has so far not exhausted this informing intuition" (p. 336). To paraphrase the early-twentieth-century physicist Arthur Eddington: something unknown in the universe is doing we know not what.

We've discussed aspects of the known and unknown throughout this book. The psychical side of our being does not behave like the physical side. In physical material reality, causality has a good chance of showing regular effects. But psyche is more fluid and unpredictable in many ways. It has inherent freedom to change and grow through imaginative processes, its plasticity, and open possibility—all cousins of infinity by any other name.

We read about Nikolai Berdyaev (Eigen, 2018g, pp. 336–7), a Russian Christian mystic, who held a view of rebirth through ultimately mysterious processes of being undone and then reborn. This is but one example of death and rebirth archetypes found throughout mythology, religion, and indigenous cultures. Other milder variations on this theme include breakdown and recovery, injury and repair, falling apart and coming together. Metaphorically, the dark night of the soul praying for dawn or the phoenix rising from ashes convey the same idea. Psychotic unraveling and its potential transformation is a deep journey because it involves the entire psyche, not just surface operations such as buttressing the ego or strengthening defenses, important as these can be. Berdyaev, like Winnicott, suggests that transformations,

DOI: 10.4324/9781003257554-14

when they occur, occur through an other, that is, through and with another person. Transformations within psyche or psychosis cannot be localized like medicines that address the physical body alone.

Winnicott elaborates many paradoxical dimensions. He emphasizes an in-between, a fluid field, a *transitional space* (1953) that is not simply unidirectional or causal. Eigen's phrase "I-yet-not-I" tries to capture this sense of paradox in psyche's relation to otherness *within* us, a separation that is, at the same time, a union. In therapy we sometimes speak of unconscious-to-unconscious communication, although no one knows how this happens. I often feel similar mysteries opening through Eigen's use of language, while paradoxically not entirely tied to his words. Eigen conveys it this way as a part of psychotherapy:

> … much of what happens in therapy, often what is most important, is non-verbal—permanently outside the reach of words. This in no way minimizes the use of words. There are people who must storm the gates with words, try to say everything … and words do lead to new aspects of reality. But in most therapeutic work, there is a tone or atmosphere or "feel" in the room that is more important. Words, after all, do not merely involve the exchange of information—they are part of the "exchange" of states of being. There is an "osmotic" aspect to therapy that must not be overlooked.
>
> (2018a, p. 4)

In Chapter 8, Eigen again brings up the term *unintegration*, touching a realm of osmotic influence *inside* the psyche. Unintegration is not simply a benign wellspring of creativity, it also has a negative side.

> Neither dissolution nor rebirth can be used as a criterion for illness or health. Whether in illness or in health, unintegration can be menacing as well as renewing. The psychotic self often lives close to a sense of rebirth. In manic moments, the self feels that all things are possible. In depression, the self feels nothing is possible. … Perhaps an element of health is the ability to work with the moods and visions that are our common lot and allow them to turn into something useful. To speak of reality-testing as the essential function that discriminates the sane from the mad is not enough. … The biblical warning that "thou shalt know them by their fruits" is perhaps as close as we can get to a sane test of who we are.
>
> (2018g, pp. 337–8)

Eigen gives examples. He depicts his personal experience with the suicides of two colleagues in New York City who were considered to be quite sane. He speculates about what motivated these men to kill themselves. One of them he knew moderately well and liked, but he and Eigen had disagreed over the years about the role of "hate" in life. The colleague emphasized love and tended to see hate as defensive, even unreal. Hate was felt to be a defense against vulnerability that needed to be dissolved by contact with a deeper love. Eigen disagreed and said that even if hate was secondary to love, he wanted to give the devil its due. He considers hate to be a real force in its own right, and learning to work with negative feelings and urges in nondestructive ways is part of an evolutionary challenge. In the case of this particular colleague, one implication I ponder is whether short-circuiting hate or treating it condescendingly may have led to greater destruction.

This brings us back to the idea that rigid or fixed attitudes often lie at the heart of mental illness. Eigen cites the dynamics of Ernest Hemingway's hypermasculine identity and Nietzsche's spiritual machismo as two examples. Hemingway was horrified and intolerant of his own physical and mental decline, and Nietzsche was overly attached to his spiritual superman. Neither of them could allow room for aspects they felt to be intolerable, and the combination of rigidity and exaggeration became their undoing.

The poet Sylvia Plath is depicted as caught between creative breakthrough that made use of madness, and her overly constricted "good girl" persona. We're told her letters to her mother oscillated between expressions of hate and her need to be good. Her mother took Plath's hate to be an expression of madness or illness and the good loving girl to be Sylvia's "real self." Everyone, including Plath's psychotherapist, seemed to side with her "sane self" against her outbursts of love and hate. Eigen goes on to pay detailed attention to Plath's conflicts and sufferings, her family dynamics and male-dominated social milieu, her creative amalgams, and finally Plath's increasing self-laceration and shattering that led to her self-destruction.

Yet another example of damage that can come from turning a blind eye to destructive tendencies is the case of Ellen West and Ludwig Binswanger's treatment of her that ended in West's suicide. This is an appalling account of a male "know-it-all therapist" who inserted his existential theories and presumptions in place of kindness, human feeling, and hope. Thank goodness Carl Rogers pops up to comment on Binswanger's failure to value West's life over Binswanger's abstract notions of suicide as some kind of crazy existential self-affirmation. Binswanger was unconscious of the effect his own expression of hopelessness had on West and her parents. There is much damage a hopeless attitude can convey. It ignores whether a more open, tolerant, accepting, and not-knowing attitude can make a difference.

This reminds me of a rebuttal by Bion to someone who asked about treating "terminal cancer" patients. Bion answered sarcastically: "what is this phrase, *terminal* cancer?" He was angered by it. Although death eventually comes for everyone, Bion emphasized this patient was still alive today and *that* is what should matter. Bion objected to the word *terminal* because it conveys hopelessness, even as the patient in front of us remains alive and breathing. Being without hope conveys giving up or giving in. Bion was against terminal anything while life is still living. He asks what we can do right now, what is possible for the patient *now* that might make even a small difference, instead of rubbing hopelessness into an already wounded and suffering soul (Bion, 2008).

Vincent van Gogh was a wounded soul yet what amazing art he produced.

> In few painters has the "dialectic" between the radiance of the capacity to feel and the darkness of oblivion reached such a peak. As he grew closer to making his choice between madness and suicide, his work grew darker. Yet the darkness itself is the more ominous insofar as it glistens with light.
>
> (2018g, p. 343)

Summarizing, Eigen says:

> In the long run ... Plath, Van Gogh, and Hemingway could not find a way to work with the basic rhythm of falling apart—coming together. They struggled against it as if it were a foreign body. They felt it should not be this way and resisted.
>
> (p. 344)

Plath and Van Gogh demonstrate that an individual can simultaneously thrive on and be destroyed by unintegration. This is where "mixtures" become dizzying. Yet mixtures are part of the complexity of our nature: opposing tendencies interwoven and influencing us simultaneously. It may be impossible to get rid of one aspect or another. We read that Van Gogh's self-hate fueled him as well as suffocated him. His creative vision and his self-attacks had something in common, but he fought to keep them separate and increased the split against himself. Plath, we are told, lacked the resources and emotional frame of reference to absorb the realization that what was alien and horrible within her was essential to her creativity. It is precisely such horrific mixtures that lend themselves to the stereotype of the tortured but impassioned artist.

When things work well enough, unintegration can be a resource of creative energy, but creative energy also has its presences and absences. We might think analogously of ancient religious mystics who felt lost and bereft when out of contact with their god, but then reborn again when contact and presence returned.

Eigen turns to Jung for some understanding of what is involved when madness threatens to overwhelm the personality. Whereas Eigen points to a kind of stubborn resistance or rigidity, Jung uses the language of "one-sided" attitudes or approaches, which, when they become infused with hostility, evoke hostility from other parts of psyche.

Jung was interested in what went wrong in the illness of those with creative passion, because Jung himself, as we know from his *Red Book: Liber Novus* (2009) and other writing, struggled with flooding from his own unconscious contents. Jung felt that one danger was the lure and seduction of becoming fascinated with the unconscious, fascinated with creativity itself. The danger was in identifying too closely with an archetype, whereby the ego becomes inflated and grandiose as it usurps the role and energy of archetypal images and their force. Some of you may know of what's called "Jerusalem syndrome" where a person in the Holy Land feels they have become godlike and starts to act erratically. Jung emphasizes that a constricted attitude along with weakness on the part of the ego can make the unconscious dangerous and intrusive.

> But what (Jung) seems to stress above all is a narrow, one-sided, and inflexible attitude of the ego ... which conditions it to be hostile toward psychic reality as a whole. In the end, the ego's hostility is mirrored by and met with hostility throughout the psyche.
>
> (Eigen, 2018g, pp. 345–6)

> The ego is caught in the grip of a relentless rigidity and is bent on sealing itself off. It neither trusts itself nor the psyche as a whole.
>
> (p. 347)

However, Eigen is of the opinion that madness is not only about a weak ego confronted with overwhelming unconscious forces, or a rigid ego unable to meet the chaos of unintegration. Eigen's model, if he has one, tends to view both rigidity, hypersensitivity and passion at work together. Rigidity and hypersensitivity are seen as pervasive throughout psychic structures, both at the unconscious level and in the ego.

"The rigidity that marks psychosis is more than insulation for hypersensitivity. It seems as basic a fact as the sensitivity itself." In this depiction of psychosis, we have an *unharmonious* interlocking of rigidity and fluidity between a dominating, rigid ego and unmodulated creative passion and obsession. Eigen says that our

> Structural restraints and the elusive, fluid responses that work with and through them constitute two basic aspects of our nature. In good functioning, the tension between these aspects of experiencing is productive. In psychosis, it degenerates into warfare or worse.
>
> (2018g, p. 346)

More important than reinforcing superficial ego defenses is a kind of wholesale replenishing and redirecting psychic life, so that the subject can become more receptive to the mystery of experiencing. The unconscious ego matrix must come to act more as a fertile womb or a container capable of sustaining the play of opposites, particularly the plasticity and determination of psychic work.

(p. 347)

Eigen asks how the unconscious might work as a good container for creative unintegration. Is not unintegration, by definition, containerless? Or is creative unintegration possible only because one trusts the containing capacity? He does not have answers to these questions, but they are important ones to ponder.

Here we come to the issue of trust … whether trusting unconscious support, trust in what arises, or trust in the unknown. Are these kinds of trust adequate to provide safe containment so that creative or reparative processes can be utilized? No doubt this varies from one individual to another, but we do know that when psychosis starts to gain momentum, everything and anything can appear threatening, from within and without.

Perhaps a lack of trust is a part of the origin of such rigidity. We know that early trauma can certainly damage trust, and psychosis often seeds itself through emotional trauma. I think of Erik Erikson's (1993) developmental model and his earliest epigenetic stage of "basic trust vs. mistrust" that needs to be negotiated successfully for sound development to take place. The artist trusts formlessness and unintegration as essential for generating creative flow. But in psychosis unintegration can feel as menacing as losing control over one's mind.

"One is terrified of disintegrating forever. One sees and feels annihilation both as impending and ongoing. At the same time, containment and containerlessness are also menacing " (Eigen, 2018g, p. 348). Internally, it feels as though there is no safe place to land. In André Green's (1975) language, psychic space in psychosis tends to feel either too stuffed or too empty, rather than being a *well-ventilated* space. "In psychosis, even a 'good' container may be felt to be a suffocating trap, although to be containerless is to remain unborn and faceless" (p. 348). One cannot bear being pinned down by definition, nor tolerate being lost in the freedom of chaotic fluidity. One fears being dissolved and disappearing on the one hand, or entombed and suffocated on the other. In well-ventilated psychic space, one tries to work with both sides, and, as these become less extreme, they may become increasingly open to modify and offset one another.

The Human Face: a "Containerless Container"

In this section, Eigen compares and contrasts the face and the breast as offering two distinct yet profound modalities of infant experience: the face as a visual merging from whatever distance ... and the breast as physical and tactile, closer than close. In early life it seems we merge with both breast and face, as infants do when they prolong their gaze at the face of mother or caretaker.

Eigen does not want to reduce one to the other, breast or face. He feels that one of the great distortions of psychoanalysis is to reduce the face to the breast, or think that the importance of the face is originally derived from the breast. In his view, the face is just as primary as the breast. They are primordial co-equals, representing simultaneous merger and separateness.

> Personal being is here felt to be distinct, yet to exist fully and mysteriously in a state of union, each pole made possible and fulfilled by the other. ... The feeling of wholeness may initially be rooted in the implicit awareness of self and other giving rise to one another, permeating yet transcending one another—a primary creative act repeated anew at every developmental juncture.
>
> (2018g, p. 349)

One of his conclusions contains a profound implication. If the face has its own equal primacy to our tactile body, then faces provide a crucial psychic reality in their own right, and the early smile of the infant is not simply defensive or manipulative as some have suggested. The profound implication is that we are born with a nonparanoid core. Even better, we are born with an essentially open and nondefensive expression of vibrant delight. Could this smile express a variant of what Eastern lineages refer to as "basic goodness"? A belief that we come into the world with eager delight, open and contactful, merged yet separate? Could this nondefensive and spontaneous smile of life be akin to Zen's "original face"?

The tactile breast-feelings and facial gaze-feelings combine to support the double or multiple rootedness of our developing self-feeling. As we've seen, no single developmental channel or process has primacy, but rather we are a tapestry of many. Freud's early dictum that the ego is "first and foremost a body ego" is modified to include psychical, spiritual, nonverbal, visual components—the primordial face of the other. The visual face conjoined with tactile bodies as co-contributors to development of self.

Eigen's Epilogue revisits important points: Freud's enterprise as an extended meditation on our responses to psychic pain ... the similarity between lying to ourselves and delusion ... and charting ways pleasure tries to substitute for pain. Eigen writes that "We must discriminate between the boundless joy rooted in the depths of our nature and its systematic deployment for the sake of avoiding and falsifying painful realities" (2018g, p. 366). He ends the book with this:

> It is hard to say, but we would not be who we are without madness, anymore than we would be who we are without death. We would be the

poorer without its truths and contradictions. But we must fight to get to a place where the mutual correctiveness of seemingly exclusive viewpoints, worlds, experiential capacities, and strategies is possible. We must keep getting to places where mutual correctiveness can become a way of life. This means not only fidelity to one's own vision, but also fidelity to the impact of the vision of others. We live in a cauldron of seething possibilities. It is doubtful that madness can be eliminated any more than death can. But we can seek an attitude large enough and open enough to encompass it. We can learn from it and treat it as a partner in evolution.

(p. 370)

Comments and Responses

Comment 1: I just wanted to echo others ... I also find myself feeling a lot of gratitude to have this way of meeting together, and that I get to meet people from all over the world that I wouldn't be able to meet if it was only in person. So, I feel gratitude that we are able to do this. And also, I can actually feel the warmth come through—even though it's not in person, I can really feel the love and warmth and presence come through, even with just the video. It comes through in the voice, in the visual, and you know, people leaning in. So, it's very surprising to connect this way, even though it is limiting. A lot can still come through.

Response 1: Yes, even though we can't all meet in person, it's been wonderful. Many thanks to everyone for going on this journey together.

References, Part One

Bagai, R. (2021). Michael Eigen and evolution of psyche. In K. Fuchsman & K. S. Cohen (Eds), *Healing, rebirth, and the work of Michael Eigen: Collected essays on a pioneer in psychoanalysis.* Abingdon, England, & New York, NY: Routledge.

Bion, W. (2008, May 6). Wilfred Bion in Tavistock Clinic [video file]. Retrieved from https://www.youtube.com/watch?v=r68oInRsFEI&app=desktop

Eigen, M. (1986). *The psychotic core.* Lanham, MD: Jason Aronson.

Eigen, M. (1998). *The psychoanalytic mystic.* London, England: Free Association Books.

Eigen, M. (2004). *The sensitive self.* Middleton, CT: Wesleyan University Press.

Eigen, M. (2005). *Emotional storm.* Middleton, CT: Wesleyan University Press.

Eigen, M. (2014). *Faith.* London, England: Karnac Books.

Eigen, M. (2016). *Image, sense, infinities, and everyday life.* London, England: Karnac Books.

Eigen, M. (2018a). *Damaged bonds.* Abingdon, England, & New York, NY: Routledge (original work published in 2001).

Eigen, M. (2018b). *Eigen in Seoul: Volume 1: madness and murder.* Abingdon, England, & New York, NY: Routledge. (Original work published in 2010)

Eigen, M. (2018c). *Feeling matters.* Abingdon, England, & New York, NY: Routledge (original work published in 2007).

Eigen, M. (2018d). *Flames from the unconscious: trauma, madness, and faith.* Abingdon, England, & New York, NY: Routledge (original work published in 2009).

Eigen, M. (2018e). *Kabbalah and psychoanalysis.* Abingdon, England, & New York, NY: Routledge (original work published in 2012).

Eigen, M. (2018f). Life kills, aliveness kills. In *The challenge of being human* (pp. 77–80). Abingdon, England, & New York, NY: Routledge (original work published in *The New Therapist,* no. 76 [2012]. https://www.newtherapist.com/eigen.html.

Eigen, M. (2018g). *The psychotic core.* Abingdon, England, & New York, NY: Routledge.

Erikson, E.H. (1993). *Childhood and society.* New York, NY: W.W. Norton, 1993.

Federn, P. (1952). *Ego psychology and the psychoses.* New York, NY: Basic Books (original work published in 1926).

Freud, S., & Strachey, J. (1962). *The ego and the id.* New York, NY: W.W. Norton & Co.

Green, A. (1996). *On private madness.* London, England: Karnac. Retrieved from https://www.sas.upenn.edu/~cavitch/pdf-library/Green_Dead_Mother.pdf

Green, A. (1975). The analyst, symbolization and absence in the analytic setting. *International Journal of Psycho-Analysis* 56, 1–22.

Green, H. (1964). *I never promised you a rose garden*. New York, NY: Holt, Rinehart & Winston.

Grotstein, J.S. (2000). *Who is the dreamer, who dreams the dream: a study of psychic presences*. New York, NY, & London, England: Analytic Press.

Grotstein, J.S. (2007). *A beam of intense darkness: Wilfred Bion's legacy to psychoanalysis*. London, England: Karnac Books.

Heidegger, M. (1969). *Identity and difference*. New York, NY: Harper & Row, 1969 (original work published in 1957).

Jung, C.G. (2009). *The red book: liber novus*. S. Shamdasani (Ed.). New York, NY: W.W. Norton & Co.

Keats, J. (1818/2002). *Selected letters*. R. Gittings (Ed.). Oxford, England: Oxford University Press.

Milner, M. (1987). *The suppressed madness of sane men: forty-four years of exploring psychoanalysis*. London, England, & New York, NY: Tavistock.

Winnicott, D.W. (1953). Transitional objects and transitional phenomena. *International Journal of Psycho-Analysis* 34, 89–97.

Winnicott, D.W. (1964). Further thoughts on babies as persons. In *The child, the family, and the outside world* (pp. 85–92). Harmondsworth, England: Penguin Books (original work published in 1947).

Winnicott, D.W. (2015). *Human nature*. Abingdon, England: Routledge (work published by Free Association Press, 1988).

Part Two

Commentaries on *Emotional Storm*

Commentary #1

Inside the Storm

I've been living in Portland, Oregon, for about 50 years now, and quite suddenly we've had a number of different storms blossom, with several ongoing simultaneously. We've had unusual Pacific Ocean currents and atmospheric weather, but also psychical and emotional weather eruptions. Murderous storms across the US have led to storms of racial protest and political extremes. We've endured the COVID-19 pandemic storm and economic shutdown storms ... and most recently, there have been forest fire and smoke storms, all occurring over the last few days, weeks, and months. The 13-week seminar on which Part Two is based began in September 2020, as the US presidential election storm gained strength approaching early November and beyond. So many storms carrying intense emotions. I first taught this book four years ago in 2016 during the last US presidential election cycle, but with the pandemic and convenience of online technology, I expanded the reach to those across the globe who wished to enter Eigen's work. I was delighted to have people from many countries, including Ireland, England, Scotland, Turkey, Canada, Germany, Croatia, India, Israel, and Australia, along with many who live all across this not-very-United States of America.

So why have I chosen this book, and why now?

Well, with so many current storms ongoing, I felt a need to offer this book as something of an antidote, perhaps for my own feelings of unreality, after witnessing increasing falsehoods, distortions, polemics, alternative facts, and toxic exaggerations each day in the news. As a countermeasure, I wanted group members to dig into something that feels more real, down to earth, and intimate, and what could be more real and intimate than our emotional life, our lived experience of body, mind and spirit? In this book, Eigen presents us with feeling storms of all kinds, infused with his sincere labor and caring devotion to the field of depth psychotherapy. His writing stimulates and challenges our thinking and feeling, while providing a hospitable shelter where feelings are not thinned out, ignored, made superficial, or commodified, as is pervasive today. Manipulating emotions has become a social, political, and

DOI: 10.4324/9781003257554-16

economic norm. I know Michael Eigen says of himself that he is not a "political person," but what he writes about in this book has social and political relevance across world cultures.

> What we do with emotional storm and what it does with us is an open process. We need to begin to learn how to make room for and work with emotional storm. Hiding or enacting it is not enough. We are challenged to learn more about becoming partners with our capacities, with who we are. Such work will not solve social or global problems, but these problems will not be solved without it.
>
> (2005, pp. 6–7)

If emotional realities are foundational to our constitution as human beings, there is benefit from paying attention to how we maximize or minimize their effects and impact. How are we to cope with our feelings in the midst of powerful storms, inner and outer? How might we engage them in less destructive ways?

> An aim of this book is to help activate, to whatever extent possible, affective potency. An alternative trope is affective digestion. To say that we swell with power in response to emotional impotence is to say that we are plagued with widespread emotional indigestion or are psychically suffocating. Psychic reality is a seemingly unlocalizable chronic irritant. The need for food, education, civil rights seem more tangible. Emotional reality may be more elusive but no less real. How we affect each other, respond to each other and use these responses—what can be more important, more difficult?
>
> (Eigen, 2005, p. 8)

When a society suffers from emotional indigestion, undigested, foul-smelling feelings and actions leak out of pores and orifices. Defensive maneuvers contribute by displacing and evacuating difficult emotions that have not been acknowledged or metabolized. Eigen highlights the importance of attending to these inner realities. He elevates qualities of spirit rather than material solutions. He values the importance of what it *feels like* to be with one another, what it feels like to be alive.

At the end of his introduction, Eigen sets up a contrast and makes a case for the voice of psychotherapy as an alternative to voices of power, money, and insensitivity. He writes about what contributes to better or worse living. He speaks of the difference between material prosperity and the quality of our felt existence, in particular our feeling life, including what is ineffable and attitudinal—all things that color our lived experience.

The importance of power, money and ideology slants our sense of the human. Ambition helps make us strong, gets us places, and I wouldn't minimize its contribution to vitality and well-being. But it also leaves us truncated, suspicious, resentful, angry, ready for battle.

(2005, p. 14)

Quality of life includes emotional quality, personal quality, quality of character. Materiality is judged in terms of what it adds or takes away from the quality of felt existence, the good we put it to.

(p. 15)

Throughout Eigen's book we'll read about different emotions and attitudes of spirit that are at war with one another. We see them writ large in the news each day but often don't realize they reflect intense inner dynamics having no good place to go. We'll explore what it's like to work from within the heart of storms, including many clinical cases and dreams. And just as D.W. Winnicott talked about reaching toward aspects of our mad or traumatized self as being paradoxically grounding and potentially healing, I find something similar happens when I read *Emotional Storm*. By going into the heart of storms with Eigen as guide, I have felt more grounded and resilient.

We learn from psychoanalysis that emotional storm does not just shatter; it spreads through experience, often unnoticed or misnamed. Sometimes outside storms are created, not simply in place of or to express inside ones, but because inside ones remain inchoate, beyond grasp, nameless, hungry. Wars and tragic events involving individuals and groups that might have been prevented give name and place to a storm hunger with roots going back at least to birth, if not before. The affective storms of infancy, acute agony or joy, provide a dim background that feeds a need for affective intensity. Individuals are driven to feel more than they can feel and groups they compose make it possible for them to do so.

(2005, p. 6)

Eigen begins the book by connecting inner and outer storms. He uses the word *storm* as an all-encompassing archetypal word, linking many aspects of what strikes, stirs, impacts, triggers, and overwhelms us. Storms incubate inside the feel of intense feelings, if we are able to sense them. Is it possible to grow our psychic and emotional receptors in tandem with greater capability for assimilating and metabolizing storms we feel brewing?

Eigen starts with external storms of the natural world and mirrors these with inner storms of infancy, including screams of birth. Inner and outer storms begin to play off one another imagistically, becoming mirrored in the social atmosphere. Today we have electric atmospheric flashpoints of protest amid the thunder of social grievance. We see political lightning storms amplify and set fire to social memes. Whether we add the power of a newborn's scream or an emotional hurricane, they all point to the meaning of *storm*.

Emotional storm points to a common affective core we all share as human beings. Intensities we observe in nature reflect and refract intensities inside us. We possess an affective core that holds a full spectrum of little storms and big ones: storms of joy, pleasure, thrill, and wonder ... along with storms of grief, rage, trauma, and catastrophe.

In addition to many strong and powerful storms, let's not forget *delicate* storms. What is a delicate storm you might ask? The conjunction of *delicate* and *stormy* might seem odd, even paradoxical. Yet poetry might be one kind of delicate storm. Poetry ... where intensity and feeling, image and metaphor, combine and condense into the art of few words. Words can be delicate but also evocative, landing a powerful punch. Eigen uses lines from Eugenio Montale, an Italian poet and writer, to prepare us for an unusual variety of storms. We are asked to imagine storms of emotion that include rainbows, eyelashes, and swamp eels, along with cyclical storms of death and rebirth. Poetry can certainly evoke feeling storms, but other delicate storms make use of music, color, art, literature, and imagery of all kinds. Any feeling or emotion can be amplified into its own storm. How might we become better stewards of these amazing capacities we have, so that we do not pose greater risks of destroying ourselves and the planet?

We are multifaceted sensuous beings as well as destructive beings, and at times our emotions are too much for us. Eigen is trying to tell us something important that we already know: emotional reality is often more than we can handle. He says it can be difficult to bear even the rise of sensation and feeling evoked by a work of art. How much more so when raw limbic affect gets stirred. How long can we stay with the intensity of feeling life ... and with what quality?

Psychotherapy and depth psychology are languages of intensity and injury, languages of emotional storm, and they contain a catalogue of assaults. Freud began with instinctual assaults from inside and cultural assaults from outside. It is for good reason we have defenses to protect us. We push away and turn off in order to modulate or take in what we can. Feeling our feelings a little at a time is one way to titrate dosage so we're not overwhelmed or flooded. One of Freud's early ideas about trauma involved flooding. As a neurologist, he thought flooding of the nervous system was equivalent to trauma itself. Back then it was sometimes called a "nervous breakdown." Today we might speak in terms of traumatic stress, emotional overwhelm, fight or flight, catecholamines and polyvagal systems. But emotional reality, however we might speak of it, can become unbearable at times. Equally, let's not forget we can also be overwhelmed by beauty, wonder, and awe. Beautiful emotions can overwhelm us too, sometimes bringing tears of joy and gratitude.

Although we'll be approaching difficult storms in this book, we won't ignore the subtle and delicate ones, the storms that move us because we are sensitive beings. Eigen feels we are all permeable beings to one degree or another, and our sensitivities need refuge at times from abrasive toxic storms and atmospheres of electric scalding media.

One of Eigen's great concerns is how we affect each other, including how we nourish and traumatize one another. He says:

> Emotional storm is one dimension of mutual responsiveness or reactivity. … Storm changes values, takes on meaning in different contexts. To parents, baby is a storm. An infant, subject to its own storms, is subject to storms of parents, who bring both bliss and tumult.
>
> (2005, p. 8)

As we will see, demarcations between storms that are somatic, psychic, social, or spiritual begin to fade, and our sensitivity is never far. Eigen says *Emotional Storm* takes forward themes from his previous book *The Sensitive Self* (2004).

Emotional storm and sensitivity go together. We feel impact from both the outside world and our inside world. How could it be otherwise? We would not feel much of anything if we were not sensitive beings, if we were not permeable beings. Someone who is heavily armored and defended against inner and outer worlds of feeling cannot be affected by them very much. More often we are mixtures. We are both permeable and armored, receptive and closed off, tough and tender; we have both sensitive spots and impenetrable ones. We will see lots of mixtures in Eigen's work, and we ourselves are a primordial mixture, composed of mind and body, psyche and soma, spiritual and material substances, all mixed together. Sometimes I wonder if our bodies are the substrate and scaffolding for lots of ineffable currents—forms of powerful electricity running through us, playing with us, and playing havoc with us too.

Eigen proposes that our psychical and emotional realities are among the most difficult parts of our nature to navigate. After all, psyche and body are the closest things to us. He underlines the "ineffable fact that psychic reality itself involves storm systems that require a responsiveness we barely sense but must grow into"(2005, p. 9). How, then, is it possible to grow into such responsiveness? Eigen suggests "a little at a time":

> The impact of reality is far greater than our ability to process it. We can't take too much reality. Our equipment simply is not up to it. If we are lucky, persistent, patient, hungry enough for the real, our equipment grows into the job, building more capacity to work with what is. Nevertheless, we are always behind the impact of the moment, at best able to process crumbs broken off from the whole …
>
> (2004, p. 8)

We are our own storm center. We are caught within our own emotional universe, and there is no objective position to take during moments of impact. We can only try to live with them and through them, trying to process and assimilate impacts as best we can.

Those of you who are psychotherapists or analysts engage each day in a kind of "emotional muscle building practice." Eigen puts the matter succinctly:

> The therapist is not outside the emotional universe. No one is. It is not that the therapist removes herself from the emotional field. It is more that she is more used to working with it from within. It is an illusion to think we get "outside" our emotional life. Even if we are feeling cold or dead, we are gripped by emotion. To be trapped by coldness or deadness is a powerful affective state. To *think* about emotion is not an unemotional business. It is permeated by a feeling perspective and passionate interest.
> Now the truth: no one gets used to working with emotion from within. To work within emotional fields is always more than one can do. More truth: one is never up to the task. Psychically, we are babies trying to coordinate arms and legs before smooth coordination is possible. We flail along in semi-blundering fashion.
>
> (2018c, p. 2)

Eigen has his eye on psychical and emotional growth in psychotherapy and life, but aspects of growth are variable, and slow going. Whether unclotting emotional blockage or catalyzing personality development, such things take time. When it works well enough, positive forces outlast and can grow stronger than self-destructive ones. But it's not necessarily a vertical or hierarchical growth that matters, nor an overarching integration of self, nor even a Jungian individuation, a Freudian oedipal resolution, or a Winnicottian "true self" that is primary—but instead something related to all of these, as when Eigen writes: "Rather than tie up loose ends, therapy pulls some threads that take the patient deeper into life" (2005, p. 12).

What might this mean, to take ourselves or therapy clients deeper into life? This is a path and practice... a practice of opening to experience, growing capacities, developing our "psychic taste buds," tolerating experience, and growing tolerance for ourselves. One paradoxical result of reaching toward storm centers is having a chance to feel more real and alive, less closed off and defended. It takes a certain kind of trust or faith to open ourselves to emotional experience. There is faith involved in allowing the impact of experience to occur at all, and even more faith needed to allow experiencing to develop—without deflecting, turning off, toning down, or turning away. By hanging in there, we practice becoming more familiar with ourselves. Eventually we might even feel safer, more durable and resilient, knowing in a deeper way we can survive the worst and remain intact.

This is not a model of trying to control feelings so much as one of "opening to new fields of experiencing." What is this opening? Wilfred Bion calls it a form of faith. Radical openness to unknown reality and unknown affective experience. In Eigen's words:

> Faith is an open attitude that lets things register. It is not the closed faith of a particular religious dogma, ready to do violence to what is outside it. The faith Bion has in mind is part of the need sensitivity has to taste life, to feel impacts and digest them in ways that lead to more life.
>
> This kind of faith is an attempt not to do violence to experience. An attempt that must fail, perhaps. But the attitude it embodies is significant—a caring, devotion, sincerity, respect, an imaginative loving objectivity, a drive to do life justice, a need to do right by experience. If taken seriously, one possible result of this kind of faith is increased ability to wait on each other, wait for each other—a sensitivity to emotional smell, spirit, affective attitude, a desire to taste each other and our mutual impacts. Waiting, patience, a certain passivity are important in order to let impacts build and unfold: sensitivity grows around them and they stimulate growth of sensitivity. It is a faith that comes back for more, that keeps opening and opening in the face of trauma waves, that registers impacts and learns to work with them.
>
> (2004, pp. 9–10)

Comments and Responses

Comment 1: I think in this book Eigen presents a different point of view, different from the spirit of Western culture. Because in the Western culture, there is encouragement for being rational, and to delay our feelings by drugs, and not to be so over-emotional. I speak about the norm of the Western culture: if you are unbalanced with your emotions, go to the psychiatrist and take drugs, as if "everything has to be rational."

Response 1: Yes, and thus the question: how to be with and work with strong feelings? When people have strong emotions, is it really something wrong or pathological? Instead of quick or promiscuous use of drugs to quell emotions, Eigen conveys the benefits of acknowledging and partnering with feeling life, not pathologizing it. I think of the poet Rumi who writes about being a guesthouse—accepting all the guests, all the visitors, all the emotions, all the feelings. And honoring them whatever they are: sadness, fear, anxiety. Emotions can be a problem, but they're a rich and human problem ... and also a challenge, an evolutionary challenge.

Comment 2: The thing I love about this book and love about Eigen the most is permission to be human, to stumble, to be a centipede. He uses this centipede example: "we've got too many limbs and we stumble over ourselves." I think we do that individually; we are clearly doing that politically, socially. We are just a mess. We are just stumbling. Too many capacities that we can't seem to coordinate. And as therapists, I think our job primarily is to be open to the experience, and to stay open and be curious with clients to help them not *have* to have all the answers. And that's what I really love about Eigen. He just steadfastly has faith in experience itself.

Emotional Storms

Emotional storm is neither health nor pathology—it is part of our birthright. Storms of emotion are part of who we are from the beginning of life, from the moment of birth. Who remembers their very first storm, a birth storm of scream and wail? Perhaps that scream of aliveness continues to this day under many guises and permutations. Can we hear or feel remnants of it? Can screams of aliveness add something to our lives in ways that do not blot us out ... or blow us up? Some screams turn into drive, commitment, dedication, engagement, and caring. Some screams run for cover or get acted out, whereas others become muffled or deadened. Some screams are never felt or acknowledged at all, remaining mute and underground, perhaps frozen.

We could say that emotional storm also comes from our evolutionary history and quest for survival. The fight-or-flight response is one example, paired reactions hardwired into our nervous system expressed in many forms: active and passive, moving toward and away, engagement and isolation, conquering and hiding, murder and escape. As we go along, we'll see other kinds of *doubles* when conjunctions and binaries appear. But not simply either/or binaries. Instead, spectrums and continua of opposites or extremes, ones that interact and form different relationships. Through this kind of relational lens, simple notions of "duality" will begin to dance and take on more complexity.

Eigen mentions that we can confuse physical and emotional storms with one another. For instance, primal fears of *physical* suffocation and starvation can become fused or confused with *emotional* suffocation and starvation. When we aren't able to process intense feelings or are disconnected from them, we risk suffocating and starving *psychically*. Horrific world scenarios arise from failure to do justice to such aspects of our emotional life. Without emotional processing and digestion, we cannot address the situation that brought forth a given storm in the first place.

In this commentary I want to talk a little about babies as one kind of storm, and about Martin Buber and Wilfred Bion, both of whom point to another important storm—namely, storms of interpersonal relationships. Later, I will

DOI: 10.4324/9781003257554-17

touch on Winnicott's *use of object* and Eigen's extension, using a larger frame of reference.

One of the reasons Eigen gives us multiple angles and kaleidoscopic views on topics such as feelings or babies, is because these are not simply one thing. They are not one-sided. Nothing is just one thing. Everything is at least double-sided if not multiply so. We might wish our emotional life to be less complex, but let's consider that complexity and its difficulty—when not too toxic, obscure, or overwhelming—provides food for growth. Complexity and difficulty can help us stretch ourselves. On the other hand, simplification narrows and contracts, often moving toward one-dimensional meaning and perspective. There are times when simplicity can be elegant and true, but it can also be used defensively to constrict reality. Growth of personality requires vulnerability and experiential opening for development to occur.

We know the meaning of whatever we say changes when its context or usage changes. Anything I say can become false or ridiculous from a different angle. The importance of context, and how something functions or is used, makes a big difference. For instance, does a particular emotional storm clear and freshen the air, or feed anger and revenge? Emotional life is neither simple nor tidy, and we must be careful with words. Words are slippery and mean different things to different people. Even when words are clear and understandable, their meaning changes in each context and with each use. As the saying goes: the bark of a dog is different from the bark of a tree.

Let's look together at one kind of storm by taking babies as an example. Eigen and Bion write about babies in multidimensional ways. Babies are seen as fresh and innocent beings as well as an "annihilating force." It may seem odd to think of a baby bringing both new life and annihilation, but there are multiple impacts an infant brings after the storm of giving birth. Pressures of a baby's needs have huge effects on parents. Babies can annihilate our thinking, our psychic flow, our sleep patterns, challenging our frustration tolerance and even our devotion ... while at the same time being an amazing gift of new life, a miracle that generates faith in the aliveness of life, the goodness of life, and the power of birth for renewal. Our very experience of a baby demands multiple points of view.

The baby's birth scream is our first emotional storm, total and all out, nothing held back. A primal psychosomatic storm fused with screaming power. But the *impact* of a baby's storm upon others depends on the receptivity and resources of the storm "receivers." Parents are primary storm receivers, and our reactions to a baby's storms depend upon how *our own* early storms were received. In one sense, this first scream of birth never leaves us. It is a scream that stays with us in different forms throughout life. Scream energy, as storm energy, is an embedded part of us from the very beginning. A little like Bion's notion of the big bang of the cosmic universe condensed into the explosion of a baby's birth scream. A portion of this book is about what we do and don't do with our many screams, conscious and not. Where do our silent and hidden screams go when they are left unrecognized or unattended to?

From another angle, screams of birth can also become storms of creativity. Something new is arising and *creative* birth can be wonderful but also painful. The baby is not just a metaphor for creative birth. Baby and birth are also metaphors for cultural, religious, or scientific birth that threatens an established order of things. New life, new growth, and new ideas often threaten the status quo. Even new forms of sensation, aliveness, or arousal can be unsettling when they arise unexpectedly or from unknown sources.

Eigen says, "Control becomes important as an ordering principle where responsiveness fails" (2005, p. 25). Failed responsiveness, whether displayed in excessive control or explosive acting out, comes about when emotional indigestion highlights a lack of capacity to respond well.

Eigen's chapter opens with Bion's rendition of emotional storm, along with Martin Buber's I–Thou formulation. Not me and you, but I–Thou ... a special form of two people meeting, a precious form of emotional storm. Bion writes "when two personalities meet, an emotional storm is created" (1994, p. 321). Buber (1970) writes "all real living is meeting," and uses I–Thou as a term for what happens when people meet *with an open attitude*. The German word Buber uses for meeting is *begegnung*. My colleague Laura Stahman tells me that *begegnung* is better translated, not as meeting, but *encounter*. The word *encounter* carries more depth and engagement, and one's *countenance* is an important part of any encounter.

The common English translation of *begegnung* misses something important. Simply "meeting" is not what Buber had in mind. What if I change the wording slightly and say, "I really felt *met* by that person"? See what happens? The feeling sense of the word changes dramatically. Now it approaches Buber's I–Thou, an encounter, a deeper sense of meeting.

Eigen often speaks about connecting with deeper layers of ourselves, a place *beyond or underneath* judging and discriminating, a place beyond good and bad, right and wrong. Meeting ourselves, our inner selves, with an open attitude rather than with judgment or critique. Can we develop an I–Thou relationship with ourselves? Not always perhaps, but maybe a little more? Something better than regularly using our harsh self-critical selves?

Eigen also begins with a reference to John Bowlby (1976). He says that long ago he attended one of Bowlby's talks, and what got communicated was a feeling of *acceptance*. Not merely tolerance, but acceptance of feelings we share or even those we undergo alone. Some form of acceptance runs through every clinical model. Bowlby, as one of the grandparents of attachment theory, moved across the ocean to be closer to his children after they were grown. He wanted to stay connected. This brings up another palette of doubles: bonds and broken bonds, attachment and separation, connection and disconnection ... all forms of being together and apart.

Eigen often models a practice of turning things inside out, giving fresh perspective... as when he says, "Withdrawal is part of interacting: we rarely, if ever, are *all* there" (2005, p. 17). Gradations of absence and presence require one another. Does evasion partly *enable* experience to survive? This is about individual needs and dosage. How much connection or encounter can we take? How much can we sustain before turning away? When was the last time you looked at a stranger and held a gaze, instead of eyes darting away? What do we gain or lose by avoiding meeting one another more openly?

From Buber's perspective, the quest for *begegnung* must have had personal significance. In Buber's early life his mother abandoned him for a love relationship. She moved abroad abruptly, and there was no contact with her for many years. Is it any surprise that Buber's search for "meeting" took on special meaning throughout his life? Needs for bonding and attachment are part of what drive human connection and survival. Some call this an instinct for human relationship, and along with attachment theory, relational drives gained prominence complementing Freud's instinctual drives rather than doing away with them. "Object seeking" is a different kind of drive. The force for bonding and attachment, human engagement and connection, shifted the focus of psychoanalysis away from the biological and neurological toward the interpersonal and relational. We now know attachments that include physical touch are of utmost importance to our early survival. Bowlby (1960) and Spitz (1946) showed this with orphaned babies during WWII. Strong attachments help us live as fuller human beings throughout life and aid longevity.

Eigen finds it important to emphasize that "emotional storm is not pathology" (2005, p. 19):

> Emotional storm is something basic—like grief, anger, fear, joy, any of which can be storm-like. It is not just that we are born more physically immature than other animals. It is more a matter of emotional immaturity. Our bodies grow up faster than our ability to digest feelings... As a human group, we are still awaiting an ability to work with our emotional life, although we may take some credit for starting to try.
>
> (p. 19)

We are a very young species when it comes to handling emotions, while technologically and scientifically we are much more developed and sophisticated. It is quite a conundrum that the closest thing to us, our feeling life, provides us with both lethal danger and utmost joy. Can we get to know ourselves from inside our emotional life... a little better, a little more?

Eigen is trying to tell us that emotional storm is real in all its many variations, and we ought not to obliterate emotional storms just because we don't know what to do with them. What does it take to stay with impacts, tolerate them, and stay with them some more? No one says this is easy. But instead, we often avoid, deny, escape, or cover over with pleasantries. Even a passing glance at someone's face can evoke a storm. Eigen asks what happens when we cannot endure another's impact? What happens if we try to escape from reacting to it? What happens if we succeed?

A lot has been written about the term *emotional intelligence*, and no one doubts that *understanding* feelings is a good thing. Mental maps can be useful. But Eigen has his eye on something else, something more experiential. Namely, the need to build emotional muscles through tolerant *exercise* of feelings, such that we experience impacts and respond in ways that further us, that help us grow rather than avoiding or perpetuating destructive storms. He writes,

> We need to grow with impacts, or around them, and let a sense of what it feels like to be together develop. ... The evolution of the human race depends on not cutting off or aborting the feeling of another.
>
> (2005, p. 21)

Too often we pathologize our feeling nature in order to escape it. Like when we say someone is too sensitive for their own good. Eigen says Bion does not call our sensitivity and reactivity either illness *or* normal, just difficult. We create storms in each other simply because we are emotional beings, and our ability to stay with it, and work with it, needs to evolve. Psychotherapy and psychoanalysis are places where practicing with our emotional life can strengthen resilience and add to life.

We are sensitive beings, and our human sensitivity is precious. Being sensitive involves vulnerability, anxiety, and fear. These come with the territory, but they do not make sensitivity less precious. Part of everyday sensitivity involves working with and metabolizing transient emotional injuries, rather than avoiding these by trying always to remain emotionally "safe." Nursing ourselves past transient breakdowns is part of this process. We do this every day by coping with irritations and disappointments. The sequence of breakdown and recovery, injury and repair, is a basic emotional sequence, a basic rhythm that colors life. No one avoids the impact of pain and suffering, whether mental or physical. We are challenged to find ways to evolve with and through these emotional rhythms, just as we attend to healthy body rhythms like sleep, food, and exercise to sustain our physical beings. Eigen says that "unconscious processing is to the psyche what air or blood flow is to the body" (2018b, p. 27). I'll change the wording for emphasis: *emotional digestion and psychical flow are as important to our psychological well-being as blood flow and respiration are to our body*. Without assimilation and metabolization of feeling life, we risk emotional constipation, bouts of explosive rage, or both.

Eigen wants to let feeling storms speak, let them have their say, and see where they lead. Can we risk this and allow storms to speak in *nondestructive* ways? He invites us to stay with him and his patients as he highlights their struggles. He invites us to stay with our *own* experience without pressing the eject button too quickly. In important ways, his writing offers encouragement to practice with our emotional capacities by exercising them.

On page 20, Eigen conveys a bias against notions of control and mastery as solutions to emotional life. No doubt control and regulation are useful for those who have impulse control problems or cannot self-regulate. But for others, attempts at control may be a way *not to* feel ... and not to experience. Eigen says we tend to stop ourselves rather than undergo important life processes. Control and mastery have been around a long time without leading to better capacities for feeling life. Control and mastery can result in blowing up or shutting down storms of difference or displeasure, rather than helping us develop further through tolerance and exercise. Mutual responsiveness without destructive reactivity is one sign of increased emotional maturity. Practicing with and expanding the inner muscles of our emotional life has practical value and is life-enhancing. It is different than aiming for control, mastery, knowledge, or understanding, important as these can be.

Eigen suggests we begin by *confessing our ignorance* when it comes to problems of our feeling life, a little like Socrates confessed ignorance about his thinking life. Confession of ignorance is part of self-knowledge. Simple understanding, insight, or attempts at self-mastery may or may not help. Sometimes we expect insight to "explain" our feelings, but at the risk of explaining them away.

With effort and courage, safety and containment, we can get to know our affective life better, experience it in titrated dosages, and try to partner with it. By doing so, we become more familiar with ourselves. We grow into learning about emotional impacts and how our own attitudes and reactions have reciprocal effects. Affective attitudes with which we meet our own emotions influence how our emotions meet and treat us. Practicing is better than erecting attitudes *not* to feel feelings, as this leaves us vulnerable to retribution from the same affective energy we shun, demean, or exile.

What is Eigen's immediate prescription for this kind of exercise? He says it is another form of *practice*. "Return again and again to the point of mutual impact" (2005, p. 21). In other words, stay with it ... practice feeling feelings together ... a little at a time. If we practice with our daily emotional responsiveness in nondestructive ways, maybe we can do a little better when bigger storms arise?

I won't downplay the difficulty. The reality is that emotional storms can be scary. They involve vulnerability and risk. Eigen says the first thing to do is acknowledge this. Grant it space, time, recognition, honor ... don't pull the plug by violence or collapse. D.W. Winnicott's *use of object* formulation includes nondestructive responsiveness aligned with containment or holding—a process that leads to maturation and a fuller sense of being.

The simplest example of *use of object* is with young children. When a two-year-old becomes aggressive, a response is called for. How much benign containment can we muster? How much of a holding environment can we provide without succumbing to retaliation or collapse, leaving the scene, abandoning, giving in, or shaming the child and inducing guilt? Instead of reacting with those responses, the challenge is to hold steady and validate their life energy without giving in or being undone by it. Winnicott believed that when the containing environment is successful, it results in the child feeling more trusting, alive, and secure. Surviving emotional upheaval intact and with decent quality brings about new feelings of security and freedom for both children and adults (Eigen, 2012).

Eigen writes in *The Challenge of Being Human* (2018a) that Winnicott's use of object formulation has much broader application for sociopolitical relations, not just children. But what it asks of us in terms of mature mutual responsiveness remains an ongoing evolutionary challenge. Along with Bion, we must ask whether our entire species is an annihilating baby or "dangerous embryo." We continue to threaten one another with forces of annihilation. Our weapons have only increased in lethality and become more sophisticated. Forms of aliveness have many disguises, including aggressive aliveness: uncontrolled, domineering, territorial, and deadly. The inner storms that drive and enliven us can also destroy us, depending on how we use them.

Whatever labels we might apply, these affective powers are asking to be partnered with and respected. They are part of the sap running through the tree of our life, and our attitude toward them often helps determine what their attitude is toward us.

Comments and Responses

Comment 1: Can I riff a little bit on that word *encounter*? I'm a Buber scholar, and what I love is the idea of countenance, the idea of a face-to-face relation. I think the word *encounter* needs to be looked at as a countenance. I think about how much happens when we can actually look at people face-to-face, versus getting caught up in ideologies; what breaks down when we actually get to dialogue with someone and honor their otherness and see their vulnerability. I think that is such a crucial piece of the notion of *encounter*, which is to be present, to be there, and to be appreciating the very differences in each other.

Response 1: Thank you, you remind me that when we get to the last chapter of the book, titled "Guilt," we're going to take up Levinas and Wittgenstein, with Buber in the surround. Countenance and qualities of human relating are important for all three writers.

Commentary #3

More Emotional Storms

In this commentary we're exploring pages 29–49 of *Emotional Storm* (2005), and Eigen has changed his format to present little vignettes that offer tastes of different kinds and qualities of storm.

We'll look at the conjunction of annihilating baby and helpless infant as they relate to "adult babies." I'll also say a little bit about infinity (if that's possible) as well as Eigen's "Primary Feeler of Feelings." We may be able to feel many different feelings, but do they belong to us?

It is odd and unusual to think of emotions as both personal and impersonal, both intimate yet not *owned* by us. We usually experience feelings encased in habitual patterns. This is different than going into the heart of feelings themselves. The clinical case of Clea will highlight this. We cannot cover all storms in Eigen's chapter, but we'll try to touch on some of them.

Primordial emotional storm can be many things: a life force, creative force, destructive force, political catastrophe, a powerful moment of birth, and more. For Bion, Buber, and Eigen, there are also storms characterized as a mystical force, an unknown force, something ineffable, ultimately unknowable. And yet all these storms are part of who we are and how we're made. We are trying to approach something here that is beyond words, using words. Not an easy task. Bion's work refers to primordial reality in terms of a mystical power or force that "cannot be measured or weighted or assessed by the mere human being with the mere human mind" (Bion, 1992, p. 371). He approaches mystical underpinnings in a radical way when he says *infinity itself* is our basic reality: "the fundamental reality is 'infinity', the unknown, the situation for which there is no language—not even that borrowed from the artist or the religious—which gets anywhere near to describing it" (p. 372).

Infinity as fundamental reality? This feels rather dizzying, maybe even terrifying. How to think about it? When I was a young child going to sleep at night, I would sometimes try to imagine being on the moon looking at the Earth rotating in the darkness of space. It was pleasant to imagine this. I would then try to fathom our blue Earth slowly rotating and rotating ... forever and ever ... and ever ... Was I trying to grasp an experience of what

DOI: 10.4324/9781003257554-18

infinity feels like? This impossible task exhausted me and I would soon fall asleep. Gazing at ocean waves, a warming fire, or the night sky can also evoke infinity.

How do we handle the great unknowns of the universe, or ideas like infinity? Do we tend to ignore the whole issue, perhaps rationalize it? Maybe try to exert control, seek definitions and explanations? The real question is why anything should exist at all, but this is unanswerable. It's no surprise we feel comfortable trying to avoid infinity and unknown forces because they overwhelm us in same way many unanswerable questions do. We avoid and tone down what we cannot handle. The same is true with our emotional life.

Bion says that religion and science have their own ways to tone down unknown forces. Religion and science both apply structures, templates, ritual, method, and interpretation to try to channel, sublimate, or explain unknowable forces, but such maneuvers become substitutes and stand-ins for whatever lies behind and underneath them. What happens if we give up the need for control or explanation and instead wait in unknowing, just feeling whatever our experience might be? Even our symbols and art, through which we try to express the ineffable, run the risk of diluting or subverting sources that give rise to them. But let's not be too dire or cynical. Art, music, and literature along with intimate connections between hearts, souls, and minds also disclose and express the primordial storms we are made of. They do not only hide or dilute them. Our cultural products are signposts, manifestations coming out of emotional storm, and our intimate relationships often live at the heart of the storm.

Eigen helps us consider that an unknown force we don't possess might be possessing us. A substrate, drive or force no words can adequately cover. When overcome by feeling life, are we borrowing from a great pool of impersonal nature? Eigen says: "We tend to mistake our formulations for the basic emotional realities they subserve, represent, misrepresent, guide, structure" (2005, p. 36).

No one is a stranger to intensity and the impact of emotional feeling. Magnetic attraction, sensationalism, emotional drama, intoxication, sports, sexuality, adrenalin rushes, and manic defenses are just a few common examples. When overwhelmed, we tone down and try to escape, or even deaden feelings in various ways. If we have some facility with emotional life, we might enjoy *playing with* storm forces at times—engaging and conversing with them, amplifying and attenuating according to taste. For many, emotional reality comes through our physical body and finds expression there.

Sensitivity preferences differ with each person— we are not all the same. Some like the intensity of impact turned up high, and others prefer it turned down low. Eigen says there are times when our ingrained sensitivity preferences color our sense of who feels real to us and who does not.

Bion's helpless infant as a growing annihilating force is an odd combination, pointing to an unknown feeling base. What do we do with powerful, dark, unknown feelings, here labeled *annihilation* and *helplessness*? As adults we've developed defenses, but babies don't have many good defenses. Babies don't know what to do with what they experience—they simply react and respond to whatever they undergo, hoping for parental support.

Annihilating force takes many forms. Life events and transitions can feel annihilating. In the previous chapter, Eigen presented the case of a man who wasn't ready to have a baby in his life because he wanted his own needs to remain primary. He wasn't willing to sacrifice his own baby needs and broke off his relationship when a baby came on the horizon. Babies regularly experience emotional storms that exceed their ability to handle. Being helpless while also subject to intense emotional energy challenges every baby and caretaker.

Adult human groups are like babies when it comes to knowing what to do with their explosive emotional forces. If this were not true, then why so many shootings, so much war, and why increasing abuse of children and one another? If we adults were not frightened and explosive helpless infants masquerading in grown-up bodies, would we have nuclear bombs pointed at one another?

The baby is an explosive, annihilating force and helpless at the same time … and so are we. The question is whether we can adequately acknowledge this about ourselves, and if so, how might we work with this dilemma? Eigen often asks that we try to partner with our darker sides and evil inclinations, rather than use denial, avoidance, or suppression. He advises partnering with inner forces to get to know them, so that we might do a little better than act them out or shut them down. Try to use the energy to be less injurious and harmful. It is not enough to give lip service or intellectual arguments. When having an argument with one's partner, how might we develop an atmosphere of tolerance, patience, and nondefensive listening? Can we foster enough benign containment to hear each other fully without reactivity taking over? Eigen says there is an enormous difference between our feelings fueling subject-object reactivity and our feelings feeding our capacity to undergo experiencing (2005, p. 48). Can we undergo more without blowing up or blowing out?

To a certain extent, the baby annihilates its surroundings with legitimate demands for its life urges and survival needs. But the baby is not only an annihilating force. The baby is also a symbol of newness, freshness, innocence, purity—but a newness that impinges and makes demands on us, a freshness that disrupts the status quo.

Eigen writes that we are composed of double psychological nuclei similar to smiles and screams, with pain and suffering, trauma and catastrophe existing side by side with joy and wonder, hope, growth, and abundance of good life feeling. He says an emphasis on the darker sides of life is not simply gloomy, but part of a necessary acknowledgment, and perhaps even a kind of mourning process for part of who we are—beings who also kill and destroy. Acknowledgment is not merely lazy acceptance. When sincere, it offers opportunity for honest appraisal for how we use the power of our emotional life.

Sustaining a focus on emotional storms also offers a chance for *digestive processes* to occur. It is a challenge to work patiently with ourselves as we grow our capacity for metabolization and balancing strong currents. To use Jung's language, we might say this is part of working with our shadow side, expanding capacity to assimilate rather than exiling or evacuating parts we would rather not admit.

To partner with our evil inclinations so they are not too injurious— what might this mean? It is part of the challenge of getting along with ourselves and others. Can we get along with those things we dislike about ourselves, even a little better? Somewhat like couples in a relationship who have ups and downs? We know that two people don't get along well together *all* the time. Families and cultures and countries don't always get along well, either. Not getting along well is always going to be part of being together. A part of getting along is also not getting along. How to make room for periods of not getting along, without destructive injury? How might we make more room for *not getting along a little better* or in better ways? Can we try this in ourselves as well as with others?

A suggestion throughout this book is to go into the heart of inner feeling storms with some courage. There are storm chasers in the outer world who track tornados and hurricanes, but far fewer inner-storm chasers are seen as adventurous or heroic. Perhaps they should be. To be filled with anger and murderous rage, but not act on it and find a better way—isn't this another kind of heroism and perhaps an evolutionary step? It seems to be important for mutual survival.

Eigen provides a thought experiment:

> An emotion surges. I interpret it as an assault, and I fight back. An emotion surges. I interpret it as an invitation, and I look for an appropriate red carpet to roll out. There is no absolute necessity that binds me to one or the other possibility. At one point in life, I fight the rise of feeling; at another, I welcome it. I become interested and begin to catch on to typical sorts of meanings I give emotional currents. I could think otherwise and rather than focus on the thinking begin to get interested in emotional reality as such.

> (2005, pp. 36–7)

Here Eigen helps us taste a form of surrender ... stripping away whatever takes us away from experience itself, felt impact, rather than adhering only to narratives about it. If we do this routinely enough, if we practice being curious with whatever arises, if we don't fight back and instead open up and listen to what is being offered and presented ... even in the midst of storminess, then we approach what Eigen's patient Clea discovered about her anxiety and panic at the end of this chapter. Rumi takes an even wider approach in his poem "The Guest House."

The Guest House

This being human is a guest house.
Every morning a new arrival.
A joy, a depression, a meanness,
some momentary awareness comes
As an unexpected visitor.
Welcome and entertain them all!
Even if they're a crowd of sorrows,
who violently sweep your house
empty of its furniture,
still treat each guest honorably.
They may be clearing you out
for some new delight.
The dark thought, the shame, the malice,
meet them at the door laughing,
and invite them in.
Be grateful for whoever comes,
because each has been sent
as a guide from beyond.

Rumi (2004)

I'll be the first to admit this is easier said than done, especially in the heat of emotional moments. But perhaps even more important than Rumi's urge for radical acceptance, is the attitude or affective framework we bring or carry with us, as we react to emotions we do encounter.

How often do we dismiss or demean our feeling life with thoughts like "I shouldn't feel like this," or "I can't stand being sad, depressed, or anxious …"? How many patients come asking for help *getting rid of* negative feelings, or think therapy is supposed to do that? What about inquiring and being curious instead? Difficult emotions offer us signals. They are asking something of us. When we defend excessively or dishonor our feelings with a negative attitude, when we frame emotion as an attack and attack back, the *encasement* Eigen writes about with his patient Clea gets stronger. The narrative, along with conjunctions of impulse and defense, become more entrenched.

We become like the heavily armored dinosaur, the stegosaurus, who was all about "protection." The stegosaurus grew hard outer plates for defense against the aggressive, predatory, sharp-toothed tyrannosaurus. But the armored plates of the stegosaurus were heavy, not flexible, and flexible defenses against everyday human insults and injuries help us adapt and get through things. But we, too, can become so armored and defended that, like the stegosaurus, we sink under the weight of our own protection. I see this as a metaphor for the crazy buildup of national weapon systems meant to protect us from the enemy *over there*, but which may ultimately do the opposite and sink us. Is there a better way to take seriously our explosive, aggressive nature and not allow it to destroy our better sides, our positive angels, our humane achievements, our joys of life?

Everything we encounter in Eigen's work is at least double-sided. This is a theme that keeps returning. Any of our creative talents can be used in different ways. We create tools that can both help and hurt us, depending. Technology is double-sided. Who would have thought that smartphones might make us dumber when used excessively, or that social media could help fight against repression and censorship, but also let lies and propaganda seep through and spread?

Eigen emphasizes that a peaceful mind is not possible until we more fully acknowledge, recognize, and work with our violent mind. Our minds create destructive tools, and yet we claim to be helpless to stop them from proliferating? Instead, we point to the instruments, the weapons themselves, and try to limit their numbers. But what about their source, the mind that created them? We haven't yet learned to work with our minds and emotions in non-injurious ways, and this reflects our lack of emotional skill, chronic indigestion of our feeling life, and the immaturity of our species. We are actually afraid of our insides, afraid of our own minds. Eigen says it is easier to organize thoughts around something external than to work with the mind constructively.

Our mind itself is a growing annihilating force and a helpless infant. "If only our minds were as easy to manipulate as video games. There are masters of games but no masters of mind or life. When it comes to the real thing, we are beginners, novices" (Eigen, 2005, p. 41).

Part of the problem is we lack *tolerance* for our insides. We want to hurry up and get over things, get past difficulties, without taking time to familiarize ourselves with what is wrong. In the realm of emotions, we want to destroy or get rid of what disturbs us without getting to know it. One of the remedies Eigen, Bion, and Levinas offer has to do with patience and waiting ... allowing ourselves time to go through things together, without cutting off and pushing the eject button too quickly.

Eigen's patient Clea had an epiphany when she discovered her anxiety, panic and fear were not something she owned or possessed, nor did they own her, but actually had an existence independent of her. Such feelings could be both part of her and not part of her.

She found they had their own momentum and rhythm. But this discovery did not happen quickly. It involved a "slow baking" of emotional work in therapy, going through many storms with Eigen. What did the trick? Can we say for sure? Eigen says a new way of approaching her feeling life appeared after years of him staying right there with her, vibrating and resonating along with her. He somehow conveyed receptivity and acceptance for wherever she was at, rather than trying to get her someplace else or better. He says this was not something that could be rushed, but instead was more like "cumulative resonance to offset cumulative trauma." They went through many emotions together, and she felt him to be an ally. Why? Because his emotional being stayed with hers, went along with hers ... wherever and however she was. And this happened without force or premeditation. It happened partly because inside of Eigen he wished her well.

This silent and ineffable well-wishing might seem mysterious, but I see it as a closely held attitude conveying a background atmosphere of support, an unconscious-to-unconscious presence and acceptance. This attitude, a variant of what Rumi's poem conveys, seemed to help with digestion and metabolization of Clea's traumatic history, and in that sense, we might also see it as an example of Bion's *alpha function* at work.

Alpha function is Bion's term for unknown processes involved in initiating and carrying on digestion of affects and life's impacts, trying to grow experience by turning it into something useable.

We can point to many forms of alpha function, with Shakespeare as one example. Eigen says that Shakespeare's work is a kind of human emotional digestive system, taking wounds of emotional storm and passing them through his literary alpha function. Shakespeare's literary alpha function includes dreaming, art, sensitivities of emotion, combined with intellectual acuity and poetic truths. Part of our challenge as therapists, and part of the challenge of diverse world cultures, is coming to recognize the importance of trying to process the impacts of destructive experience ... to digest, elaborate, discover, and create what else is possible between us.

Comments and Responses

Comment 1: I just had a thought about welcoming the stranger—whether sitting with nothingness or depression or darkness, there is something about the attitude in welcoming this. I've heard Michael Eigen speak before, and he really embodies that—of just being very welcoming, very accepting. I think when one embodies that, it really helps the patient to develop an attitude themselves to be more welcoming of the stranger within. And how that can make all the difference.

Response 1: "The stranger within ..." I like that. The stranger, the other ... So much has been written about how we meet the stranger, how we meet the other ... whether the other is within us, strange emotions, "not-me" states, a person from another country, culture, religion. So many kinds of otherness. How do we meet them? With what quality do we encounter forms of otherness? Lots of spokes on that wheel, thank you.

Smiles and Screams

In this commentary we'll explore *smiles* and *screams*. Approaching this pair of words, we could add common analogues, like joy and suffering, happiness and pain, peace and turmoil, comfort and catastrophe.

Eigen begins his chapter writing about reversals—swings from one feeling sense to another with blends of both. For instance, Ivan Ilyich, in Tolstoy's masterpiece *The Death of Ivan Ilyich,* having a moment of joy that offsets years of suffering as well as examples from Kurosawa and Fellini movies. Often, we tend to separate feelings into opposites or binaries, like sad or happy, sweet or sour, and at the extreme we sometimes speak of euphoric highs and suicidal lows. Such extremes are usually rare emotional states of being. More commonly we feel mixtures rather than purely one thing or another. Eigen's work gravitates toward mixtures and combinations in emotional life, asking us to consider complexity. With emotional mixtures, I think of words like *bittersweet, or agonies of love.* Dead spots within aliveness can also be viewed upside down—sparks of life still glowing within ashes of destruction.

Eigen emphasizes a point of affirmation after going through something difficult, even traumatic, and coming out the other side to feel a renewed sense of life. He highlights that life *can begin again* after living through despair and traumatized hopes. This is a variation on ancient themes of rebirth or renewal, a journey that goes by many names. It points to a process and rhythm that easily gets overlooked, especially during times that feel difficult and hopeless.

I want to approach Eigen's chapter by talking first about rhythms and fluidity as natural and healthy parts of both our emotional life and physical life. Rhythmic movement is with us at every level of life. We tend to speak of mind and body, physical and mental as separate. However, these distinctions are somewhat artificial because we are spirit beings and material beings simultaneously. We experience mind and body as interwoven with one another. For instance, the habits and practices that come out of our thoughts, emotions, and attitudes affect our physical health to some degree, just as the good or bad health of our body affects our mood and spirit. Even a thought or belief about a medicine can affect its physical manifestation inside us, which is why

DOI: 10.4324/9781003257554-19

drug testing for efficacy must use double-blind placebo-controlled studies for validation.

There are rhythms in both our physical body and our emotional body. We are part of nature, and nature has her rhythms too, from day to night and season to season, tides of the oceans and phases of the moon. Our bodies and emotions are no different. We are rhythmic beings. We breathe in and out rhythmically; we digest by taking in nourishment and eliminating waste rhythmically; our hearts beat rhythmically circulating blood. We have circadian rhythms, menstrual rhythms, sleep and waking rhythms ... even rhythmic cycles during sleep itself. Our individual cells and organs are rhythmic, with cells being born and dying throughout each day. Our moods are also rhythmic, but perhaps not so regular. Even so, feelings and moods rarely stay the same for very long. We can go from being downcast to upbeat, or the reverse, with even a little bit of good or bad news.

Eigen's work often puts an emphasis on the screams of life, the emotional pains, the traumas and catastrophes. Why this emphasis? In my view, it is because navigating the darker difficult sides of life, the injurious sides of life, are among humanity's biggest challenges, and one of Eigen's callings is to try and help a little. For most of us, it's easy to be happy, expansive, and embracing of life when things are going well. It is much more difficult to engage with our pains and troubles when present, let alone try to use them as potential sources of growth or learning. Indeed, we are lucky if our responses and reactions to trauma do not lead to further injury, as when trauma binds and constricts us, feeding on itself. Our emotional reality on the screaming side of life is among our biggest challenges, and Eigen notes that we are beginners, novices really, at knowing what to do with our negative emotions, impulses, and reactions.

There are therapists and psychology writers today who elevate and put a premium on the positive side of life, believing that health comes from spending as much time as possible avoiding the bad and remaining close to the good. Some even try to concentrate *only* on the bright side of life, while ignoring, deflecting, or tiptoeing around difficulties. In the early twentieth century psychoanalysis developed a language of wounds and trauma, focusing on psychic and emotional catastrophes of many kinds as well as defenses we use to cope with them. Birth trauma, abandonment trauma, intrusive trauma, war trauma, suffocation anxiety ... annihilation dreads of many flavors. We learn that sudden shocks to the personality or lack of emotional nourishment very early in life can have long-lasting effects on growth and well-being. Like Eigen's patient who "died inside" at age 18 when his father suddenly went into a rage at the dinner table. We met him in Eigen's previous chapter where he explains how qualities of personality in this man's mother and father during his upbringing had remained glued to him, even following him into adult relationships (2005, pp. 53–4).

Eigen also writes about his own emotional difficulties when young, an important background for understanding his attraction to emotional tumult and dead spots. Eigen, who so poignantly writes about emotional reality and his work with patients, went through his own life traumas, helping him to become a depth psychology poet able to find *our* inside struggles and touch us where we live (2005, pp. 52–3).

Why are healthy rhythms so important for emotional and psychological well-being? One reason is that if we get stuck, if flow or fluidity become obstructed or clotted, a constriction of emotional life and growth takes place. Emotional digestion and circulation stop. Eigen reminds us that emotional digestion is to the psyche what blood flow is to the body ... a circulation of affective energy that can nourish or remain undigested, festering, stuck.

As human beings we could be said to vibrate rhythmically, just as all life on Earth vibrates rhythmically. If, in the natural world, we have rhythms of seasons, of moon and tide, why wouldn't rhythms also be operating and reflected in psychic life? I'll use sleeping and waking as one example, where conscious life reflects a rhythm of fading out and coming back. We might refer to this rhythm as a mini-death and rebirth. Sleep as a miniature death and waking as a form of rebirth or renewal.

Babies offer another example. Infant rhythms consist of extreme variation in states of being. Babies do not just physically sleep and wake, eat and poop; they also exhibit moments of extreme distress and satisfaction. One moment turbulence, the next moment comfort. We might even say that babies seem to alternate between states of heaven and hell. The feeling life of a baby reminds us of our original smiles and screams.

If both smile and scream are with us throughout life, what can we say about their rhythm in the adult world? And what happens when we become stuck in a smile or a scream that does not go through changes or show nuance?

Have you even known someone who always seemed to be smiling ... nothing but smiles? As though their face is frozen into a smile and does not flex or bend into any other expression? It doesn't appear natural, does it. On faces of some people I've seen, this smile can begin to look more like a grimace, with clenched teeth and tight facial muscles that do not seem to relax. In such cases, the plasticity and back-and-forth flow between feeling states has been lost. One wonders about obstructed screams underneath such fixed smiles. Eigen condenses one theme of this chapter into a single sentence: "The smile that grows out of the scream is not the same as the screamless smile, one that makes believe no scream is there" (2005, p. 51).

In different books, Eigen uses pairs or conjunctions pertaining to rhythms of psychic and emotional life. These rhythms are amplified by metaphor and psychologically real. They go beyond simple reversals of happy and sad, adding more complexity. For example, consider rhythms like continuity and disruption, fragmentation and cohesiveness, opening up and closing off, disappearing and coming back, contraction and expansion, blockage and flow, falling apart and coming together, breaking down and building up, wounding and recovery, injury and repair. There is feeling out of one's mind, gone, distracted, somewhere else … and then feeling right here and very present. At the extreme, we might speak archetypally in terms of agonizing despair and perennial hope, or crucifixion and resurrection. All such phrases are umbrella notions that frame and contain thousands of variations in experiential life.

Often, we tend to separate these rhythms and their flow into distinct binaries or opposites. When any emotional state becomes one-sided, polarized, overly hardened or rigid, fluidity stops and rhythm itself freezes or goes awry. In a way, we could say it is just this fluidity or flow, with its balanced or flexible rhythmic movement between states of being, that is one marker of emotional and psychological health. Some of you will remember similar ideas from Part One of this book.

In addition to binary polarization, we also seem prone to defend against the *worst* with ideals of the *best*. Eigen references hyper-aliveness embedded in themes of the immortal self, the eternal self … life ever-after. These forms of hyper-aliveness tend to deny their counterparts, like forms of deadness, emptiness, and nonbeing.

Religious conquest of death (as in everlasting life) or quests for the fountain of youth are themes that aim for something similar. But cults of extreme aliveness, by attempting to banish anti-aliveness, betray our more natural rhythm of activity and rest, striving and quiescence.

Aliveness as an absolute, an idealization, a maximizing process can become so extreme and one-sided that it brings about reversals and swings to the opposite extreme. (I think of the story of the Tower of Babel or the Garden of Eden.) To always be fully alive, productive and driven with no counterbalance? This becomes a mockery of basic rhythms. We need to sleep every 24 hours, but some try to cheat this need, and it is said Americans are chronically sleep-deprived people. How about resting as a value in itself, not just as a counterbalance to aliveness? How about downtime and doing nothing as positive resources in their own right? Such things are to be respected and embraced for the fertility they can provide. Farmers do something similar when they let the soil in their fields rest and regenerate.

In different ways, Winnicott, Bion, and Eigen all address the importance of quiet states, slow states, and rest. There are some close cousins too, like meditative stillness, not knowing, reverie, passivity, emptiness, open receptivity … surrendering ego and agency.

Can we allow for balance among these two aspects of life, active and passive, the smile and scream? Can we allow, accept, and even foster more downtime, deadtime, dead spots within us, or must we defend against them? The current COVID pandemic is giving us an education in slowing down and resting, even as many still fight against it.

Eigen writes that when *total* aliveness becomes an ideal or ideology, it becomes tragic, involving deception and incurring costs to oneself and others—a little like utopian societies that crumble because they cannot sustain the pressures of their idealizations.

A clinical example of unhealthy rhythm is bipolar or manic-depressive illness, where manic or hypomanic activation is meant to ward off depressive affects that feel intolerable. A supervisor during my training many years ago used to say that manic defenses, including action-oriented discharge, are used "to stay one step ahead of emotional life"—defenses to avoid what one feels by keeping active, not stopping to slow down or feel things more deeply.

Totalizing, absolutizing, idealizing ... these have the power to take us over, as they contain mixtures of strong affect and belief, wish and hallucination. I want to apply these to the clinical case of Pam and her analyst to address some of what went wrong in that therapy couple.

Eigen says there is something he needs to tell us that we may already know. There are many variations to it, but his words are: "we hallucinate a *woundless* state around a *wounded* core" (Eigen, 2005, p. 56). Other ways of saying it include pretending things are fine when they are not, or covering over inner vulnerability with outer appearance of strength.

Bringing together thoughts on rhythm with wishes for more or better results, we start to see the different ideas, visions, or "hallucinations" that Pam and her analyst had for one another. For Pam the therapy was good enough, maybe better than good, but her analyst's superego wanted something more, different, or better.

> The point where this therapy relationship failed is precisely a crux in analysis today. Part of what analysis does is open a situation where the patient can break down (partially) and recover over and over (partially) as part of sessions. The individual gets practice in falling apart and coming together, injury and recovery—part of what happens when two human beings are together. Pam and her analyst enacted feeling good and getting wounded, but did not bring the two together as part of the rhythm of their relationship. Rather than becoming a [rhythmic] nucleus of the work, each phase became a rigid totality. As alternate hallucinatory states, they did not modulate each other.
>
> (Eigen, 2005, p. 57)

Here we see their hopes and expectations as not open to modification—a not-so-hidden expression of hallucinatory wishfulness. "We are hallucinatory beings striving for truth and truth-oriented beings striving for hallucinatory perfection—and the two intermingle ... in strange ways" (Eigen, 2018f, p. 47).

We see similar "hallucinations" in political movements, religious cults, and utopian visions that often end badly. Hallucination cannot stand up to reality for very long, and today we hear of some who hallucinate the COVID virus as not being real, or wearing a mask as not really necessary. In other instances, hallucinatory wishfulness can take the form of a drive or quest for purity, for total oneness, absolute enlightenment, or eternal life. Whatever it is that affords no room for difference, no room for anything other than itself, becomes suspect, because it refuses modification or modulation by ever-changing realities of life circumstance and thus risks becoming ossified and partly dead—not open to change, development, or growth. Breakdown is necessary for new forms of life gestalts to appear. Asian cultures long ago realized that an apex or high point contains within it an inevitable descent lower. When something reaches full ripeness, the beginnings of decay are not far away. Balancing such rhythms becomes part of the practice and art of living.

"The smile that grows out of the scream is not the same as the screamless smile, one that makes believe no scream is there" (Eigen, 2005, p. 51). If we can allow and admit and honor our screams of life, instead of dodging them, we might be surprised by transformations that can occur.

But the smile that denies the scream is hollow, a covering over, perhaps a frightened smile. A smile wishing for a sense of security using defensive means. Bion says there is a part of the personality invested in maintaining safety of the status quo. But there will always be new thoughts, feelings, and events that arise to threaten the status quo. The birth of something new typically upsets conventions. Eigen and Bion seek a different kind of security that comes from our ability to go into, suffer through, and stay with what feels difficult or too hot to handle. They believe this "staying with it," and staying with it some more, offers a different kind of security. A security born out of greater self-contact and the ability to come through life's travail. A security that includes the likelihood of feeling more real, alive, and grounded.

There are times when trauma binds us to it. It has a force of attraction, a power, a radiance, a magnetic pull, as we see in this chapter with Eigen's patient Shula. Force fields of intense affect and dissociation are often part of the work with trauma patients.

There are also people for whom oblivion, deadness, and "not being there" are what feel most real about living. They know little else, perhaps due to severe wounding in early years. We know that very early trauma can freeze growth and development. It can also inhibit openness, exploration, and curiosity. Trauma can freeze the rhythmic movement of beginnings and endings, coming together and falling apart, starting anew and letting go. When natural rhythms get disrupted, one cannot "complete" their movement because psychic fluidity and flow are not allowed their natural gradients.

Comments and Responses

Comment 1: I really love this chapter ... it addresses so much. I think of what a lot of my patients face struggling with ideals and perfection and how it causes a lot of problems. I mean, it's good to have ideals, but to literally have to achieve it? I think that's impossible. But there is this kind of hallucination trying to achieve what's impossible. I was thinking about this dominating attitude in our society that "I deserve to be happier, so I should get it." I've had patients tell me, "I work out, I eat healthy, I do all the right things, why am I not happy?" But we are really talking about rhythms of life ...

I feel love or joy is like grace; it's something that can't be forced. It's something that surprises us. I think our society tends to want to force things to happen. That's part of the problem, this dominating attitude and also a sense of entitlement to happiness or love or joy ... and then being angry why one doesn't have that. So, I think there is this sense of entitlement and a controlling wish too. Wanting to avoid failure, or avoid mistakes, but those are also a natural part of living. We try things and sometimes they don't work out, but we figure it out and try again. But still, there seems to be this real fear of making mistakes or failure.

Response 1: Yes, I was just thinking about your word *entitlement.* The United States is such a young country, young culture. The drive for perfection, or thinking we "deserve" this or that ... Good heavens! The back and forth of failure and achievement is also part of a "faith rhythm." We meet obstacles and sometimes get crushed, then have to start over. It's a rhythm of faith, if we can persevere and stay with it.

No Amount of Suffering

Eigen's chapter "No Amount of Suffering" describes an emotional storm in slow motion, a difficult chapter that requires fastening one's psychical seatbelts. It is unsettling and depressing to grasp the kinds of suffering portrayed in the lives of Leila and Vance. It is difficult to consider how invisible forms of early trauma can have such insidious effects.

An international colleague who has English as a third language asked me about this chapter's title: "No Amount of Suffering," and I interpreted it as something like "no end to the amount of suffering" or "endless suffering … suffering without end." This puts the spotlight on Leila and Vance. Eigen's poetic writing style allows feelings that gather around their early life traumas to be even more graphic and wrenching.

My first and abiding reaction to this chapter was a feeling of helplessness, as though there was no way to assist, let alone alleviate Leila's and Vance's emotional pain. I felt depressed and hopeless by the end of the chapter—with no chance of redemption for either of them. I also felt an impulse to protect group members from how hard it is to absorb such things. But that's not possible either. So I felt helpless a second time. And then I thought perhaps not everyone had my same difficulty. My reactions were a signal that this chapter hit home. It did its job, landing with impact. It left me feeling helpless and hopeless to think of ways to make a difference in the lives of Leila and Vance, were I to be in a therapy role with them. And I believe this might have been one of Eigen's intentions—that the reader feel a sense of no escape, no making things better, no solutions or fixes … even though Leila and Vance are said to have decent enough lives in other ways.

I've known medical colleagues who will try anything to save a patient's physical life. They go the extra mile, bringing all their knowledge and care to prevent death. And yet, physical healing is not always possible. People's bodies give out and give way, and sometimes people die even when young. I remember how horrible these physicians felt when they lost a patient … when, in spite of everything, they too felt helpless to save a life. That's from the physical side of life and illness.

DOI: 10.4324/9781003257554-20

Here, we have psychical and emotional life injuries, and those of us who are therapists have been trained to try to help with emotional life. We are dedicated to emotional health and well-being. But if we take on patients like Leila or Vance, what is our responsibility? And what are our options? Such questions will generate different answers among us. There is no standard of care I know of, for the kinds of early life trauma Leila and Vance experienced, no evidenced-based protocols to go by, no uniform templates for these traumatized psyches. Yes, we have tools that can soften and help regulate our nervous system functioning; we can alleviate cycles of flooding and vegetative symptoms with medications, or try to change thinking patterns and synaptic firings that affect mood. But if the death of a young physical body can defy a physician trying to cure illness, how much more uncertain are our methods with psychical and emotional bodies that have been crippled by chronic relational trauma from early life?

What exactly went wrong with these two people when they were children? Eigen directs our attention to what can be invisible about trauma, or rather, it was Leila who directs our attention by recounting her story of the Israeli doctor after a bomb had exploded. That doctor found a shaking, crying woman who showed no mutilation and no external bleeding, but whose lungs had been invisibly destroyed by the impact of exploding air. She needed immediate treatment even though no one could see anything visibly wrong. Here is a poignant metaphor for invisible early trauma whose effects are sometimes observed only later in life, after damage has been done. Leila's emotional insides were blown away by forces her parents were unaware of, resulting in chronic self-attack on her innermost self. By contrast, Vance saw evils of life everywhere in the outside world, while his father's self-importance hypocritically preferred to see only the good stuff, or else not look at all.

Eigen tells us there was broad overlap between both fathers' negative emotional impact and both mothers' emotional absence. Eigen summarizes this by saying that each had experienced holes in mothering and floods of fathering. Fathers were described as extraverted and shallow, critical and hypocritical, rageful and not capable or caring enough to observe and tune into their children. Mothers were described as poisonous, absent, hollow, unavailable, while also exhibiting "beautiful exteriors," even while Leila's mother physically deteriorated. Perceptual reality and emotional reality were constantly at odds with one another and, in combination, gave toxic contradictory appearances. Everything was fine, except it wasn't. Everyone was supposed to be happy, except they weren't. This disjunction, this gap, and these lies, could not be covered over, and together they fed confusion and rage, self-doubt and shame, terror and hate into the emotional core of Leila and Vance.

As I considered my own reaction to this chapter, I noticed it partly felt like a black hole, almost as if my own feelings were being sucked into a hole of hopeless darkness. Eigen says that terror and hate were a large part of

Leila's and Vance's experience: Leila's terror and hate being more inner-directed toward judging herself; Vance's more outer directed, finding fault with the world and seeing the lie in everything. They both shared much seriousness and severity as part of their personality. Eigen says he has never heard Vance laugh.

> For Vance and Leila, everything was organized and collapsed around their mothers' illness and filled out, inflated around their fathers' energy, self-importance, self-centered outpourings, depressive exuberance. One balloon that never was fully inflated and another always about to pop.
>
> (2005, p. 65)

One thing I tend to do when I become emotionally stymied with clients is try to think more. I look for causes, try to discover patterns, and use my intellectual defenses to explain things. I try to find a way to help through better knowledge and understanding. Knowledge and understanding are all well and good—actually they are quite wonderful. But the essence of this chapter is not about offering knowledge and understanding. It's about sitting with and experiencing helplessness ... and what we do, or don't do, with such feelings in the room.

I want to consider two broad realms—cognitive knowledge and experiencing our experience—and highlight some differences. I want to bring understanding and experiencing together as a pairing, but also a distinction. I could use different words, like knowing and being, or intellect and impact, abstract distance and intimate closeness, observation and immersion. These contrasts give a sense of what I'm aiming for. Clinical questions haunt the therapist in such cases: Is there a way to help with helplessness? Are there useful ways to *be with* helplessness?

We will return to these questions, but first please indulge my intellectual defenses as to what may have gone wrong in the early lives of Leila and Vance.

From an object relations perspective, we know that parental figures are all important during infancy. Let's imagine for a moment what babies might experience. In another book, Eigen writes:

> One thing that gets projected into the object is the baby's object-seeking drives. The very urge to be with another enters the other, seeks another to go into and be a part of. One goes into another to create a response, to have a place in another person ... and one needs the other's thoughts and feelings for one's own psychic nourishment ...
>
> In order for object-seeking feelings to thrive, or even feel real, they have to be projected into another who works with them. The drive to make contact with the other needs to find the other's insides and stimulate

thought, feeling, imagining. One needs to feel who one is elaborated in
the mind of another ...

(2018b, pp. 64–5)

But what if the baby is thrown back on itself, meets a wall, or more anxiety or hostility? What if, to use Bion's locution, the object is intolerant
of projective identification? What if the caregiver cannot let the baby's
feelings affect her or reacts destructively? What if the worst a baby can
feel cannot get into another person for modification or psychic reworking?
What if the other person refuses the input, evacuates it, cannot bear it,
or does not have the equipment to process it? What if the baby's feelings
have nowhere or very hurtful places to go?

(p. 64)

One can imagine such things happening to Leila and Vance. As infants, the
responsiveness we receive from caregivers, both the caring responses and the
absent or lacking ones, take place *before* we are fully conscious.

By the time we awaken to ourselves, we have an entrenched sense of being
excluded/included with regard to the desires of others, partly as a result
of whether and how we found our way inside another and what became
of us there.

(Eigen, 2018b, p. 65)

In the 1980s there was a lot of writing related to French analyst André Green
and his understanding of "the negative," variants of vacuum and void in
early-life parental responsiveness. One of these he called the dead or emotionally absent or vacant mother. Of course, any parent can have this profile,
but at that time Green concentrated on the relationship between infant and
mother.

We can imagine that both Leila and Vance suffered from just such an early
emotional absence with their mothers, while at the same time being at the
mercy of extroverted fathers who filled the void with an atmosphere of self-
centered critique and hypocrisy. Eigen says Leila's father

was as filled with life as her mother was with death. But it was the wrong
kind of fullness, to match the wrong kind of emptiness. The baby and
child was lost in a space that vanished and filled with noise.

(2005, p. 65)

Sounds pretty awful, doesn't it? Perhaps all the more so because both Leila
and Vance were sensitive people, and traumatized sensitivity is a compounded
injury.

Eigen says Bion, Freud, and Melanie Klein come closest to understanding what Leila and Vance go through when they speak of a destructive force within, a force against recovery (2005, pp. 69, 71). Proof of the power of this destructive force is that it never lets go. There is no final victory over it, and Eigen gives examples of being a rager and self-decimator. What is it about trauma that binds us to it?

> Nothing is more binding than damaged bonds, more mesmerizing than toxic nourishment, especially when ecstasy merges with rage and terror.
>   One of the great secrets of trauma is that it trades in radiance ... Pain and something beatific inextricably fuse, creating a more intense, endurable bond than either alone.
>
> (2005, p. 70)

We seem to be left with an unsolvable problem ... and questions haunt us.

What can be done when it feels like nothing can be done? Where might there be help within helplessness? How is it possible to find hope within hopelessness?

Eigen begins his chapter contrasting suffering that is redemptive and suffering that crushes life. Suffering that can play a role in both opening and closing worlds as well as suffering that is simply a fact of life in every social system and every human being—something that will never be eliminated. Another contrast: ordinary suffering that one gets through and around in daily life, and more severe, chronic emotional wounds that need closer attention. Some people live their waking lives in a state of emotional vacuum or worse, while others cannot stop attending to what feels wrong or damaged. For people like Leila and Vance, daily pains are not simply daily pains but much larger, and depending on one's sensitivity, these become soul pains and world pains that must be thought about and never let go.

More often, though, we try to soften our suffering, deny it, ignore it, dispel it, distract it or ourselves ... all of which is natural enough. But Eigen asks about the costs to this.

He says our culture is phobic about helplessness (2005, p. 73).

Still, we are powerless against many things. We are powerless in infancy, powerless in the face of whatever era and culture we are born into, and powerless in the face of mortality. Yet we go on ... we adjust and adapt to life circumstance as best we can. The dominant culture today seems all about becoming more powerful, more successful, more acquisitive, and one wonders if all these maneuverings are partly unconscious efforts to defend against helplessness. If the existentialist writers of the last century believed we were primarily driven through life by unconsciously defending against death, perhaps another variation today is defending against feelings of helplessness and powerlessness.

I'll move now from cognitive understanding to emotional immersion, letting the intellect rest a little. Let's approach something more experiential by trying to contact places that Leila and Vance live in, with, and through—places that theories about growth and wellness don't really touch.

Eigen uses the poet Rainer Maria Rilke to open sensitivity and let raw experience speak (2005, pp. 75–7). He says that Rilke holds onto nothing, gives himself over to the impact of the moment as it builds and transforms, opens and shatters. Rilke stays close to the terror of opening, the moment of helplessness when experience itself tears us open, burns us, stings, ripples, and vibrates through us. Some people live for such moments. Can we stand this, endure it? If not, if we always remain defended, what sort of being do we become? Without terror of opening to the unknown, what sort of beings are we? Is this, perhaps, what patients like Leila and Vance are asking of us? To let the worst speak and not run from it? To let helplessness speak and not leave it behind? To let traumatized sensitivity speak and not turn away? Eigen proposes that we do more tasting and waiting within these very moments before jumping into action … and through exercise, let our faith muscle grow.

Here's an example Eigen gives from a web post a few years ago. It's about moments of therapeutic paralysis.

> There are people you work with who do well and others who stymie you—with the ones who stymie you, there seems to be no way to succeed no matter what you try. Yet even in these cases, I have found that something may happen … not what was hoped for or expected, but something that makes a difference in ways that had not yet been imagined. This may sound strange, but there is a place of no-hope that can be freeing. Give up expecting to be a helper and just be there. Sometimes you are forced to give up trying to help. There is nothing you can do except be there, yet something happens in your paralysis, a resonance happens. There is a difference between evacuated paralysis and resonant paralysis. When you can't do anything else, mutely expressive resonance has a chance to grow. You can't find a way to be helpful but you find a space of no-help or it finds you. If you sit in a place of no-hope/no-help, something happens and the person feels it. It is very freeing. It partly frees us from ourselves.
> (Eigen, online post, 2019)

Here, Eigen offers a path or exercise of staying with something difficult and uncomfortable, and then staying with it some more. Instead of trying harder or trying different things, instead of knowledge, insight, or understanding, he points to something else: leaning into an experience of raw resonant being. Eigen is proposing we stop trying to get anywhere other than the place our patient is living, breathing, and experiencing … even if this is a place of no hope and futility. This may feel like surrender, but it's also a profound joining with the patient in their emotional suffering. No agenda, no critique, no suggestions or distractions … just an open respectful waiting that joins with an attitude of radical acceptance, evoking a "resonant paralysis." Something else or different can happen in this new space over time, and we don't know how it will go, how it will unfold. Not knowing is important. It touches Eigen's notion of faith: an open attitude of unknowing, a receptivity without desire for change or expectation of progress. Simply a resonance with the patient wherever they are. Others have different ways of saying this. Some call it a form of "witnessing," but this feels a step removed. Some call it "presencing" (being fully present to the emotional reality of the moment). Ofra Eshel (2019) calls it *with-nessing*, a deep form of being with, a special kind of meeting akin to at-onement.

Eigen and Eshel both suggest that when we move into these difficult feeling states, when we abide in them *with* our patients, something helpful can happen in the helplessness. If nothing else, it's not so much that the patient feels understood, as it is feeling fully met and unconditionally joined in their suffering.

Comments and Responses

Comment 1: A few little quotes that relate from pages 73 and 81 (Eigen 2005).
"Our culture is phobic about helplessness. Helplessness is bad, associated with being a victim … One should be proactive, fix things, work to make things better, redress injury and wrong, be an active agent of choice and desire." "Mastery is not always the best model when it comes to emotional meaning and transformational chances." On page 77, about being a therapist during moments in therapy when we feel out of control and an urge to do something:

There's a moment of helplessness that stops our breath, a quick shock, before we jump into action. I propose we do more tasting of that moment, sifting it, letting our faith muscle grow, as building tolerance for the fleeting shock begins to transform us.

So, that's what I wanted to share.

Response 1: Thank you.
Comment 2: I'd like to draw attention to what Eigen (2005) writes on page 74:

[Bion] saw that precocious activity often made matters worse and suggested that passivity in the face of evil could be more effective. This was not a matter of nonresistance but more a waiting on reality, letting impacts build and transform, becoming familiar with what one is up against, opening to unknown possibilities.

What caught my attention was *"becoming familiar with what one is up against."* What are we up against? And later in the same paragraph he says, "What one confronts are ways personality responds to its traumatic plight" (p. 74). Self-destructiveness is part of what Bion calls the psychotic personality in us. I just wanted to note that in this area of waiting, being with, there can also be the observation of "What is going on? What is happening that I am doing this to myself?" You know, observing this in a passive stance. This is also part of waiting.

Response 2: Thank you, even in our passivity we can be active. We are actively observing, we are thinking, we are discovering what we are up against. I like that because it's a kind of double. We might allow ourselves to experience destructive elements and difficult feelings while also observing and waiting, if we can. It doesn't mean disappearing or going numb, even if those kinds of passivity are sometimes needed. Finding out what we are up against is important. It is a big part of what therapy is about.

Comment 3: It seems to me we are all living in the unknown at this moment in our democracy. And we are all waiting for election day in the US (November 2020) and what that is going to bring. But it's an opportunity, I guess, to have faith. Because we don't know what's going to happen. Our basic values have been abandoned—what's truth, what's not truth? And it's quite challenging, I think we are all being very challenged at this moment. So, I think having faith is very important at this time.

Response 3: Every day it seems we are hit with challenges to staying open. Faith in the unknown, faith in the future is difficult. Everything feels topsy turvy, upside down … lies are truth, truth becomes lies. It feels horrible. We could go to a lot of places with that. But let's stay in the unknown and exercise our faith muscles. I think that's what you are asking us to do, and thank you for that.

Somatic Storms

In this commentary we'll be discussing Eigen's chapter titled "Somatic Storms" (pp. 80–95). I was struck by how Eigen begins this chapter talking about his difficulty transitioning between the kinds of exchanges we have in psychotherapy and the kinds we have in everyday social interactions. Those of you who are therapists may have experienced introducing yourself at social gatherings only to find that mentioning psychotherapy tends to stop the conversation. This has been my experience. It seems to be an occupational hazard and alerts me to how wary people can be about emotional life and therapy. How odd it is to have a profession that alienates people in one setting and draws them closer in another.

Somatic refers to the physical body, our somatic substrate, our physical house. As we might expect, Eigen feels it too simple to make neat and tidy divisions like mind and body, psyche and soma, as though we think we know what these things are. We speak of psychosomatic illnesses, physical symptoms that are somehow connected to or caused by psychological-emotional states of being. But is it really so simple?

Bodies are not only physical. They are not simply objects for medical attention, nor solely material substance. So much comes through our body that is ineffable: soothing and abrasive touch, irritations, aches and pains, joys and sufferings, some with no clear bodily location ... all kinds of feelings, sensations, affects, and twitches. We often blend mind, body and feeling together. For instance, we say I have an upset stomach after a difficult meeting at work, or my head aches so much I can't think, or my brain feels fried. My heart is broken because I've lost a friend, or someone was hurtful and stabbed me in the back.

There is someone I know who talks about getting a "mental stomach ache" when she feels anxious or worried. Her mental worry finds its way to a special place in the tummy. Or consider Stacey, the woman in Eigen's chapter who could not "swallow" the toxic effects of her mother. She literally could not swallow when talking about her mother. Eigen spontaneously proposed that her mother was stuck in her food pipe and was

DOI: 10.4324/9781003257554-21

indigestible. A simple statement that had profound effects. How do such responses come about? Was Eigen's intuition accurate and his statement well-timed? Was Stacy ready to hear this in a way that mattered? Whatever else we might say, Stacy's pause and pondering the word *indigestible*, and her recovery shortly after, provide a good example of how "opening new experiential fields" can be therapeutic. Not ready-made solutions or expert advice, but a surprise opening that speaks to the individual's unique situation in the moment.

Yes, we have a palpable physical body. But our body both does and does not exist separately from how we regard it and treat it. Paradoxically, our physical existence both is and is not under our control. The body functions independently and separately, and the body also responds well or poorly to good or bad treatment from its owner. Some people are more distant from their physicality, and some view their body as burdensome. Some even think of it as a mechanical apparatus that must be fed and kept clean on a regular basis. Others regard their body as a sacred temple of heart, soul, and life ... and treat it accordingly. Still others obsess over every little thing their body does or doesn't do. For the most part, bodies don't exist in a vacuum without minds and attitudes that relate to them in one way or another. There are always exceptions too. Like someone in a coma, where the body is kept alive by mechanical means. Bodies can outlast minds that used to belong to them, as with severe Alzheimer's disease. Yet even those with various forms of dementia, whose bodies keep living while minds have slipped away, can suddenly come alive when music is played, reaching their insides and sparking spirit. Our spirit and body are intricately interwoven and affect one another in mysterious ways.

Do we really know where to draw the line between the two? Emotions can be felt as embodied, and emotions can be felt as having no location at all. When we say I was touched by a poem or piece of music, where is the location of that touch? Where does that kind of touch reside? When we say we felt moved receiving a personal letter, what is it in us that gets moved? Can we locate it? Weavings of psyche and soma are interesting to think about ... and anything but simple.

Are we one being or two? Are we both a oneness and twoness simultaneously? As conjoined psychical-physical beings, we are both split and fused together. A mind and body, a psyche and physical substrate that are separate and together at once. Are we also, like the poet Walt Whitman, a "multitude?" I believe we are multitudes, and in the commentary below I offer different models, past and present, that highlight our complexity.

As prelude, here are some contrasting attributes of mind and body, experiential awareness entwined with our fleshy substrate. Consider the following two columns that highlight differences between material and mental realities:

Body	Mind
Matter	Spirit
Physical	Nonmaterial
Brain	Psyche
Measurable	Nonmeasurable
Bounded	Boundless
Finite	Infinite
Visible	Invisible

Hippocrates in Ancient Greece developed the four humors. These were combinations of physical and temperamental traits. The four humors originally referenced bodily fluids but were later associated with personality traits.

- *Black bile:* related to earth, having cold and dry properties, associated with Melancholic traits.
- *Yellow bile:* related to fire, having dry and warm properties, associated with Choleric traits.
- *Blood:* related to air, having moist and warm qualities, associated with Sanguine traits.
- *Phlegm:* related to water, having moist and cold qualities, associated with Phlegmatic traits.

Another model combining physical and spiritual components is from Jewish mysticism. The tree of Kabbalah is sometimes shown superimposed on the human body. Its ten sephirot point to inner tendencies and capacities that are interwoven, balance, and play off one another.

Another model is the Indian Chakra system of energy centers, interconnected up and down the spinal column and resonating throughout our psychophysical being.

In addition, Chinese medicine uses circulation of energies through 12 body meridians known as *Qi* or *Chi* energies that have various properties and functions.

What do all these different models tell us about who we are as psychophysical beings? They tell us we are many different things, and they tell us we are not any *one* thing.

Moreover, what kind of beings are we if we are always changing and developing while also remaining the same? Perhaps this is an impossible question and paradox, given all the different models above. But it can be fun to consider impossible questions because we have the kind of mind that makes it possible to ask impossible questions.

Instead of mind-body or spiritual-material, Eigen makes a different kind of separation, a different pairing. He puts "emotional body" and "physical body" together in this chapter. Feelings, attitudes, emotions, and felt senses exist in and through us, but they are also separate from us. We don't own them and perhaps only "borrow" them. Feelings and emotions predate us and were around long before we were born. Some believe that feelings and emotions have an even more radically independent existence—they hover in the atmosphere waiting for our particular use of them.

There is so much we don't know about these things, so much that affects our body and its functioning. We know, for instance, that thoughts themselves can affect our body. We can, for example, intentionally induce a "relaxation response" that is measurable— lowering our heart rate, respiration, and blood pressure. To a certain extent, knowledge and belief can also affect how chemicals react in our body. We see this in the *placebo effect*, where belief alone can affect a chemical outcome or result. Connections between our unconscious mind and body remain baffling, just as early hypnotists were baffled by the power of suggestion in connection with the unconscious. Hypnotic states led Freud to question temporary symptom relief being tied to transference phenomena and suggestion. Were these merely variants of "seductive influencing" rather than something more durable?

One could also point to the history of cults and cult phenomena as well as "psychic contagions" going on today. Such phenomena highlight the danger of rigid idealized beliefs and belief systems containing hallucinatory wishfulness masquerading as absolute truth. It doesn't matter if we speak of political systems, religious beliefs, or even schools of psychology and psychoanalysis. When strong emotional juices combine loyalty and idealization, any religion, national flag, sports team, rock star, or politician will become subject to and evoke megalomania, with all the psychotic vulnerability that entails.

At bottom, we are mysterious beings. Our emotions come and go, and we remain partly hidden from ourselves. This is rather odd because we're also very intimate with ourselves. There is no greater intimacy than we have with ourselves ... no one else is privy to our inner depths. Simultaneously, we are our own greatest mystery. How can both be true? There seems to be mystery within intimacy and intimacy within mystery. If we ask, who are we? What makes us real? One of Eigen's responses is: "We are all the more real because we are mostly unknown ..." (2016b, p. 8).

Think about that for a moment ... being unknown makes us more real. What if we turn this around and play with it a little? What if, instead of being mostly *unknown* to ourselves, we were mostly *known*? What would it be like if human beings could become mostly known and predictable, everything laid out? How then, would we ever change, develop, or grow? What would happen to creativity and imagination? What would become of surprise? If everything were known and predictable, the world and our experiences in it would be flat, gray, and boring. Thank goodness we are a mystery, even as our knowledge and expertise increase in many areas. The additional question Eigen likes to ask is: how do we *use* our knowledge, for what purposes? Physics and chemistry are necessary for architecture and space travel, but they also give us nuclear and biological weapons. Medicine is wonderful, but can also be lethal when used wrongly. Or, in the case of the man at the beginning of Eigen's chapter (2005, p. 81), psychotropic medicines used promiscuously can help us get back on top of things quickly, but we might miss the chance for fuller self-knowledge.

Eigen says something important about this man who suffered a personal defeat at work.

> Whatever it is that connects him to living runs through body, emotions, attitudes, relationships. Learning about this connecting thread may get lost or downplayed by scurrying to feel better and get on top of things as quickly as possible.
>
> (2005, p. 81)

The interplay of feelings, attitudes, and relationships are all experiential states of being, not abstract or theoretical. Eigen contrasts physical injury with wounding of one's spirit:

> It is a natural reflex, trying to right oneself as one falls or get up as soon as one can, if one is not too injured. But when injury comes from the emotional meaning of events, when the bruise or fall is to one's ego, vanity, image, getting on top as fast as possible may cause one to miss an opportunity to ponder and grow. Mastery is not always the best model when it comes to emotional meaning and transformational chances.
>
> (p. 81)

The experience of being hurt emotionally can be met with different responses and reactions. But whatever these might be, they also carry an *affective attitude* alongside.

Affective attitudes are subtle and not so obvious. We respond with hidden attitudes toward our own feelings and emotions. How often have we heard patients say, "I shouldn't be feeling this way ..." or "I hate having these feelings, I wish they'd go away."

Not only is such a person close to an unwanted experience, but already there is another feeling, attitude, or judgment present—a foreclosure, a dismissive attitude posing as defense or escape. When such affective attitudes become chronic, emotional *indigestion* gains traction because feelings remain unacknowledged and disrespected.

What's the alternative to pushing away feelings we don't want to feel or acknowledge? Poets and sages throughout history, along with Eigen, invite us to sit with them, play with them, inquire ... walk around our fears and wishes, turn them over, examine them, talk to them ... have a conversation with our unwanted feelings. Pierre Janet had conversations with the unwelcome hallucinations of his hospitalized patients in the late 1800s. Janet had an attitude of curiosity, and curiosity can help set the right tone. We might ask our unwanted feelings or hallucinations directly: Why have you come to visit? Tell me your story. What are you asking of me? What is it you really want, and is there something I can help you with?

Eigen uses the word *magic* at least twice in this chapter when referring to the effects of psychotherapy on physical ills, and he uses that word to highlight how interconnected we are, how permeable we are, and how we affect one another, especially in the intimate setting of the therapy room. What can we say of this magic? Is it the effect of spirit on body? The impact of insight and understanding? It is a great mystery how permeability and connection with one another and ourselves can influence us for better or worse. It's a natural impulse to try to understand these things, try to pin them down with formula or method, but I'm not sure this is possible or desirable. My own sense is that therapy relationships foster various underlying attitudes of approach, receptivity, or "posture"—an overall orientation toward unknown aspects of ourselves that help create an atmosphere for further development, even though we cannot quantify or make formulas for it.

Eigen presents the case of Amanda, her going along with others, or going the easier way rather than something gusty. She then finds a more genuine or authentic part of herself that needed challenging to feel satisfied. Not fluff and icing, but a melting into what she experienced as a truer part of who she really was. How did she get there? At first, I thought Eigen's comment about her father's penis pushing into her head causing migraines was a little crazy. But as I considered more and thought about Amanda's conflicts to go further in life than her mother and father had, as well as the connection with thinking and headache, I got a different sense of how Eigen's unusual interpretation, while opening up a can of worms and a hornet's nest, actually assisted Amanda's own thinking, allowing her to make links to life hesitations and conflicts about using her mind more fully. Not only blinded by the pain of headache, but also able to see by the light of insight, she allowed her mind to swell with intensity and grow large enough that she became a neurologist.

What about the patient Hardy, who was so "hardy" that he buried himself in work to distract from aspects of his life and marriage that were not working well? Instead of blaming everything for his chronic and irritating illnesses, he eventually came to feel that what was missing and broken lived *inside of him*, and this brokenness, this "something wrong," had steered and colored his life since he was a teenager. Eigen writes:

> It is good to have this feeling, to connect with it, express it. We wreak horror on ourselves, others, and the world at large by making believe we are whole. To be whole, we break others. No accident "total" is the root for "totalitarian." Humility is missing in pretensions of wholeness.
>
> (2005, p. 85)

By the end of this case presentation, Hardy was not cured and had not "solved" anything, but instead had started to clarify important pieces of his inside and outside lives. He was left pondering how to make the best of it, whatever that might come to mean. He had arrived at a deeper feeling about his life, better self-contact, and more genuine knowledge of his situation and what felt wrong. This deeper contact and feeling of aliveness, this ineffable psychic sense that runs through our lives, is very real. It is an elusive sense, but precious.

> There are no formulas. It is not true that people doing body work are dis-ease free, any more than people working with emotional states through words are. Therapy is no panacea, no escape from death and mishap. It does not solve the problem of pain and illness. But it is not without value. There is something to be said for growth in self-knowledge, awareness of one's personality makeup, one's patterns, and an ability to work with, if not control, those patterns, although this is not the main thing. More important than "knowing," is opening fields of experiencing, building a taste for life, for experiencing, problems of psychic taste buds. ... a feel of aliveness that has its own quality and tone. One is driven back to the feel of a life, to an elusive "something." An elusive something that is precious.
> (Eigen, 2005, p. 93)

Comments and Responses

Comment 1: What about somatic countertransference?

Response 1: Another mystery ... Why do we vibrate physically with one another in the room sometimes? There are therapists who try to match their breathing rhythm with the patient. That can be powerful. Others feel things in parallel. One of the interesting things in neuroscience is "mirror neurons." How do we know when someone is feeling something? Because it activates our own mirror neurons. When someone is sad, I feel sad if my mirror neurons get turned on and I'm receptive. There's been much renewed interest lately in somatic therapy and paying attention to bodily feelings.

Comment 2: Once when I was in my own psychoanalysis, sometimes my analyst's or my stomach started rumbling. And the other one entered too. And we basically made a symphony. [Laughter] It was so loud, it was symphonic! When people say, "What's important about a therapy, what do you remember?" that would be one of them. And how can you explain it, you know? It doesn't always happen. My stomach growled other times, but we've never been able to re-create that.

Response 2: That's wonderful, thank you. In my very first analytic sessions decades ago I was pretty nervous, and in the first or second session, I could hear my stomach rumbling. It was quite loud and I was embarrassed. I thought, "Oh no! What's he going to think?" And what was his response? He said very quietly, "You know, therapy is like that … there's something about being in therapy that stirs up a person's insides." And that's all he had to say … I calmed right down. The *way* he said it was very reassuring and gentle.

Dream Images

In the previous commentary I sketched several historical models depicting mixtures of psyche and soma—diverse cultural conceptions mapping human complexities, such as Indian Chakras, Kabbalah, and East Asian energy meridians. Each model says something important about our nature and constitution. Yet none have the final word—no one system can cover everything. We humans are always growing, developing, and evolving—we are always becoming more or other than we are today. Our conceptions of who we are change with us. Our minds and imagination play at the edges of infinite possibility, and it is partly our dream life and dreaming that have significant roles to play in personality growth and life feeling real.

Here, we peek into Eigen's nighttime psyche and dream life (2005, 96–119), where he shares thoughts and feelings about his own dreams. Some might think these too disclosing or intimate to be publicly shared, especially his sexual dreams. I felt similarly at first. I don't know of any other psychologist or analyst who writes with this kind of self-disclosure. But after my initial shock, I found it refreshing. It is as if Eigen is saying: this is real, these dreams are a real part of me, and dreams tell us something meaningful about life and selfhood. One of the ways dreams do this is through their multidimensional nature. Dreams almost always have more than one meaning. Dreams are not unidimensional, although some can seem obvious. More often, dreams are "multiply determined"—they have multiple sources of influence converging to create them. Freud and Jung point to dreams being *condensed*. Dreams pack a lot into a little, sometimes condensing into just a single image, feeling, or atmosphere. Dreams ask to be unpacked, fleshed out, and amplified for potential meaning. Wilfred Bion believed the meaning of dreams lies primarily in their emotional quality, their emotional impact or nucleus, their feeling presence. How the dream feels *is* the dream's meaning. Because dreams are condensed, we bring associations to them, elaborating and discovering possibilities of what they bring. Some dreams are clear, some subtle, some chaotic and convoluted; some are bizarre; and some are complete mysteries. Most dreams may never

DOI: 10.4324/9781003257554-22

be remembered. Dreams are mysteries that add other voices and views to our mysterious lives.

Here, I want to highlight dreams in their personal and impersonal, or non-personal, aspects. I also want to say something about Eigen's "rhythm of faith" and giving birth to ourselves as a life-long process. First dreams …

We've talked about different kinds of doubles and mixtures beyond simple binaries or dualities, and there seem to be several kinds of doubles happening within dreams. One is they look both backward and forward. Dreams try to work with what has happened during the day, but dreams also bring something new and look ahead. They are a source of potential birth as well as a way to process recent and older feelings and events.

Dreams and dreaming are also a form psychic and emotional digestion. Bion used the term *alpha function* for this process, and in endnotes at the back of *Emotional Storm* Eigen explains that "alpha function is Bion's term for whatever work is done to begin digesting life's impact on us and our impact on ourselves. Alpha function overlaps with *primary process* and *dream work*, which help initiate the processing of affect" (2005, p. 228). Bion chose this vague term *alpha function* "to keep things open, to remind us we don't know very much about how we digest experience or make life feel real" (p. 228). In one talk Bion called alpha something like *a nest where birds of meaning might alight* (Bion, 1980, p. 73).

Eigen and Bion both consider dreaming to be one important way we try to process and metabolize emotional experience. One of the themes that exercises Eigen is precisely this mystery of emotional digestion. We know that emotional processing is problematic, because individually and socially we suffer from chronic indigestion. More commonly, we use words like unresolved feelings, emotional baggage, or unprocessed trauma. These continue to reverberate through us whenever their underlying impacts remain unattended to. Effects of emotional indigestion come out in various ways: miscommunication, rage outbursts, emotional abuse, violence, various addictions, suicide, war. Wouldn't our lives be better off if we grew more tolerance and inner resources to address and process feeling life? Without engaging emotional life more consciously and fully, it tends to go underground and create all kinds of mischief, pain, and acting out. Our feeling life, the closest thing to us, is one of our greatest challenges.

Eigen's ideas about emotional digestion touch parallel metabolic processes in our physical body. The more we taste, chew, and digest little bits of feeling life, the more we allow assimilation of affect to occur and grow our psychical-emotional muscles. This leads to increased capacity for a broader range of emotional and life experience. The more practice taking in life, the more life becomes available to receive. Our psychic taste buds and resilience grow together. Another benefit is feeling more grounded and real to ourselves through stronger self-connection. Perhaps with enough practice a virtuous circle arises, where openness to life and experience becomes second nature, rather than defensive closing off, shutting down, or deadening in order to survive and get by on crumbs.

Dreams allow us to have emotional experiences not possible in waking life. We see this in Eigen's homosexual dreams, ones that startled and frightened him at first and made him question himself. But he does not try to push these away or discount them. He remains curious even though unsettled. He gives these dreams respect and interest. He turns them over and around, looking at different sides ... and lets himself feel them. Such things are all part and parcel of emotional digestion. After staying with this process, Eigen comes to sense an inner structure that forms and guides him. He says that when it comes to sex, he might be able to cross his own fear boundary, but it's really women he likes, and he knows this about himself. Even so, the dream experience provides another set of inside feelings and new ideas about warmth and wetness, and these do not stop just because he is essentially heterosexual and likes women. He says these new ideas and feelings about men add something. This reflects Eigen's ecumenical embrace of life, even when encountering intrusive otherness and fear. What is foreign adds to his life, and there is a great lesson in this if we can build some tolerance for it. Not that we need to identify with or act on our dream messages as they act upon us, but that we don't simply exclude or banish them out of hand. Instead, the lesson is to remain curious about what they offer, even when we're not sure, even when they seem alien. Sometimes dreams can be so strange we have no idea what to make of them. Mystery is part of their nature.

Freud talked about what he called the *dream navel*. The dream belly button is a cute image. In *The Interpretation of Dreams* Freud says,

> There is often a passage in even the most thoroughly interpreted dream which has to be left obscure; this is because we become aware during the work of interpretation that at that point there is a tangle of dream-thoughts which cannot be unraveled and which moreover adds nothing to our knowledge of the content of the dream. This is the dream's navel, the spot where it reaches down into the unknown.
>
> (Freud, 1900, p. 525)

The known and the unknown, our conscious and unconscious mind, rational ego and irrational id ... these are formidable conjoined doubles in constant exchange with one another. Instead of valuing one side and being suspicious of the other, why not close this split by seeing what each has to offer?

It used to be accepted that the ego needs protection from the id, the rational mind needs protection from the irrational. Primary process was best contained and controlled by secondary process. The id was characterized as unpredictable, containing instinctual drives that needed safe channeling through the work of a rational ego. The word *id* is a translation from the German *das es*, or the "it," which was couched in nonpersonal language, a force of nature, a "seething cauldron of energy," outside of time and logic, a little like the pregnant old lady who seemed unstoppable in Eigen's first dream (2005, pp. 96–106).

This impersonal or nonpersonal force, like so many things discussed in Eigen's books, is ambiguous in its double-sided potential and functions in different ways depending on how we use it and approach it. For instance, instead of being an adversary, is it possible to think of the id and unconscious forces as sources of support and nourishment to the ego—places where imagination and creativity gestate? All too often we think of id's instincts and drives as destructive, and they certainly can be. But it seems more accurate to think of the id as being both generative and destructive depending on how it is channeled and used.

What if we flip the question around and talk about protecting the id from the ego? That is, protecting the wild and irrational side of us from domestication and control by our rational side. Protecting the sacredness of mystery and the unknown from dominance by an egocentric or all-knowing intellect. Freud's ego and superego, if given free reign and left unchecked, often try to exert control and usurp psychic territory. But what if we consider our unconscious mind as a benign resource to be left unmolested, rather than exploited, condemned, or banished?

Freud (1923) was not so trusting of unconscious process. He wanted to tame and transmute the id, as when he said, "Where id was, there ego shall be ..." Freud's idea was to progressively transform instinctual drives into something more usable, more socially acceptable. In other words, a variant of making the unconscious conscious, a process of sublimating drives and instincts. But when overdone, this represents an attitude of conquest, an elitism of the ego or superego trying to dominate the id, rather than seeing it as a potential resource in its own right.

We could also cast the issue a little differently, in terms of exploiting unconscious resources for cultural benefit. One aspect of *sublimation* is using id energy to squeeze out juices of creativity: art, literature, philosophy, and more. Most would say these are a legitimate plumbing of psychic depths, a creative use of the unconscious. But consider the following contrast, where Eigen talks about Bion's different models of approaching the unconscious.

> Bion has many models. Pillage is one state, opening to the unknowable is another, the first involving greed, the second a modicum of sincerity. Perhaps akin to selfish love on the one hand and love beyond grasp and graspingness on the other, e.g., Spinoza's *amor dei*, or the biblical love of the unknown-unknowable, ineffable, infinite God with all one's heart and soul and might and mind.
>
> (2016a, p. 99)

It seems to me that part of this love for life and its source, for life's living waters, is precisely this opening to the unknown and unknowable. To do so affirms a faith that birth never stops, life never stops, being born goes on throughout one's lifetime, even when chronologically old. Eigen's pregnant old lady dream conveys this message. We are perennially pregnant with life, and we are pregnant with many births throughout life. Continually being born is one of Eigen's touchstones.

I often like to elevate the feminine and refer to this as an "ovarian" model. Or perhaps a Hindu model, in that we hold "uncooked seeds" within us waiting for the right conditions to sprout and grow. Eigen writes somewhere that he once tried to go by the adage of "living each day as if it's your last," but that never worked for him. So instead, he lives each day as if it's his *first*. What would that be like? Each day, each moment, each breath a new possibility and gift? Grateful to be born again when another day begins. Grateful for this mystery of living we call life and awareness, even with all it brings. One variant I've experienced: not a year goes by that I don't discover something new or different about myself, or find something or someone that calls to me, brings me into new territory of living.

> Pregnancy does not stop with old age. Simply, pregnancy does not stop. ... If we treated ourselves and each other as pregnant beings, murder might become a less addictive solution to problems. Imagine, pregnancy and birth a possibility of every encounter. The will to power might lose some of its appeal if its energy had better things to do. Emotional storms are here to stay, but we may have some input as to how we undergo them.
>
> (Eigen, 2005, p. 102)

Eigen's perpetual motion old lady is one kind of force, a force without dominance. And in his next dream Eigen puts the old lady alongside the young girl dream, where fear, dread, and death suddenly and unexpectedly transform into renewed life. A gripping sequence with a surprise ending!

> It has long been my belief that a kind of rhythm involving injury-recovery is part of a faith structure that is part of the foundation of experiencing. This may involve processes of renewal, rebirth, regeneration in many forms, always partial and tentative, although too often felt or conceived as totalistic and absolute.
>
> (2005, p. 103)

The old lady and the young girl express two different life forces: one as relentless and enduring, the other as part of a sequence, whether we call this death and rebirth, injury and recovery, wounding and repair. We see this rhythm in nature's progression of seasons and in the darker and lighter seasons of our own lives. Both dreams use surprise, startle, and shock as part of their method. And the lesson? There is more to life than we might dream. Dreams literally wake us up and make us take notice.

I will end this commentary with a few thoughts on the paradox of dreaming, involving personal and nonpersonal aspects of dreams. I want to entertain the question of who authors or creates our dreams. Dream authoring itself is something of a paradox containing doubleness.

James Grotstein (2000) titled one of his books *Who Is the Dreamer, Who Dreams the Dream?* It seems there is some kind of doubleness involved in authoring dreams. On the one hand, dreams come out of our personalized self-matrix. They involve remnants of our daily lives, the events and people in it, filtered through our personality. Yet there also seems to be a hidden, unknown element or intelligence that is not ours alone, or perhaps does not belong to us at all. We don't know what this other element is. It is a mystery. It may be more impersonal than personal, more not-us than us. Some have called it "wise mind" or "greater self." Jung's archetype of the Self and collective unconscious come to mind. The paradoxical formulation in dream authoring might be some combination of me and not-me, something like a dual-union or "I-yet-not-I" (Milner, 2011; Eigen, 1983). Although such phrases seem awkward, one gets a sense of the personal combined with something impersonal—myself as author, yet something other than me adding to the creation of the dream. Something unknown, embryonic, undiscovered, hidden, or greater than the "I" of my personality is playing a role in dream life. If this were not the case, how could anything new or different arise from dreaming?

Freud's famous "iceberg" was a structural metaphor of the mind, where most of the iceberg is submerged under water, representing the unconscious, and our little ego and conscious awareness is the upper tip of the iceberg peeking out above the waterline. What if we extend this metaphor and ask about the waters below the bottom of the iceberg? How might we think of *those* waters? They are below or beneath the *unconscious* mind, yet also in contact with the iceberg's bottom. What shall we call these waters? A realm of Jung's collective unconscious? A pregnant void? Realms of dreamless sleep? An unknowable resource?

Eigen approaches this mystery when he writes:

> We sleep not only to dream, but to allow contact with places dreaming cannot reach, that reach *towards* dreaming. ... Sleep enables experience outside the reach of waking and dreaming to move towards dreaming's reach. ... Shall we call this a wordless, imageless unconscious, a portal through which our lives are fed impalpably and ineffably by experience that accesses us in dreamless sleep? As though God or nature or evolution has safeguarded something from our use of it, a special form of

contact that we cannot ruin with our controlling narratives, or our lust for power, or our fears, which gains access to us when our ordinary focus and selective attention, even the foci of our dreams, are out of play…

(2014, p. 2; italics added)

I love this quote because it expresses and affirms value in the unknowable birth of experience, the value of unknown resources tied to deep dreamless sleep. It conjures the ancient Hindu saying: waking life is the past, dreaming is the present, and dreamless void the future…

Comments and Responses

Comment 1: I so appreciate Eigen and what you said about the generosity in him. And when you said also how you can identify with him, it is like that for me too. I grew up very close to where he grew up, and also being a working-class immigrant, I am a first generation. And there are so many things he says … it's like he is speaking to me and my personal experience, which I find profound. What Eigen said about his parents—that he moved away and didn't want to be in contact, I did that as a young person too. There is so much that I can identify with him. And there is a way he makes himself available, a generosity of spirit, that shows this human experience we live. Not a blaming, not a judging—just us, living this human experience.

Response 1: Thank you.

Comment 2: We had an earthquake here in Turkey today, a big one. And it's still shaking once in a while. And as the evening was falling, I looked outside the window. You see the sea, the mountains … it's so beautiful. And you think, how can something so beautiful like this all of a sudden make this huge shake and everything would collapse! And I thought, this is so beautiful, and at the same time wondered, is it cruel, is it indifferent? Like Eigen is talking about in the book. But it is not cruel. It is not indifferent. It just is. Nature is—like dreams are. Is-ness made me think of that. It is not cruel… it is just that way.

Response 2: We're glad you are okay and could join us today! Yes, we personalize nature and call it cruel. But it is not personal. It just is … and wonderful you can see it that way and also see beauty at the same time, even in the midst of something potentially catastrophic. Thank you, please stay safe.

Commentary #8

Killers within Life and Psyche

The seminar on which this commentary is based occurred on November 8, 2020, five days after the US presidential election. That week was one of the most difficult and tense weeks many could remember. Beyond fears of the COVID pandemic, sporadic violence at protests in the town where I live, remnants of toxic smoky air, and a crippled city center, beyond all that, on Tuesday, election day, a much greater fear was in the air as initial election results started coming in. The fear was that we would be stuck with four more years of a presidential killer, a dream killer. It was a terrifying moment when I wondered aloud for the very first time if I could continue to live in the United States with Trump reelected as president. And so we waited ... and waited ... for four uncertain days. Remember, this was a president who first denied COVID was a real threat, then suggested injecting bleach into our veins as a remedy. Some actually tried this and died. This is a man who lied so many thousands of times that people lost count, a man who surrounded himself with criminals who went to jail, a man without any compassion or moral compass, possessing merely a self-centered drive for power and money.

Among the voting public, very few realized on election night that some US states were counting mail-in ballots last, after counting those who voted in-person first. Other states did the opposite, counting those who voted at the polls last and mail-in ballots first. We waited days before enough votes were counted to declare Joe Biden the winner. Due to the pandemic, millions more paper ballots had been mailed for the first time, so counting them took much longer.

As I said to my seminar participants that day: if you survived both the US election and Eigen's chapter "Killers in Dreams"—and it seemed most of them did—then I have good news for you: Coming through all this means you are more resilient, sane, and psychologically mature than you thought you were. It is nearly unfathomable to imagine the emotional resilience needed to tolerate and process all that went on that week. An emotional rollercoaster to say the least. What happens with the future transition, whether it goes smoothly or not, we don't yet know (written in November 2020). More

DOI: 10.4324/9781003257554-23

evidence of resilience comes from our colleague in Turkey, who endured aftershocks to her life from an earthquake that damaged her home in the midst of the pandemic, and yet still found a way to join the seminar. And speaking of that part of the world, I want to return for a moment to Ancient Greece, where Plato wrote about the nature of time.

Plato's idea was that time is not linear as we often think it to be. Instead of a linear progression, Plato thought time was cyclical. And whether for an individual or a civilization, there are not only periods of growth and development but also periods of decay and decline. Periods of building up and periods of breaking down. The myth of the Tower of Babel is one example. Here in the US we've seen this cyclical pattern during the last few decades with elected presidents. It feels a little like a pendulum swinging back and forth. In the mid-1990s, Bill Clinton was president; he was followed by George W. Bush; and Bush was followed by Barack Obama, who was then followed by Trump. Some thought we were progressing in our American experiment of unity within diversity by having a Black president. But the pendulum then swung again, and the last four years have been a regression into further polarization, distortion, fear, blame, and anger. But with a new president we now have a chance to swing back toward more sanity. Yet a larger question remains: Is it possible to have progression without regression? Is it possible to have life forces without destructive forces (Eigen, 2018e)?

Freud theorized a life drive or life instinct, sometimes called *Eros*—a building up of greater unities and preservation of life. Freud also added a concurrent and opposing death drive, sometimes called *Thanatos*. Eigen and Winnicott, in this chapter, wonder about the need for a separate death drive, since the life drive itself can do much damage.

Eigen, along with Bion and Winnicott, stay close to our emotional and experiential reality. They often highlight our insufficiency in the face of emotional life, an insufficiency that is a source of social and individual difficulties. From Freud onward, psychoanalysis has shed light on the power of our conscious and unconscious idealizations and wishes. When these combine with feelings of lack, deprivation, and fear, there is often a need to project blame onto those who are "other." Such dynamics are seen in cultural and religious wars. That's one possibility.

From another side, we have examples of psychic and social democracy. Psychic democracy was something Winnicott (1950) wrote about, where inner tendencies offset one another rather than rigidly dominate. William Blake in the nineteenth century had a vision of heaven where different voices and agendas are at war with one another, but each adding to, rather than damaging the others. Rather than being destructive to one another, each voice, each difference, contributes and adds to the whole. This is more like a *partnering model*, a "horizontal" exchange that acknowledges different but valuable contributions (including competition) all contained within a larger whole. By contrast, prevailing *dominance models* exert power and control from the top down, with the loudest and strongest obscuring and diminishing others. Some call this a "vertical" hierarchy.

Can we imagine the kind of emotional tolerance and capacity it would take for more democratic exchanges, for inner and outer worlds to explore differences that contribute to one another rather than dominate or try to destroy each other? If we follow analytic lines of thinking, part of the difficulty can be located in our emotional life and what we do with it.

In past commentaries we've talked about ways our affective realities can add to or take away from life. How we approach and experience psychic pains, or evacuate them, can help develop or impede our capacities. I'll repeat something Winnicott said about emotional suffering, because I find it somehow oddly soothing. He said, "Probably the greatest suffering in the human world is the suffering of normal or healthy or mature persons" (Winnicott, 1988, p. 149). Eigen asks why. Is it because such people can take more? Is it because they feel more? Do they expose themselves to more life? Likely yes to all of the above, because that is what sensitive, open, engaged, resilient people tend to do. But I also want to imagine mixtures—both tough resilience *combined with* sensitivity, robust life impulses *guided by* judgment and control, risk-taking mixed *with* discernment. Such blends or hybrids may have evolutionary potential for better survival and life quality.

Which brings us back to what is problematic about humans and human groups. It's the thing we don't want to admit about ourselves: we are partly killers. We are partly a destructive and explosive life form that does great damage. Not just physical damage with weapons, or damage to the Earth extracting natural resources, but also *inherent psychological dangerousness* due to our needs for survival, esteem, belonging, and egoic pride ... impulses that merge with aggression and competition, with fears of deprivation, coupled with a desire to get ahead and be on top (Eigen, 2018e). In Eigen's chapter we read that when such forces combine and spin out of control, they lead to explosive ecstasies of destruction. They lead to psychopathy in everyday life. Eigen asks if we can do a little better.

Even the US national anthem celebrates war and victory, the beauty of explosive colorful destruction, Fourth of July fireworks, bombs bursting in air. We might survive destruction, but with what quality? And even when basic survival needs are secured, humans always seem to want *more*. Wanting more doesn't stop, even if it is a murderous more, like making a financial killing, or crushing political and business adversaries. It's a terrible truth that destruction of others can bring satisfaction, even pleasure. Revenge ethics and top-dog attitudes have a long history, with no known vaccine or immunity yet developed. We have only ourselves to work with, and "we never recover from being human."

Here, Eigen covers many sources and faces of our killer psyche, from pure life energy itself to conflictual forces rubbing against each other, from id energy to murderous superego. One particularly difficult idea is that aliveness itself is often murderous.

> The life drive is not wussy. It is allied with desire and aggression. One kills to eat, injures to gain and secure territory, competes for mates. Predator-prey relations are on the side of life, death as a result of appetite and need. In human social life, ambition takes over this function and skyrockets. Traditionally, Eros is allied with disturbance, war, rage and injury, as well as intense satisfaction. The Western literary canon begins with the word Rage, Homer's story of war as the result of erotic theft. It did not take Freud to point out that human beings are inept at handling life forces or ins and outs of difficulties with aggression and passion.
>
> Today, our economic system is fused with the taste of power and feeds on its own ambition. Henry Kissinger called power an aphrodisiac, a kind of life drive gone wild. For the sake of gain, it destroys—poisons air and water and land and psyche. The life drive, once productive, once in service of survival, has itself become a menace, a threat to life. There is enormous resistance or incapacity or unwillingness to take in and work with what we are doing—*denial of violence* inherent in our sense of life. Addiction to gain, dominance, power promotes more addiction to gain, dominance and power and inability to let in and counteract the negative effects of this spiral contributes to its momentum.
>
> Attached to this cycle is fear of the psyche. As if letting in psychic awareness would be suicidal to one's ambitions. As if letting in awareness of a fuller psychic reality would undermine one's desire or, at least, slow one down. Epidemic child abuse and suicide are among discountable side effects of the lust for power.
>
> (Eigen, 2018a, pp. 77–8)

In this chapter, Eigen highlights Leila's bulldozer dream. He uses the bulldozer metaphor as an entree into many kinds of psychic killers and dream killers. The bulldozer image seems extreme, but was very real for Leila. She could not escape the pain of early life that kept scratching at her mind and body.

Eigen also uses bulldozer language for thoughts about psychic energy, life energy and forms it takes as different kinds of killers. Too much or too little can do us in. Excessive tension or not enough tension. Eigen says we can reach a kind of emotional death or zero point from either end of the continuum: too much tension and flooding of affect and we are put out of play. Too little and we can also fade into psychic death. Loss of self with loss of tension, loss of self with too much tension. Either extreme may not only feel like a death but also mediate a dread of murder, which gets expressed in dream killers.

What is the real difficulty here? Can we say? Everyone blames everyone else for difficulty, but Eigen says that difficulty is an *independent entity* and has a life of its own. Difficulty precedes us and is embedded within living. Wherever difficulty is located, anxiety about it remains. Eigen says we survive as partially murdered beings. We think that getting rid of difficulty will get rid of pain, but this strategy backfires. The fantasy of "getting rid of" becomes hope of trying to destroy the thing that pains us, trying to destroy forms of destruction themselves. Wish fulfillment adds another layer to this. "There is always hope that fulfillment of wishes will do the trick. No parent, no pain. No child, no pain. No rival, no sibling, no pain. No people, no pain. No self, no pain" (Eigen, 2005, p. 139). But perhaps we can do a little better than getting rid of any particular X of disturbance, including ourselves?

It is naïve and simplistic to try to destroy destruction, to think we can completely get rid of bad stuff in life or in our nature. Psychologically, it has never worked to get rid of anything. Whatever is denied, remains unprocessed or repressed, eventually returns and can reappear in strengthened form. Doing a little better requires greater tolerance and more resilient capacities. In particular, Eigen and Bion focus on overlooked aspects of self-relation, like the ability to question oneself, the capacity for doubt and uncertainty, an ability to wait and hold back, without moving into immediate action.

Shakespeare offers one example of waiting in the midst of doubt and uncertainty. I'm thinking of Hamlet's agony of self-reflection at the moment he wants revenge. It is his *pausing before acting*, his pondering and ambivalence about whether to proceed with retaliation and revenge killing that is interesting. Revenge was a strong force attached to his family honor and lineage, one that evokes the age-old question of whether to adhere to tradition or rebel against it. Eigen cites Hamlet as pausing, waiting, pondering, reflecting, agonizing ... rather than immediately moving into vengeful murder expected of him (Eigen, 2002, p. 3).

The ability to wait, to think, to reflect, to agonize ... to feel one's way into conflicts. These pave the way for another step, an ability to interpose word and symbol in between impulse and action. These are developmental accomplishments and perhaps evolutionary steps, even though never completely safe from regression and undoing. Although Hamlet eventually succumbed to the pull of murderous revenge, there is a sense that his pausing to consider the futility of killing, while knowing damage would continue to ricochet into the future, is a step. Hamlet's pause itself, as Eigen relates it, can be seen as a gift to us, even as Eigen jokes that Hamlet wasn't being Hamlet *enough*, that is, he didn't pause or wait long enough for further development or perspective to occur. The same could be said about the ending of Romeo and Juliet. Tragedy born from an inability to wait, or not waiting long enough, for more to emerge and unfold. We might also apply this to psychotherapy during moments when we feel pulled by clients for quick answers or urgent action. Why not wait for more unfolding?

Whether inside or outside therapy, patience and waiting are also doubles. There are times when we need to act quickly and decisively as well as other times when we act too precipitously rather than giving time for further development to occur.

But to stop and reflect rather than immediately act or evacuate feelings, to digest and metabolize difficult emotions rather than project these and hurt others or ourselves, isn't this a more difficult but more sustainable path signifying growth of capacity and a potential step in the maturity of our species? (Bagai, 2021). We grow from changes in our self-perception, in how we view ourselves and what we do with these new perceptions. Perhaps deeply acknowledging destructive and self-destructive impulses as a real part of who we are is necessary. It seems each new generation must arrive at this insight for themselves and struggle with it.

> The vision of destructiveness (like destructiveness itself) can never be fully integrated, transformed, metabolized, processed, converted into something useful. Our ability to injure ourselves and others never ends. It is cruel to rationalize all destructiveness as secretly useful, as hidden good. I think we must make room for the possibility of destructiveness as such. Making room is not indulgence. Making room for the possibility of really being destructive without precociously rationalizing it, makes room for spontaneous growth of protective measures. If one confesses one's viral (virulent) self, one's touch may soften.
>
> (Eigen, 1998, p. 103)

> ... there is a seed of unquenchable optimism in our sea of pessimistic realism. Are we not catching on that it is up to us to work with the equipment we have been given, to partner our capacities, not just exploit them, to learn and keep on learning about our make-up? Is that not what we have been trying to do for thousands of years, probably longer? Is that not where evolution is taking us—closer to opposing our need to murder (whether physical, economic, social or spiritual)? Closer to embracing the struggle with our make-up and trying to do better?
>
> (Eigen, 2014, p. 8)

Comments and Responses

Comment 1: When I first read this chapter, I had such difficulty ... I ordinarily assume there is something wrong with me when I have that level of difficulty. But then, listening to you talk about it, once again I am just astonished at how you can weave it all together in conjunction with other authors, other experiences, and with this week's US election!

Response 1: Well, this is only my particular weaving … but thank you. I sometimes have to read Eigen's chapters over and over before they sink in. I can only get a little in one reading … it's tough and many agree. Someone just wrote on the chat window that they "felt helpless" with this chapter. I feel that way a lot too.

Comment 2: I haven't been getting a lot of sleep actually this week. I've been on pins and needles, like everyone else … I was hopeful when I heard Biden say, "The other is not our enemy." You know, we have to work together. And so, to me, that's a life function—when we hear things like that. And the refusal to concede … because I think part of life is also being able to lose … The refusal to concede seems like a destructive death force. So I look at it more as life force and death force within each party. Not one being bad or right or wrong. If the two could come together with the life force, it could be really good. I'm feeling hopeful, and I am glad that democracy has prevailed, and people's voices have been heard.

Comment 3: Well, on the other side of the ocean, I was feeling the intensity of this week too. I think a lot of Europeans did. And there was talk here about "the president of the world"—kind of, you know, jokingly. What I want to share is something that has been on my mind since last week, when you talked about pregnancy, and then my mind went to Polish women's protests. Not just women, men too. It has been going on for weeks now. Because the government has increased the prohibition on abortion. And listening to you now, I had those moments in mind, where people have to be resilient defiantly, when they have to kill—either an animal, or a wounded soldier, or a patient who is dying and not just wounded. So, it is clear that you are either going to let the person suffer for some more time or you relieve him from it. And if I think about mothers, animal or human mothers, who would calculate that they wouldn't have enough food, or it would be impossible for another child to survive … I was thinking that this is resilience, and I would say … I am not sure about death or life instinct, but I am leaning toward life here … definitely love.

Comment 4: As I read Eigen over the years, there's this idea that we have the killer in us; this destructive force in humanity and in all of life—that life is destructive, and we need destruction to have life; we can't have it without destruction. It has taken me quite a long time to really wrap my head around what that means. A lot of emotions and reactions come up. I am kind of horrified by that reality, and afraid of it, afraid of what that means in terms of our killer instincts within ourselves, within me, within all of us … And I also feel relieved that I don't have to run from it or deny it, but I am responsible for owning it and figuring out what killer instinct is in me … hoping to come to a place of healing and being inclusive. Somehow we need to turn our destructive capacities, come to terms with them in some way, and it made me think of women's role in this US election, women of color in particular, and how they've stepped up. How they've endured a disproportionate amount of murder and destruction, and they have stepped up—which is so inspiring—and being able to turn that into inspiring action showing resilience.

Killers in Dreams

We continue to explore doubles in this commentary, in particular those paired conjunctions of life and death tendencies that play off one another in emotional life. Examples include feeling more deadened or enlivened, more shut down or opened up. These reflect alternating currents and rhythmic tendencies with many variations. Eigen's psychic palette reflects many colors.

Deadness can be an escape from too much life, a toning down or shutting off. Mania can be an escape from deadening or depressive feelings. Emotional deadness can be stifling while also claustrophobic, triggering a need to break out and break free of the downward pull. Other forms of deadness can actually be pleasant, like feeling oblivious or comfortably numb. Deadness can also be a reaction to fear of aliveness, a hiding from life. Or deadness can be simply low life energy, a lack of drive or capacity for living. When preferred and habitual, a safe but only partly alive life results.

If we return to the division between physical body and mental psyche, one distinction concerns being physically finite. We die physically only once, but psychically, emotionally, and mentally we can die thousands of times and continue to live, or at least appear to live. Forms of psychical death have infinite variations and can continue throughout a lifetime. We form defenses to help soften these psychic blows, and if we're lucky, early life nurturing gives us something important—a holding, containing, loving substrate as bulwark against inevitable emotional injuries.

For many who did not receive early support and nurturing or worse, every insult and slam, every "ghosting" or unsympathetic look, every cold shoulder or misunderstanding can feel like murder to their emotional insides. Much depends on one's sensitivity and thickness of psychic skin. Each time we experience a moment of shame, we cringe and tighten. Shame itself feels like a mini death. We are vulnerable to being cut open and wounded by others, but we also do this to ourselves. The more sensitive we are, the more vulnerable to emotional wounding. The more permeable we are, the more easily feelings can be hurt. We need our defenses, our shields, our coping mechanisms, but how do they continue to serve us? At what point do we become servants of

DOI: 10.4324/9781003257554-24

them? Some defenses are flexible and work well. Others are rigid, engrained, and overused, shutting down possibilities of new life. Eigen refers to this kind of shutting off as a murdering of our embryonic nature. It's a place where growth stops because life rhythms freeze up.

Bion writes about the paradox of being murdered *into* life. This is an odd phrase, and a counterintuitive idea. Yet, even if we are emotionally murdered in various ways all lifelong, don't we also continue to survive, adapt, come through, cope, and grow ... even if emotionally gnarled and malformed? Isn't being murdered, coming through, and then being alright again a sequence that is basic in our emotional life? Or at least partly so?

The question becomes, how do we actually go through this sequence ... with what quality? How do we react in better or worse ways to feeling emotionally wounded or murdered? There are many possibilities. Sometimes it is necessary to withdraw, escape, shut down emotional life, try to sedate ourselves. We close off and hide. We might also attach ourselves to comforting others or belief systems in a parasitic way. There are many defensive strategies. At times we might become reactive, strike back, go for revenge. It is difficult to let emotional pain be, without doing anything to it. Difficult to let suffering run its course, stay with it, be curious and see whether there might be something useful that comes from it. This is not meant to champion pain and suffering for its own sake. Nor is it promoting masochism. One of the points of this chapter is about dreaming our experiences (even destructive ones) by *imaginatively engaging* them.

Several summers ago, Eigen reported he was busy repairing a patio table in his backyard when unexpectedly stung by a bee. He shared this story with an online group, detailing the way he watched the entire sequence unfold over a few hours—the initial sting, growing pain, swelling of the skin area ... and then also watching the slow eventual subsiding of swelling and pain over several hours. He tried to stay open to the experience rather than closing off— one of many responses to physical pain, a bee sting. Emotional injury is more complex and often not as visible. When injured feelings accumulate and agglutinate without adequate capacity for assimilation and processing, they halt developmental growth trajectories. Deformations can result.

Opening and closing, injury and recovery, wounding and repair as basic rhythms offer something important if attention to their flow can be sustained. Rhythms are ubiquitous: contraction and expansion are part of the pulse beat of our physical heart and emotional being. We are never just one side or one thing. The heartbeat of life requires exchange between twoness.

Rhythms in emotional life are also reflected in daily physical rhythms. We sleep by surrendering or dying into our unconscious nighttime self, followed by awakening and renewing our daytime conscious self. It is amazing to think that everyone on the planet does this consistently every 24 hours.

If emotional pain and traumas of everyday life are a given and unavoidable, what's our best strategy? Closing off and shutting down seem to make things worse in the long run. Bion and Eigen think a better strategy is to develop resources, approaches, and attitudes to engage, metabolize, and digest what is difficult. The inevitability of suffering is not going away—emotional pain is universal. It's what we do or don't do that offers a universe of possibilities and outcomes.

Perhaps a certain kind of surrender to the fact of suffering is helpful, even necessary ... a form of surrender that does not try to negate or prematurely fight off pain or psychical murder. But what kind of surrender is this? Eigen says, "In Bion's account, endurance and persistence lace surrender" (Eigen, 2005, p. 141). Tasting, meeting, enduring, and becoming familiar with what Bion and Eigen call the "murderous superego" is important (pp. 141–50). The murderous superego is part metaphor and code word for anonymous destructive forces that cannot themselves be destroyed. Such forces may not be anything personal, but they reach us in intimate ways, find us where we live, and sometimes where we are most tender.

Doesn't a certain symmetry exist between positive and negative? If we believe that basic goodness is part of us and that such goodness is indestructible, then how can we deny "basic badness" and "basic destructiveness" too? Aren't both sides embedded within life?

Is it possible to endure and even thrive while persisting through the bad stuff? This might seem counterintuitive. But the world does not have to be perfect in order to live a decent life. Most people prefer to avoid suffering, outmaneuver pain, circumvent tragedies, and at the extreme some do this by joining groups that provide insulation or profess to have all the answers. But as we've learned in Part One, utopian visions and idealized societies are more likely wish-fulfilling castles made of sand. History tells us utopian visions of purity and pain-free living are hallucinations, signaling danger.

If defenses against the pain of life go to extremes of denial or dissociation, life's fullness breaks down and we lose contact with reality. Some have taken their last breath denying that COVID-19 is real. Chronic denial and defensive numbing are dangerous and, at a minimum, result in feeling less fully connected to ourselves. That said, there are also times when surviving as best we can means retreating, hiding, and cutting ourselves off from toxicity.

Psychological danger arises when psychic and emotional flow stops ... when life rhythms become stuck or frozen. Wounds and injuries then tend to recycle themselves endlessly because assimilation of traumatic impacts cannot be fruitfully reworked, processed, and metabolized. Kernels of these injuries give off sparks that continue their sinister glow, even as psyche stops or goes on pause. When feeling life freezes, less energy is available, and there is less imagination and endurance to engage what feels wrong.

Sometimes we sleep more as a way to restore ourselves. Sleep is wonderful ... and like any resource it can be over- or underutilized. Americans, in particular, seem to be a sleep-deprived bunch—always on the move, in a hurry, trying to achieve more or better. Not that most of the rest of the world isn't similarly inclined. Whatever happened to the luxury of slowness and rest, time for reflection, lengthy consideration, and thoughtful contemplation? What happened to stillness and quiet that allows us to hear ourselves from the inside, fostering an environment for mental reflection and digestion?

In nighttime dreams, the fears we suppress in daily life come back in predatory dream characters disguised as killers, rapists, invaders, kidnappers, shadowy figures. Eigen conveys hazards of too little and too much, when he writes:

> Too little feeling can be imagined as killers because of the threat of depletion, emptiness, nothingness. Too much feeling can equate with psychic blood bursting and splattering: too little equates with psychic blood gone. We are dangers to ourselves by *being* feeling beings, although without feelings we may be even more dangerous.
>
> (2005, p. 147)

And yet somehow, even with all these dangers, we still find a way to survive and even dream ourselves continually into being. Dreaming as part of becoming, as part of development. Dreaming as part of digestion and creation. In Commentary #7, I mentioned an ancient Hindu saying that waking life is the past, dreaming is the present, and dreamless void the future. Let's try to imagine what this means.

The present moment is "past" because this very moment is always slipping by, always receding to make room for future moments. We can't stop this moment-by-moment flow, but we can try to hold still and experience it more fully by savoring moments and turning them round. We can try to work with this particular feeling or that pain by engaging it imaginatively, which means dreaming it more fully through reverie and reflection, paying sustained attention as we are able. The more we focus and sustain attention, the more we see. Dreaming signifies fluid movement, linking past, present, and future moments. Unknown future moments hold surprise. I take the phrase "dreamless void" to be akin to "pregnant void or emptiness," a lovely phrase used by Marion Milner (1987) for unknown and unknowable mystery that is an infinite resource.

Eigen references Freud when he says our conscious awareness, or ego consciousness, has contradictory tasks expected of it. The ego is tasked with "quite a balancing act, an executive function modulating passion, morality, and the need to survive" (2005, p. 147). Eigen says we are never really free of psychosis, nor are we totally without curiosity about our psychotic minds. And in stressful periods like our era, we see wishes and fears merge into powerful amalgams across political spectrums. We witness how difficult it is to deconstruct and defuse delusional elements in various subgroups of "true-believers" like QAnon— those who hold entrenched combinations of paranoid fears and unrealistic wishes along with the hubris of self-certainty and unshakable belief.

Any of our capacities can go awry and be used destructively, and any can be used constructively and creatively as well. Freud's superego was originally allied with conscience and morality, a self-regulating part of the ego, a system of checks and balances. But what happens when feelings of guilt and reparation have never been allowed to fully form? Are we doomed to become self-centered and sociopathic, where superego turns into immoral conscience, a negative reversal from its original purpose? Another scenario is when the rise of life-feeling is itself experienced as threat and fought against. Chronically beating down life drives or beating back emotional feeling as threat produces its own anxiety and exhaustion.

In clinical work as in life, we find hyperbolic states and must navigate different kinds of doubles: idealization and disillusionment, over- and underestimation, deification and demonization of self and others. We have the kind of minds that can magnify and minimize, infinitize and reduce to zero. These days, we have something called "cancel culture," a form of annihilation by fiat. Ghosting or giving a thumbs-down icon on social media are quick and easy forms of emotional murder, done with a single click. Who knew that psychical annihilation via displacement and projection of fear or hate could become so easy, enacted with impunity in our digital age?

The rhythm of being murdered and then being alright again is not popular today. Remaining emotionally "safe" is often idealized and expected. Even if this were possible, it is not realistic or sustainable to circumvent the emotional rhythms we've been discussing. We usually get practice with these rhythms early in life, when things go well enough and are not too traumatic. For example, a baby is hungry, cold, or needs a diaper change, and lets us know with a scream. Help usually comes and relieves the distress. The baby "goes on being" without undue trauma, a relatively benign cycle of disruption and continuity, a mini-trauma with subsequent repair. Another example might be a two-year-old child's tantrum, when allowed to be expressed but also safely contained. The aliveness of the child's anger is given validation, but is neither indulged nor punished. Transgression of boundaries is met with firm but safe limits. We convey to the child, "No, you cannot go running out into the street alone ... I will catch you and hold you and keep you from endangering yourself, even as you flail about." In this instance, both a life impulse and good enough containment go together without damaging the spark of aliveness, without punishing the life force being expressed.

Our sense of self and others mixes hallucination and delusion with perception of real impacts. I like to think of ego as the guardian of hallucination and of fact, performing a double protective function, since we need and value contributions of imaginative extravagance and everyday perception.

(Eigen, 2005, p. 148)

This is another example of mixtures contributing to psychic democracy. It's not that one capacity is bad and another good—we're saddled with both. It's a matter of how they are used, how they are employed. The biblical saying of being known by one's fruits is as good a measure as any. The test of the pudding is in the eating.

All rigid structures defend against alternative points of view, and the antidote is to develop capacity for multiple points of view. I'm reminded of the common housefly, an insect that has exterior eyes that can see in many different directions. Perhaps we should emulate the eyes of this ordinary fly for its diversity, scope, and vision. Eigen sometimes talks about our having many different inner eyes, many kinds of receptors and senses. Perhaps this is another way of talking about psychic taste buds.

> Bion suggests exercising our ability to see life, world, body, personality from many vertices or "viewpoints": how life looks from the "viewpoints" of eyes, ears, breathing, skin, digestion, etc. Marion Milner suggests contracting (expanding) into one's big toe to get a different sense of being. To imaginatively sense the world in many keys of experience requires growth in respect for diverse experiential domains. In life across the globe, few things are needed more. Attitudes in dreams and toward dream figures carry over into waking life. Waking and dreaming consciousness structure each other. Killers and menace in dreams reflect and constitute dangers in relationships, whether dramas of injury and repair or cycles of spiraling injuries. The kind of psyche that is involved with murder while asleep is involved with murderous tendencies when awake. It is the same psyche in two states, and it is up to us to work with it.

(2005, p. 149)

Commentary #10

Training Wheels

This commentary focuses on the chapter titled "Training Wheels" (pp. 154–67), an extended case study involving Eigen's therapy with his patient Eva. It is another of Eigen's self-disclosing chapters where we get an inside look at his thoughts and feelings. What can we learn from these two as they engage with one another?

I want to start by sharing the initial paragraphs on page 154. Eigen begins by having a feeling that something he said was wrong, and he knew it immediately but needed to think about why. He says that Eva dreamt about a bicycle with training wheels, and she shared the dream with him in their session. Often, in an intensive therapy or analysis, a dream offers commentary on the therapy itself, among other things. Eigen responds by saying he had never thought about therapy being like training wheels, but now that she dreamt it, he saw it and it made sense. This "... sounds OK enough from the outside. But I knew immediately it was a wrong thing to say or a wrong way to say it" (2005, p. 154). Why?

A few days later in their next session, Eva tells him what he said had felt distancing to her. There are different feelings that words carry, depending on how they are spoken, their affective tone and texture. The important thing here is how Eva felt receiving his words and how his words made Eigen cringe as well. He reflected more deeply at the point where Eva made him pay attention.

Next comes a confession. Eigen writes:

> The truth is I felt touched inside, a heart feeling, when she told me the dream, because of the delicate and deep connection in therapy, the emotional threads that knit us together. I betrayed my true feeling by making a sort of pleasant, affirming, objectifying remark. A remark *about* an image, not an expression *from* the feeling, perhaps an expressive gesture once or twice removed.
>
> (2005, p. 154)

DOI: 10.4324/9781003257554-25

Eigen wonders if this is the best he can do? He says he has a hard time linking up with himself, perhaps especially when touched in an emotionally tender spot. He says, "Getting affect to words is another matter. A lot gets lost along the way" (p. 154).

I have often experienced this same difficulty. As a youngster growing up, I remember having emotional reactions from impact by others, but it was not obvious what my feelings were. In those moments, I didn't really know what was being evoked. Often, I would need time apart from the situation in private reflection to explore my reactions and connect with my feeling self. Did I feel angry, afraid, misunderstood, hurt … perhaps shy and unsure? Was I too sensitive, too vulnerable? I didn't know during the moment of impact and felt a need to hide from others in order to find myself, to discover what was really true, what my emotional experience actually was. And because I often watched others around me react very quickly and easily with their own emotional responses, I felt I was somehow deficient needing extra time to go inward and sort things out. What a relief in my early 20s when I started reading Carl Jung, who wrote about introverted people and how their emotional need for processing was very different from extroverted people. Maybe I wasn't so weird or different after all?

Over time, linking up with my emotional self became easier. Even with practice I still get stymied at times, but I've come to think of it as a normal part of self-reflection. It takes time for feelings to find words that give proper expression. As one example, when I was doing live seminars on Eigen's work in my office setting, the 15 or so people present would sometimes remain silent for what seemed like a very long time after my introductory comments ended, and at first this made me anxious. What did their silence mean? Why were they so quiet? Had I said something stupid or incomprehensible? Did I go on too long? But then I realized they were absorbing silently— something I still do, and I grew to appreciate those deep silences because they come out of respect for psychic digestion, which takes time and quiet reflection.

Back to Eva and Eigen. I experienced Eigen softening as he writes about his feelings in reaction to Eva's comment that *he* was her training wheels. At some level he knew this. He says he had a heart feeling, he was touched, and his heart feeling was deeper and more vulnerable than what came out of his mouth in words.

> A heart feeling. How much heart? One can't exactly measure, but there definitely are variations in intensity, fullness, range, depth, totality. In the heart region there are relative totalities, now more, now less. No sense in ordinary logic but real enough for heart logic.

(2005, p. 154)

Eigen highlights another double when he writes:

> Of course, there are no regions when it comes to heart life. The physical
> heart has a specific place, but the emotional heart can't exactly be located.
> But let's talk a bit as if the heart is findable just to make communication
> a little easier.
>   What is it to say one's heart is moved in therapy, *my* heart, with *this*
> person? The hour ends, we go our ways—but the emotional moment is
> real. It has effects, irradiates in our lives and beings. It can be affirmed
> and betrayed and our—*my*—relative openness *and* defensiveness is not
> confined to one moment, one person. Even a little heart opening has
> consequences, especially when compared to a little closing. One develops
> sensitivity to the relative opening-closing that characterizes micromoments
> and to an overall sense of fluidity-rigidity that tones personality.
>
> (2005, p. 155)

Eigen says he

> ... felt relief when Eva fingered the distancing place. She felt set aside by
> me just at the spot where she touched me. Calling my evasion enabled me
> to link up with what she knew I felt. She felt a subtle jolt when my real
> feeling hid away. Why did I hide? Perhaps out of embarrassment, fear,
> shame, feelings she well understood. I think, too, a quiet sense of being
> on top feared being toppled. Hiding is a baseline habit.
>
> (2005, p. 155)

Eva had said it clearly and simply: Eigen was her training wheels and having
strong feelings for him helped Eva feel like a human being.
    The intimacy of that moment was too much, and Eigen made his distancing
remark ... a remark "about" rather than "from or within" their emotional
connection. This difference, if I stretch and magnify it, might also relate to
the psychoanalytic pivot from so-called one-person to two-person models.
Said differently, the turn from a classical subject-object model to a relational
subject-to-subject model. With this turn, no longer was the analyst or therapist safe by hiding behind neutrality, expertise, or being once-removed, like
a medical doctor treating symptoms. No ... instead, the relational turn meant
that each member of the therapy couple swims together in the emotional
sea between them. Both are affected and each touch the other's insides. Jung
characterized the therapy relationship as a kind of chemical reaction. Jung's
alchemical elaboration meant that both therapist and patient are necessarily
changed during the process of their encounters. The therapist is neither outside of nor exempt from impact. Maintaining distance and objectivity could
no longer be valued in the same way.

Other aspects of the therapy relationship remain vitally important: holding the therapy frame steady and consistent, maintaining good boundaries, and putting the needs of the patient before one's own, along with offering a safe environment or "container" to receive and hold whatever arises. These aspects continue to form the bedrock and scaffolding from which a person can continue to examine their life, explore, stretch, and grow.

In contemporary language, Eigen and Eva were having an *enactment*. The cringe and twinge that each one felt signaled something important to pay attention to. Eva was the braver one in this instance, as she brought her hurt feelings back into focus during their next session. She called Eigen out, and he was able to receive her message and respond. Impact and response is an important part of the atmosphere we breathe in psychotherapy.

This example tells us it's not just friends, partners, or marriages that have to negotiate issues of closeness and distance, but therapy couples as well. What shall we do as therapists when we have a twinge telling us we've said the wrong thing at the wrong moment? These days I find myself prompted by intuition in therapy sessions. Strange associations can arise, and what I say can feel off or wrong at times. But such risks are worth it if there is underlying good will and clarity is sought. Both parties can learn something from such episodes, as we see with Eva and Eigen.

Many years ago, Philip Bromberg came to give a talk here in Portland, and during the Q&A he became upset with a question I asked him. I was not getting his idea that there can be benefit from getting into misunderstandings, messes, enactments, and stuck places with therapy clients, and that these can be fruitful if we're able to hang in there and work with them together. Not just as a side benefit either, because Bromberg emphasized the view that working through enactments was an essential part of therapy, that deeper work could not be accomplished without such messiness. He felt there were golden kernels hiding within enactments. But at that time, I was pretty young and naively optimistic, holding out hopes for smoother therapy rides.

Over the last 10 to 20 years lots of attention has been paid to enactments between therapist and client in the clinical literature. Getting into muddles, conundrums, misunderstandings signal our interacting sensitivities at work, often under the umbrella of transference and countertransference language and creation of "thirds." Eigen brings us a different language—growing capacity and resilience for emotional experiencing by going through difficulties together to build and strengthen inner resources.

One of the difficult things Eigen and Eva went through together was dealing with Eva's sexual intensity. This brings the question of what to do with sexual intensity in the room with our patients. Eigen gives little soliloquies in this chapter about his inner thoughts and reactions to what Eva presents, including her family rages, sexuality, and guilt feelings. Not many therapy writers talk so openly and candidly about their fantasy life with patients, let alone write about their own sexual musings. At one point Eigen seems to peer over the edge of a sexual cliff, and we wonder if a slippery slope will proceed to *physical* enactment with Eva, one that would destroy the therapy and reverberate with ripples of injurious repercussions. What are we to do with an attractive and insistent therapy patient who sits there telling you what they'd like to do *with* you and *to* you? Perhaps more often we are the recipients of anger, frustration, and disappointment in therapy sessions. Those are more common and maybe even less taboo. But sex? It's no accident that Freud pointed to sexuality and aggression as primary components of aliveness that can also have destructive consequences. Sex and aggression as libidinal twins.

But Eigen did not jump off that cliff with Eva. He waited … he considered. He checked in with the whole of his being and with Eva's history. I think also his sense of responsibility to "do no harm," to remain therapeutic, was an embedded calling, and he survived to write about it. Eva may have expressed her fantasies and desires for wanting everything from Eigen, "but what she most wanted was a healing experience" (2005, p. 160).

I want to say a word about the benefits of constraint and containment of wishes and impulses, but with a twist, a difference. There is a type of rigid containment that can injure, and another kind of containment that can further. Actually, there's a whole continuum of these. In the moment we're focusing on, Eigen said a distancing remark that hurt Eva and was off-putting. Yet Eva's previous therapist had been judgmental and used harsh criticism. He was said to have punished Eva for perceived failures, while refusing to look at himself. She needed to break out of his confining container. By contrast, Eigen did not criticize Eva's ongoing sense of guilt, or her repetitive patterns, or her sexual life. He did not punish or reject her. He affirmed her life force and her sexuality without indulging it, ignoring it, or inducing guilt. Yes, he felt a need for more distance at times, and these were felt by Eva as slights and abandonments, but they were both able to use these moments, process them, and learn.

This latter quality of respectful containment has two important components: one of these is a radical acceptance and openness along the lines of Harry Stack Sullivan (1953) who reminded us of the Ancient Roman playwright Terence's phrase "Nothing human is alien to me." But such radical receptivity and acceptance must be combined with safety of limits and boundaries as well as not pretending to know everything. We might even think of this doubleness as a variant of D.W. Winnicott's *use of object* formulation: that is, affirming life energy (even or especially when aggressive or sexual), affirming desire and wish, while also not indulging, ignoring, punishing, or giving up. Instead, it is important to keep the frame consistent, as a paradoxical "open container," so that everything can be spoken, put on the table, symbolized and discussed, rather than acted out or in.

Another contrast I want to mention is when Eva and Eigen are thinking aloud about two kinds of "feeling sorry," or two kinds of guilt feelings—one that bears fruit and one that makes things worse.

> Eva says: "Sorry when you're in contact with real hurt leads to change. Sorry when super ego makes self the victim doesn't." Eva thinks of her children. When she feels sorry for injury she inflicts, she thinks about damaging consequences and works on herself. She feels the hurt of others. ... This kind of sorry inflicts inner pain that is useful, related to her actions. Feeling this pain is motivating.
>
> (Eigen, 2005, p. 159)

By contrast, Eigen says Eva's superego self-victimization, as when we punish ourselves for not being this way or that, or put ourselves down for not being better, spins and goes nowhere.

> Useless pain mounts. Eva can be sorry from now to kingdom come, but the only thing that happens is feeling worse ...
>
> Feeling sorry while in contact with the other's hurt is something else. It spurs Eva to do better. She tries. Scratching wounds and falling deeper into holes is unsatisfactory in comparison with the real thing. She longs to get the job done, to have a good effect on others and herself. How to go about it? It is a sorry that asks to learn more about contact.
>
> (p. 159)

Eva's early feelings of deprivation are important ingredients. Deprivation that evokes acting out seems to go hand-in-hand with the hardness of Eva's sexual desire. A deprivation that could not be filled or satisfied. No matter how much aliveness or how great her embrace of life, nothing could take away from Eva's deeper sense of deprivation. Her previous analyst recommended a life of gratification to compensate for Eva's felt sense of lack, but this only made things worse.

I think it's important to highlight that therapy with Eigen did not "solve" the bottomless sense of lack or deprivation Eva felt. One thing I like about his writing is the *absence* of final or permanent solutions. Solutions often get valorized by other writers who put neat ribbons and bows around case studies, declaring entrenched problems have disappeared, or the patient is cured and leads a happy life. To me such storybook endings do not feel real.

What did happen with Eva that shows therapy helped? For one thing, Eva says she is able to feel more tender. Tenderness with her husband and from her husband is new, and growing, rather than the hard stuff. Sweetness, too, has come to their relationship. She tells Eigen she knows her increased tenderness comes from him, from their time together. "She is not trapped in single-eye hardness. Her dreams mark the difference ... leaves a door open for mixed tendencies. ... She is linking up with the dangers and opportunities double tendencies provide" (2005, p. 166).

In another book, Eigen muses about what makes for change in psychotherapy:

> How does change happen ...? I'm not sure I can say ... And in psycho-therapy? What is it that draws us on, leads us on ...?
>
> Even if we are hard put to say exactly why this happens and not that, why or how this person benefits a lot or a little, we best follow Buddha's advice and keep practicing. Keep on doing it, this mysterious process in which one being touches another and one touches oneself. As we do it something grows richer. *We* grow richer. More keeps happening. Paths, dimensions, experience open. There is no answer, only more to do and feel.
>
> No tricks. Just working, finding, feeling, thinking, communicating, keeping at it. Sometimes it feels like we're monkeying around in the basement or sometimes working with the flow the psyche is. Psychic res-piration, circulation, digestion. How a person affects another or affects oneself. Quality of attunement is only a start. It's a treacherous business. So much can go wrong anytime and if we are lucky, we work with what goes wrong. I think of Asian carpets weaving errors into art.
>
> (Eigen, 2016a, pp. 142–3)

Comments and Responses

Comment 1: I think of working on ourselves as something eternal.

Response 1: I agree, it never stops. Referencing Buddha's life again, people asked him: "How did you achieve enlightenment?" And what did Buddha say? He said it took him thousands of lifetimes, that was his message. Thousands of lifetimes ... and even then ... well, I no longer believe in enlightenment as something "final" because life keeps challenging us. One thing Eigen says, perhaps learned from D.T. Suzuki, is that even if you reach enlightenment or *nirvana* ... *samsara* does not go away. But our attitude toward it changes. That's rather profound. Think about that. The pain and suffering of life will always be with us, but our attitude toward it can change.

Comment 2: Ram Dass has said exactly that, and it's wonderful. He says, all the years of practicing psychotherapy, being in analysis, years of medi-ation, working with his gurus, all the psychedelic trips he did, all of that, and he still is who he is— he still has the same neurotic pieces, but it's different. He has a whole different relationship with his "schmutz" now. But it's all still there.

The Binding

This commentary focuses on Eigen's chapter titled "The Binding" (pp. 168–81). Such a loaded word, *binding* ... being bound *to* something or *by* something or someone. There are many associations to the word: a contract, a covenant, a calling, a commitment. What do we bind ourselves to, and who or what binds itself to us? There's the expression "bound to our duty, our obligations ..." and in many cultures, "bound by our ancestors." Long ago during my first trip to India to visit relatives I had never met, I was surprised to see young men and women committed to and bound by tradition to follow in their parents' footsteps, whether through role, career, or station in life. At that time there seemed to be very little freedom or unbinding from cultural and familial expectations. I was in my twenties then and found such attitudes quite foreign, even suffocating, as I had grown up in the excessive freedom of Southern California culture.

In this chapter we read of bindings between Abraham and God and between Abraham and his son Isaac—a binding as close as skin, like observant Jews who wrap Torah verses inside *tefillin* around their arms and skin. But in this rendition, we have a commandment from God to sacrifice a loved one, for love of God. A mad request. There is emphasis on rage and destruction, side by side with its opposite: caring for the life of others. It begins with God commanding Abraham to sacrifice his son Isaac.

This is not just about Abraham and Isaac, or God and Moses. In different ways one asks, who or what is being bound? Who or what is doing the binding? Many threads get opened up and none are exhaustive ... there is always more. We are again left with the prospect of taking little nibbles from these big subjects, like little fish taking small bites.

There are many different kinds of bindings: having our hands tied, being overburdened, feeling bound even when we are immersed in something creative. Then also, being bound in the sense of feeling hamstrung, befuddled, confused, conflicted. A different sense than being bound by loyalty, oath, contract, or bound by word and deed. Binding is not only tied to something other, but also conjoined with self, as in bound by my thoughts and feelings,

DOI: 10.4324/9781003257554-26

a conjoined closeness within self. It is probably no accident that words like *binding* and *bound up* are so tied etymologically to words like *bonds* and *bonding*, relational closeness that binds.

To be bound is also related to *legal bonds* (as in, your bond is your word) and being *bonded* (to be bonded financially means one is trustworthy and reliable), but we also think of attachment and relational bonds. Even bondage and restriction of freedom that comes from traumatic attachments. Eigen's book *Damaged Bonds* (2018b) has a lot to say about early attachments and the relative success or failure of such bindings.

But the emphasis in these pages is a focus on destruction and fury, side by side with love, loyalty, and fidelity to God's word. Why such a crazy command from God, testing Abraham's faith? One can feel Eigen is quite exercised by all this. He often explores what is most difficult and troubling, the horrific stuff. I like to think by focusing on such subjects he opens up further thought, sheds light on core conflicts, so that alternative possibilities might be imagined. And isn't *this* sort of focus precisely how psychology might be of cultural value? To become familiar with parts of ourselves and dynamics that contain impossible problems, parts we cannot get rid of and must learn to work with.

We are bound by so many elemental things from nature. By our longevity on Earth, by gravity ... and by time itself. We bind ourselves by habit and repetition. Existentially, we are bound by forces large and small. Even birds are not totally free. Paraphrasing troubadour Bob Dylan, they are bound by the chains of the sky.

In the east, Dharma and Karma are two forms of binding. One of my Indian uncles used to say that Karma is one's deeds, and Dharma is one's duty. In the Bhagavad Gita, Krishna tells Arjuna that it is his duty to fight on the battlefield, but Arjuna observes his loved ones and cousins on the other side and does not want to murder them. Some see Arjuna's reticence as an evolutionary step, a turning away from the binding force of caste and duty toward compassion, perhaps a pivot point from Hindu "fatalism" toward Buddhist compassion and nonviolence. Yet we also know that Buddhists murder other Buddhists, too. No human is immune from murderous potential in the midst of murderous storms.

Aren't we also bound by our physical anatomy, as in Freud's dictum that anatomy is destiny? Not as much these days, perhaps, in cultures accepting of more fluid gender orientations. The late Oregon writer Ursula K. Le Guin wrote a novel of speculative fiction called *The Left Hand of Darkness* (1969), about people whose sexual organs change and morph back and forth every few years into the opposite sex. I wonder if rotating our anatomy like this might help us be more compassionate with ourselves and each other, less hierarchical. We could no longer deny or be phobic about forms of otherness, even within ourselves.

Lacking such fluidity, we remain relatively bound to our anatomy, just as we are to neurology or personality. What about being bound by guilt, conscience, and ethics? Physicians are bound by the Hippocratic oath to do no harm, and as a psychologist I'm bound by ethics and standards of practice.

Eigen's chapter is partly about the binding quality of delusional thinking and hallucination, seeing or hearing things not present. Did Abraham receive a command from God or hallucination from somewhere inside himself? Does location really matter? Why are some people bound to act on such commands, whereas others can refrain and question them?

My first encounter with binding in Judaism was years ago, while flying to Israel for a conference in the Spring of 2000. It was a long overnight flight to Tel Aviv, and I remember being half-awake as first light came through the airplane windows, surprised to see men in black coats praying quietly in the aisle, davening at the back of the plane. *Davening* is a rocking and bowing motion during prayer. These men had tefillin with leather straps wrapped tight around their upper arms with scripture inside little boxes—a ritual of binding self to God, a physical reminder tied to one's flesh. *Akedah* is Hebrew for *binding* and comes from the binding of Isaac to the altar. A concrete and literal binding to God's word as law. Which raises the question and dilemma from the opening pages of Eigen's chapter: How do we know whether the voice that commands us to do anything is not a godless voice, a psychotic voice, a devil's voice? Especially a command to kill a child?

I have a softer association from outside my window at home. Each day I'm reminded of davening prayerfulness when hummingbirds come to feed at their tray of nectar. Each little bird has its own unique rhythm of bowing and dipping into the sugar water.

As I think about it, that's another kind of binding. I feel bound to the hummingbirds, a bond I have with them to provide nourishment, to refresh their tray. Do they appreciate it? They seem to visit often. Then I begin to think we are bound to each other in a reciprocal way, a symbiotic way, because we nourish each other on physical, spiritual, and aesthetic levels. Thankfully, we don't try to murder one another, that's not part of the deal. I provide food, and they provide color, joy, awe, and wonder ...

But in this chapter, after the opening salvo between God, Abraham, and Isaac, Eigen says what must sound quite heretical to many orthodox people: that God's command to sacrifice Isaac is *a psychotic command*, that God himself is full of rage and partly psychotic, and psychotic commands are mesmerizing. Those of us who have worked in psychiatric hospitals know that commands from auditory hallucinations are both terrifying and compelling. There is no room for perspective, no room for weighing alternatives, no self-reflection, no questioning. Delusions possess one completely. Delusional thinking loses the ability to self-correct or offset itself with another view. It becomes totalizing and absolute, convinced of its own truth. Thank goodness Abraham listened to the angel, God's messenger, and at the last moment averted the human sacrifice of Isaac.

For better *and* for worse, the word *binding* can refer to psychotic demands to kill others as well as an ethical duty to love and care for others. We are bound in so many ways to so many others: our children, patients, spouses and partners, our parents and friends ... just as we are bound to the earth, nature, and animals in our care.

Eigen relates the *akedah* to other stories from antiquity:

> Cronus kills his children; Oedipus and his father try to kill each other and one succeeds. It almost does not matter who wins. The murderous impulse works both ways, parents killing children, children killing parents. Murder goes in either direction within and across generations. The impulse is a constant, while subject and object reverse, oscillate, shift roles. Infanticide, matricide, patricide, fratricide—among the great themes of literature. Literature turns the flashlight on destructive desires, part of a vast, ongoing attempt to see and feel who we are. One would like to think that awareness of our makeup plays a role in the evolution of sensibility, but that remains to be seen. We do not appear to tire of murder.
>
> (2005, p. 170)

> Whatever else the *akedah* means, it expresses a drama between destruction and care that plagues the psyche, constitutes the psyche, in some sense *is* the psyche.
>
> (p. 181)

The drama between our destructive nature and our caring nature—what can be more important to wrap our heads and hearts around, and what can be more difficult?

How are we to think about destructive energy that binds us? Are we ever free of destructive energy? Must we be forever bound by the destructive side of our nature? Freud depicted an incessant struggle between Eros and Thanatos. But Freud also suggested sublimation as a way of transforming destructive energy that could potentially be turned to better use.

It is not just our instinctual and aggressive drives that bind us, but our perceptions and attributions as well. We often feel bound to our perceptions and judgments as true and valid, but can we also consider they may be distorted, partly hallucinatory, partly made of our own fantasies and projections? And if so, how do we tell the difference? One difference between delusion and realism is a measure of flexibility. We are fortunate when able to question ourselves, check things out, test reality ... then change our mind when new developments point in different directions. Flexibility and questioning are themselves forms of *unbinding* and can free us from unconscious habits. Eigen's notion of *faith*—receptivity with an open attitude, is another form of unbinding. Faith in coming through periods of catastrophe, rhythms of faith supporting resilience to survive destructive currents and pressures in the zeitgeist.

> Bonds are packages of intense feelings fusing excitement, hate, caring, warp, frustration, injury, striving, longing. Bonds suffocate and nourish. An aim of murder is freedom, to break away, to clear out, but, Freud points out, guilt intensifies bonds.
>
> (Eigen, 2005, p. 169)

It is not lost on Eigen that

> Most murders by individuals are of lovers and family members and, also, of oneself. … Proximity plays a role in murder between national groups as well. There is often some kind of bond with the other that one tries to kill.
>
> (p. 169)

And yet Abraham manages to swerve away from murdering Isaac at the last moment, although this did not become a permanent solution. Human destruction of humans continues to this day. "There is always some portion of humanity that conceives an irresistible urge to take control of death by perpetuating it"(Eigen, 2005, p. 171).

Which brings Eigen to ask deeper questions: Can people bear themselves? How much of ourselves and others can we take? Any intense feeling, reaction, emotion, or impulse can create an emotional storm. Do we hold back, stuff it down, repress rage and destructive urges until the energy becomes irrepressible and explosion occurs? Do we instead ventilate our emotions, safely release the energy to try to regain equilibrium? Do we deaden ourselves to tame destructive energy, circumcise our aliveness, opiate it, disassociate ourselves from it? A major challenge is whether we can we learn to harness and use destructive energy in generative ways. What Eigen sometimes calls *creative destruction* (where real injury is held to a minimum and in the service of further development) is perhaps similar to "creative waiting" or "creative guilt" that can lead to new learning and growth, something Eva experienced with her guilt feelings toward her children in the previous chapter.

God's destructive surges run throughout the Bible, with flooding and plagues wiping out whole peoples God is angry with. Is the binding of God's destructive energy another allegory for evolutionary attempts to bind our own? Or is it also the other way around? Part of a human responsibility to help God *within us*, the "superego" within us, to temper his or her own rage?

> The Bible is littered with broken bodies and hearts. God, the parent, is ever grieved, destined for disappointment, righteous rage. The Bible

alerts us, if we can take it in, to the rage that parents and children share, that courses through humanity. God is the aggrieved and injured parent par excellence, writing large with cosmic lettering the story of wounded parental narcissism. Fury and forgiveness are two of God's horns that gore us, as we try to dive through the space between them.

(Eigen, 2005, p. 180)

Binding and going beyond binding. Is this like rhythms between bondage and freedom? Struggle, tension, and conflict alternating with breaking free, clearing, and perhaps grace? Another rhythm of faith? The pain of struggle and upheaval ... followed by being alright again?

Yes, our destructive elements can and do bind us, just as they bound the God of the Old Testament. But Moses and God, even while both raging, at least engaged in dialogue, had a discussion. Perhaps analogous to a parent angry at their child for disobeying, but talking it through with them instead of resorting to rage and punishment. How we go about wrestling with ourselves makes a difference.

> The sheer force of wrestling with oneself is important not only for growth and ethical behavior but for filling out one's sense of how life feels, what is possible and, perhaps, a little beyond possible. We push edges of experience in many directions, including poles of indulgence and severity. Some people favor physical exercises that pit muscle against muscle, muscle against barriers. Exertion reaches a maximum at which muscle gives way, leading to strengthening. There are times one needs to exert this kind of pressure on oneself psychically, with the paradoxical result that experience gives way, opening previously unavailable dimensions of experiencing. The capacity to pay attention does amazing things. Whatever it burns into opens. We use this gift to make money, weapons, art, medicine. Is it possible to become the kind of persons that can use entrancing physical, mental, emotional, and political gifts in less deforming ways?
>
> (Eigen, 2005, pp. 176–7)

I'll end this commentary with excerpts from Eigen:

> What we have with Abraham and Freud's Moses is a momentary victory through struggle with oneself. Both point to a crucial dimension of experience that needs cultivation, a sore spot in human nature that needs every ounce of strength we can muster: the perennial challenge to oppose oneself. A kind of self-strengthening and growth through self-opposition.
>
> (2005, p. 175)

> Conflict is an important tool for intensifying subjectivity. Without intensity of conflict, personality remains jejune. In my version of Abraham

and of Freud's version of Michelangelo's Moses, emphasis is on intensity of struggle, holding back but not simply holding back. One develops a holding environment for one's own being, a frame for waiting. Waiting on a feeling is not simply waiting a feeling out or putting oneself on hold, important as these are. To wait on a feeling allows reverie, imaginative reflection, a "feel" for oneself and one's situation, to grow. At the height of impossible struggle, one holds the self like a mother holds a baby. Holding as a prayer for development.

(p. 175)

Comments and Responses

Comment 1: I also want to highlight this, where Eigen talks about self-opposition:

... a crucial dimension of experience that needs cultivation, a sore spot in human nature that needs every ounce of strength we can muster: the perennial challenge to oppose oneself. A kind of self-strengthening and growth through self-opposition.

(p. 175)

Self-opposition ... So, it requires a dialogue within ourselves. In another part, he highlights dialogue and destruction—that the Bible oscillates between dialogue and destruction. So, if we can have room for dialogue within ourselves between different elements, different parts of ourselves, it may be an ability to oppose destruction a little bit.

Response 1: Thank you, to my mind you point to part of what development and evolution of psyche and our capacities are about. Some people never ever question themselves, let alone engage internally in a dialogue and opposition with themself. So yes, absolutely. Many of Eigen's themes are rich with visions of how we can grow. Dialogue with self, struggle with self, opposition with self. Can we learn to do it more, or a little better—without going to the extreme of beating ourselves up with self-persecution or self-tyranny?

Comment 2: One of the things that I really appreciate about Michael Eigen's work so far is the fact that he brings to light things we feel that we don't want to say we feel. We are in the process of raising a puppy right now. And I can't count the number of times I've wanted to murder him. And this is something I feel I shouldn't acknowledge, and I want to bury it. But bringing it to light seems critical. Right? And reading this, you begin to feel it is okay that we want to murder our puppy. But you get to the edge, and you don't. And as a result, you learn from that. Eigen says, "Meditation on what it means to suffer human personality is part of lifelong stretching processes." That word *stretching*, I really felt that word in particular.

Response 2: Perhaps we should give you the nickname of Abraham? [smiling]. Right to the edge and you don't murder the puppy. Good for you. I can relate ... I think we all can. We all have surges of intense anger, rage, murderous impulse at moments ... but can we hold back, hold off ... wait? It's so important. And then a dialogue with self: "What's going on?" Yes, I have this intense feeling, but it's not all of who I am. I might try to modulate it, or offset it with another view ... or simply wait it out to see what the next day or next moment brings. Thank you.

Comment 3: So, actually, just one other thought. In the sentence that was mentioned, "the perennial challenge to oppose oneself." There is also a perennial challenge to accept oneself.

Response 3: Yes, both are needed by different people in different proportions. Thank you.

Guilt, Suffering, and Transformation

In this commentary we explore one of the biggest emotional storms through the ages. It goes by the name of guilt. Here I'll be focusing on pages 182–200 of Eigen's book. Guilt is a huge topic, and one that is impossible to completely wrap our heads and hearts around. It's simply too vast.

But Eigen's chapter is not about guilt alone or by itself, but rather how guilt gets combined and mixed. How it is allied with life, with suffering, with inner struggle, with conscience. Guilt as opening and closing doors to torment, care, and redemption. Guilt is an emotional storm that permeates our lives even as we try to evade it. Are we guilty just by being alive? Some feel this more than others. Those who do hope for absolution, relief from tyrannical guilt.

On the other hand, some people never feel much guilt at all, and Eigen highlights this by saying we all approach, engage, and utilize guilt in different ways. Herein, we read about a range of different responses to guilt, from Lady Macbeth to Wittgenstein and Levinas.

Eigen turns his powerful kaleidoscope onto guilt, viewing it from many points of view, inner and outer. He makes pairings that conjoin guilt with faith and torment with wonder. He tells us that, historically, guilt was associated with bad deeds and crimes, like injuring others, theft, and murder. In a word, guilt for bad behavior. But he also points to more recent kinds of guilt, an inner sense that is not tied to outer injury. Inner guilt as feelings of failure, unworthiness, not living up to how one should be, or not becoming all that one might be. Isn't this universal? Don't we always wish we were more or better than we are? Is there anyone who doesn't suffer from such disparity? I sometimes wonder if humans are the only ones who feel guilt. If you've ever had a dog, you know that dogs can appear to feel guilty too, or at least exhibit guilty behavior when they've done something wrong.

Eigen begins by telling us guilt can act as a barrier against emotional storms, but it also creates them. Guilt as a part of *conscience* can keep us from doing bad deeds, but when magnified it creates inner obstacles.

DOI: 10.4324/9781003257554-27

More recently, guilt is associated with transgressions against self, as well as against others. Not simply bad we do, but good we fail to do, especially with regard to living the fullest, best life possible. We speak of existential guilt, failure to actualize potential, guilt over unlived life. A strange but powerful bird, this newish guilt, life not lived, a person one failed to become. More broadly, guilt is suffered over failure to do others or self justice, to do life justice. It connects with the ability to enrich, deplete, or damage the life of others or oneself.

(2005, p. 182)

Guilt is one of the great themes of literature. ... It is not simply that we are guilty for the things we know we do. We are, also, guilty for actions that escape our attention, that we fail to relate to or understand.

(p. 182)

Guilt through blind ignorance ... a powerful reminder from the story of Oedipus.

How do we talk about guilt as basic or primordial? Is there such a thing? Eigen conveys this in his short book from 2006 titled *The Age of Psychopathy*. There he begins by fingering a terrible truth ... marrow in the bones of guilt:

We are all killers. Thus, we are all guilty. We are all guilty killers. There is no way around it. We cannot get out of it. We kill to live. We kill each other to live.

Killing is part of living. It is built into life. But like light refracts into so many colors, aliveness is alive with many tendencies and counter-tendencies, many emotional colors. We kill but are not just killers. We love, we are curious, we wonder, we explore, we drink life fully, we appreciate ourselves and each other, we appreciate the world. We care about life. We want to do life justice.

(Eigen, 2006)

While it is true that aliveness and eros are part of our makeup, and we cannot escape their destructive aspects, it is also true that "... guilt and reparation, deeply felt, *can* open unsuspected dimensions of personality, lead the way to uncharted areas of experience. Guilt as discipline, spur, penetrating agent into something unknown" (2005, p. 183). Although those might be functions of guilt at its best, this was not so with the likes of Lady Macbeth or Hitler. Neither could bring themselves to be penitential, nor were they ever humbled from within. "If repentance fails in its developmental function, weakness collapses in on itself and takes us with it. [Lady Macbeth] could not undergo the deeper psychospiritual suicide Oedipus tasted, which makes living possible" (p. 184).

Eigen recounts that as a young man, he felt guilt was offset by positive aspects of life.

> What seemed to me more primordial than guilt was the felt realization that we were alive, precious, amazing, thrilling—capable of injury, joy, caring. This was not a matter of guilt but an immediate, positive apprehension of reality.
>
> Similarly, the injunction to love God with all your heart and soul and might. An experience of loving God that permeates one's whole being is translated into an objectified, exteriorized commandment.
>
> (2005, pp. 184–5)

But exterior commandments and laws cannot substitute for, or replace our lived experience—the preciousness and precariousness of being alive. Laws and commandments might bind and preserve something of original importance, but this is not the same as encounters with life experience itself. One example Eigen gives is about efforts to "renew the days of old," the way things were at the time of the ancient temple. It dawned on him that this message was also about returning to something life-giving within, returning to a sense of divinity itself. Not a law or commandment, not an angel or messenger, not a temple, but …

> A life of renewal as such, the thing itself, an affair of quality. Not turning back the clock. Turning to the breather of life, transformational tuning in. A challenge to remake life, to make life better. A moment that opens everything.
>
> (p. 185)

I wonder if his moment of epiphany was instrumental in planting seeds for Eigen's future writing, where he elaborates themes of rhythm, return, and renewal as aspects embedded in life and faith. Here he is highlighting the importance of getting back to lived experience rather than representations or rituals that become codified and miss something essential.

An important contrast we've touched previously: the value of lived experience and feeling life, side-by-side with abstract ideas and representations we overlay. Such things can never be neatly separated. The immediate felt sense is what Eigen calls "the thing itself" or the "goal region."

Although Eigen says going through God can open a heart smile that never ends, a heart smile is not enough when it comes to daily living. We have laws as containers, putting the brakes on potential transgressions. Laws work up to a point, but transgressions do not stop.

> No law can take the place of immediate experiencing: O my God. We are precious. Life is precious, not cheap. How can we murder, steal, envy?

How can we live without a primacy of love? Guilt signals something less than love. As a signal, it keeps us growing, aiming for better.

... But guilt, like law, can become cancerous, lose touch with basic vision, basic goodness. Lose touch with the fact that it mediates something more, something beyond itself. Guilt, like law, can take on a life of its own, turn into an idol. Guilt becomes a kind of god one worships, trapped in guilt.

An instinctive reaction to traps is to break free.

(Eigen, 2005, p. 186)

At their best, law and guilt sustain and renew each other in positive ways, even if they are easily degraded.

Yet a moment of loving God—loving anyone—is its own reward. Love is intrinsic, the thing itself. Nothing exterior to it is necessary. In reality, we need to incarnate love, make it daily bread, live it with real others. Law from the outside and guilt from the inside act as signals, as guides, help us steer. Still, the moment in which the heart sees God or feels the heart of another person is a privileged reference point. No stick or carrot can take its place.

(p. 186)

Eigen writes about *originary* dimensions, things that precede us or are deeper than our individual lives, larger than our particularity. Guilt and love are prominent among these.

In my translation of Bion, guilt has no head or tail or legs. It is an emotion or state or intention or disposition awaiting subjects and objects to form it. It is part of an emotional field we are born into, an emotion awaiting experience, awaiting an experiencer. Like thoughts in search of a thinker or characters in search of an author, feelings are sometimes in search of a feeler. We are inserted into guilt as we are into language or a social field. It is part of a field of experience we cannot step out of, anymore than we can breathe without air.

(2005, p. 187)

Can we find origins of guilt or love? Some like to look for causes, but Bion (2005, p. 121) reminds us that the idea of "cause" belongs to criminal investigations, not emotional reality. Still, there is a tendency to suppose that if guilt appears, then a person or thing must have caused it, be antecedent or prior to it. This forecloses the possibility of an emotional field without ownership, a field we all share.

We look for causes for what we go through, but maybe the idea of finding solutions for emotional reality is not the right search? What if emotions we experience do not lend themselves to being solved? What if emotions like guilt or love have no cause, but are part of an interactive field we share and co-create? Not a linear cause and effect paradigm, but one that is more rhizomatic, like mycelium. Guilt, like many emotions, is part of something larger that the notion of "cause" precociously tries to organize and obscures by doing so.

In contrast to causality, there's another view that keys on that word *rhizome, rhizomatic*—both as a literal bulb or tuber under the soil, and as metaphor. Eigen references John Heaton characterizing Wittgenstein's thought as rhizomatic:

> A rhizome (bulbs and tubers) ... has diverse forms ramifying in all directions. Any point can be connected with any other. There is no ideal point closed on itself that serves as a foundation. It changes its nature as it increases in connections, but follows lines. It can be cracked and broken, but starts off again following another of its lines. It is not answerable to any structural or generative model.
>
> (Heaton, 1999, pp. 128–9; cited in Eigen, 2005, p. 191)

Eigen likens the rhizome to emotional fields, including guilt. No beginning or end. We get inserted into them. They await our use, and we are always in the middle. Fields of emotional experience grow in us as we grow in them. We are interwoven with what predates us.

If there are implicit generative processes at work in rhizomes like bulbs and tubers, are there also implicit generative processes at work in guilt?

Neurologists tell us something similar about implicit work in preconscious activity of our brains, so that our conscious awareness is almost like an afterthought. And this doesn't include all the "work" our minds do at night while sleeping and dreaming. Perhaps in the rhizome we have a model of emotional reality that reflects a model of mind. Instead of a causal or linear view, a rhizomatic one, at times proliferating wildly such that we often feel a need to package or frame our experiences in more manageable ways.

It is interesting to consider Freud's "dream navel" as rhizomatic. The common view of Freudian dream interpretation, that dreams are disguised wishes of sexual or aggressive drives, goes only so far. Freud also conceived the dream navel as "a tangle of dream-thoughts which cannot be unraveled," and which does not "have any definite endings," branching "out in every direction into the intricate network of our world of thought" (Freud, 1900, 5:525; cited in Eigen, 2005, p. 191).

I think of mushrooms popping up out of soil, growing out of underground mycelium we cannot see with eyes of consciousness. Nevertheless they make their presence known to us in dreams, sudden insights, intuitions, and feelings we sense but cannot name. It is probably no accident that Freud hit upon the idea of free association as a method for tapping into unconscious thoughts and feelings. When my patients say they've lost their train of thought in a session, have forgotten where they were going, I tend to say, "It's still down there underneath awareness, not completely lost, just resting. If it's important enough, it will return at another time."

Eigen's recurring theme of double-sidedness has another iteration called *Janus-faced*, where one face has two expressions looking in different directions.

And so it is with guilt as Janus-faced or double-sided. Guilt as cruel, perse-cutory, inhumane, pitiless, demoralizing. And guilt as humanizing, allied with caring and wanting to do better. How can guilt be pitiless *and* caring? Eigen says guilt can contract us, pierce through our heart, torment us, but also bring us to deeper places.

Here Eigen begins to link guilt and suffering, and torment with redemption and faith. He says he does not want to speak about meaningless suffering that is a byproduct of illness or exploitation of power, but something deeply personal and individual.

> My wish is to paint a picture of an amazing fact of suffering—at least for some people, some of the time. My aim is not to celebrate suffering but to bear witness to a possibility.
> Suffering opens worlds. Not always, not with all people. But frequently enough to warrant appreciative regard.
>
> (2005, p. 194)

He goes on to describe personal experiences of suffering that were, for him, transformative. Experiences that resulted in "an ethical commitment to bettering life, living better, or, at least, sharing appreciation for our amazing experiential reality" (p. 194).

But even after transformative moments, struggle does not end. Even after coming through suffering that opens the heart ...

> Such moments subside, and the work of love requires real living, setbacks, fresh tries, scraping shells, more suffering, more struggle.
> ... The fight with one's nature is never-ending. Yet struggle interacts with grace, with good feeling, beatific feeling, with faith. So that neither feeling good nor struggle has the last word.
>
> (p. 195)

As Eigen says elsewhere, "... the fire that never goes out meets the wound that never heals" (2018d, p. vi).

We now come to Wittgenstein and Levinas. Hard to do justice to these two giants with only a few words, yet:

> Few writers other than saints express links between guilt, self-opening, responsibility, and caring for others more intensely than Wittgenstein and Levinas. The latter two share a sense that guilt engenders

open-heartedness, open-handedness. Living engenders guilt as a caring about the life one lives and the lives of others.

(Eigen, 2005, p. 196)

For Wittgenstein, Christianity is not a doctrine, not a theory about the human soul, but an actual occurrence in human life. In a similar vein, he is less interested in the Gospels as literal or historical narrative, but instead as a "force that changes living." Wittgenstein says we should make a very special place in our lives for the Gospels—they not just another historical narrative:

And faith is faith in what is needed by my *heart,* my *soul,* not my speculative intelligence. For it is my soul with its passions, as it were with its flesh and blood, that must be saved, not my abstract mind.

(1984, p. 33; quoted in Eigen, 2005, pp. 197–8)

Once again, we are directed toward flesh and blood experience, where life reveals itself more fully. Not theory, not speculation, not abstraction, not even wisdom. Wittgenstein is quoted as saying: "Wisdom is passionless. But faith by contrast is what Kierkegaard calls a *passion*" (1984, p. 53; quoted in Eigen, 2005, p. 198).

Passionate faith is not the same as belief (although Wittgenstein seems to use these words interchangeably). Eigen contrasts *faith* and *belief* in his other books, viewing belief as a closed system and faith as open, something deeper than belief. Faith receives storms of emotional impact, remains vulnerable, not-knowing, suffers without assurances. No escape into comfortable ready-made answers. It is precisely the torment of guilt for Wittgenstein and Levinas that offers possibilities of transformation.

"This is a thread not everyone experiences or wants to: torment gives rise to faith, gives rise to an open heart" (Eigen, 2005, p. 199). An open heart that cannot exclude others. Yet how to live such reality with the inevitable tension between self and other? We cannot all be saints, but many try to give what they can.

We are included in this self-giving. No one can give herself like we can. It is *our* self-giving, *our* waiting on the other that counts. No one can do it for us. In this, we are irreplaceable ... We give ourselves, our unique beings, our self-substance, our abilities, our personalities, and it may be precisely this, exactly this the other waits for and needs. The other waits for and needs—*us.* And in this, no one else will do.

(p. 210)

Allow me to paraphrase a story related to this irreplaceability and our inescapable responsibility, as we conclude this commentary ...

Rabbi Zusha was a great Chassidic master, who, as the story goes, lay crying on his deathbed. All his people were around him. His students asked, "Rebbe, why are you so sad, why crying?" "After all the mitzvahs and good deeds you have done in your life, surely you will get a great reward in heaven!"

"I am not sad," said Zusha, "I am afraid!"

"Why afraid?" they asked. "Are you afraid God will ask why you were not more like Moses or King David?"

"No, that is not my fear" he replied. "When I get to heaven, I'm afraid God will ask Zusha, why weren't you more like Zusha? And then what will I say?!"

Comments and Responses

Comment 1: I would like to mention another aspect of guilt it seems to me wasn't mentioned. And I would like to use Buber who speaks about "existential guilt," and I think it is crucial to mention, because he describes a passive dimension of guilt. Not an active dimension, not because we do something, but the very fact that we are a witness to the sufferings of others—that's the baseline for guilt, the primordial of guilt. The very fact that we are a witness to the sufferings of others and we can do nothing. And if we think of birth, for example, from the beginning the baby is crying and came into life from suffering, and we have to be a witness to it. And I think that it is the existential foundation for guilt.

Response 1: Thank you for bringing existential guilt, babies, and Buber back into our discussion.

Guilt, Care, and Afterword

We've arrived at the last commentary on *Emotional Storm*, and these ten chapters of Eigen's book have been intense and storm-filled. Michael Eigen dedicates this book "to storm survivors, storm transformers, and those who live and work in storm's heart …" I feel the storm's heart can be found wherever emotionally sensitive people live, including all of you reading this book.

We've come through lots of storms and will no doubt practice coming through many others.

In the previous commentary we talked about forms of guilt—that we are all guilty killers in one sense or another. If this is unavoidable and true, it is also true that we are not *only* guilty killers. We are much more, even if some harm is unavoidably done as part of living. Buddhism tells us that doing harm in this life is a given, adding that we should try to do the *least amount* of harm through our choices and actions. But trying to assess what is least harmful can be complicated. Sometimes we know intuitively what this is. We might also ask what is the opposite of a guilty killer? What's at the other end of that continuum?

Emmanuel Levinas believes it has to do with being a saint. Those two poles form quite a conjunction, quite a continuum—guilty killers at one end and saintliness at the other, with lots of mixtures in between. Eigen takes up Levinas's idea of the saint as an ideal or aspiration. It comes out of our human capacity for valuing others. And not just a capacity witnessed now and then throughout history, but a capacity needing further development today. Levinas and Wittgenstein believe that an essential part of being human is about putting the other first. Putting the other before oneself. As counter-intuitive as this sounds in today's world, would that we try it more. After all, there was a time very early in our life when someone else put us first.

When we put ourselves first, above all else, when, at the extreme we make ourselves the center of the universe and don't care about others, when the other becomes invisible or an object to manipulate for gain, what happens? It seems we crush a small kernel inside us that is, or might be, saintly. Martin Buber adds an important piece with his I–Thou formulation, contrasting it

DOI: 10.4324/9781003257554-28

with I–it. Relating to another person as "Thou," a precious being, an end in themselves, holds a difference that is in short supply today. What are some aspects or components of this saintly vision Levinas writes about?

Forgiveness might be one aspect. Let's have a little fun dissecting the word *forgive*. "Fore" plus "giving": we could hear it as "giving before," giving ahead of time; or "forward giving," giving to others before being given to, giving without first "getting." Can we find parts of ourselves that ask to be saintlier? To forgive, to sacrifice for others, to put others higher and self lower in some way, in our own particular way?

> The saint as an image of the soul or model of aspiration is an explicit part of Levinas's portrayal of a fully human being. He touches a place where guilt is associated with failure to put the other first or "to put oneself in the place of the other." As Bion and Wittgenstein suggested, this call, this guilt, is in place awaiting us. We grow into it, meet it, but it is already there inviting, urging, demanding us to grow into more caring, responsive beings. Responsibility is here associated with responsiveness, particularly response to the vulnerability of the other.
>
> (Eigen, 2005, p. 201)

> Levinas writes of this call, this order, as being older than thought, older than words … This is not the life of being, of will, of desire, the élan of vital power. It is an awakening into a life beyond chronic self-interest, triumph, survival, and pleasure to something Levinas believes more fundamental for who we are or can be.
>
> (p. 201)

The call of the other asks for our responsiveness and caring, and this call comes to us through the human face—the appeal, the vulnerability, and raw nakedness of the human face. This is something universal we share: the face as portal to our insides, a transcendent doorway to psyche and spirit.

Where does the saintly call originate? Where should we look for this appeal to put the other first? As psychotherapists we naturally put our patients first. Someone somewhere in our early life put us first, or we wouldn't be sitting here right now. Eigen says babies are a good place to start when it comes to putting the other first. We return again to babies as conveyers of important truths. Earlier in the book we talked about babies allied with basic emotional rhythms, their stormy ups and downs. Here babies are allied with an appeal that speaks to us from their helplessness and vulnerability. And are we not all emotional babies?

Taking care of infants requires sacrifice, giving, putting the other first. Eigen says this doesn't mean all parents put the baby first, but that there is a call to do so. For myself, I find babies to be amazing creatures, and not just because I've raised one. The face of a baby opens this call, the appeal Levinas is referencing. Have you ever fallen into the face of a baby? Held the gaze of an infant? It's one of my favorite moments. Baby's faces are magnetic. To gaze at the face of a contented baby can open a sense of infinity, an openness that contains fresh aliveness, perhaps even divinity. The appeal of the face as an infinite moment. Levinas makes this into a universal ethical truth, embedded before existence, before time, before words.

Years ago I made many visits to New York City to hang out with Eigen, sometimes in his office and sometimes in his home neighborhood. At that time, I was reading these passages on the New York subway, the call of the other's face, and this flashed open new impact from faces that I had never experienced before. Unexpectedly, all faces became amazing. I remember walking the streets of Manhattan where so many faces pass by, and it was actually a little scary suddenly to see so deeply into a face. Like a new channel of perception had opened up and I could look through faces into peoples' inner being: seeing something of their character, their pain, their insides. Sometimes even a momentary glance could be too much. For whatever reason, faces became doorways or portals and certain qualities stood out, like their relative softness or hardness, more open or closed, more enlivened or deadened. In New York, like most big cities, people don't like you looking at them too much or for too long. It can be dangerous to give people too much facial contact. I learned to be discrete, respectful. On the subway most people hide their faces in cell phones, reading material, behind sunglasses or closed eyes. These days, of course, with Covid, we wear masks and are practically faceless. A lot more comes through a whole face than one with a mask on, even though the eyes are said to be windows to the soul.

What besides the face does Levinas point to as important for the saint within us?

> Waiting and patience are important for Levinas—to wait on the other, to be patient with the other. Sometimes we do not know what else to do. This waiting and patience is a gift. We rush each other today. Impatience is the rule. We push each other to do this or that, fill each other with advice, like modern Job's comforters. So much of our pushing and rushing is tied to nervous energy, fear, irritability, the need to quickly get on with or on top of things. Levinas's valuation of passivity and waiting may seem strange, but it is a tribute to the other, a caring for difference, giving difference time.
>
> (Eigen, 2005, pp. 204–5)

Giving difference more time … and here Levinas uses language that gets a bit difficult. He speaks of proximity as being guarded by *in-difference* and *disinterest*, terms Levinas uses that are the opposite of how we usually think of them.

> For Levinas, caring for difference is a kind of proximity, nearness ...
> ... not an impatient taking upon oneself, taking control, not a taking hold of.
>
> (Eigen, 2005, p. 205)

This is an important distinction. "Taking hold of ..." conveys action, an agenda, possessing the other, which can be forms of distancing when such things do not allow fuller openness, developing familiarity, the time it takes to get to know more, the time it takes for further unfolding to occur.

> In-difference takes on new meaning, the opposite of ignoring, brushing off. A very special "in" arises and becomes important. The in or out that protects difference is the core of proximity. Disinterest guards proximity, enters into a form of proximity in which the other's good is infinitely valued.
>
> (Eigen, 2005, p. 205)

Can we remain *within* difference (*in-difference*, that special kind of "in") and not flee, distract, or turn off? Can we be with difference from within? Can we be with difference and not run away, not *dis-associate*?

The Other, the stranger from another culture, the one we avoid or look at askance ... doesn't such dismissiveness also occur toward those "strangers" within us, our own otherness, emotions we dislike? And don't these two realities, inner and out, mirror each other? If I fear and want to avoid my own inner strangers, how easy to project these fears and avoidance onto outer strangers, and vice versa. Here's a place where psychoanalysis and psychotherapy help us become more ourselves—filled out by inner strangers, whether these are labeled opposing tendencies, conflicts, or unwelcome difficulties rubbing up against one another causing pain and confusion within. Inner "others" can help us grow—if we're lucky.

One approach Levinas uses is differentiating *totality* and *infinity*. These two terms form the title of one of his books. We often think of *totality* as allied with wholeness or completeness, referring to good qualities. But here Levinas offers an opposite view of totality. He means, instead, absolutizing, constricting, defining, and foreclosing ... a totality that allows no room for more, no room for difference, no possibility of further elaboration. Eigen explains,

> Squeezing other or self into packets, totalities, wholes with positive and negative valences justifies war. I am this, you are that—defined,

rationalized. I respond to my interests, my images, my identity packets, and if war is in my interest, I shape the situation accordingly—and you do the same. Levinas's difference is perception of each other beyond definitions, totalities, and identity sums.

(2005, p. 203)

By contrast, *infinity* remains open to new possibility. Totality forecloses and shuts it down. Similar contrasts come to mind between mystical unknowing and rational certainty, raw perception and absolute judgement. Perception without judgment remains dumb, open, and receptive, a form of infinity waiting for more, whereas absolute judgement acts as totality, sealing the deal prematurely, without giving *time* for another view, a second look, reflective thought. *Totality* and *infinity* as umbrella terms hold tendencies that give rise to very different outcomes.

Sometimes we do need to take quick action and urgently fix problems. Here in the US, our zeitgeist is all about speed, action, and results. But results with what quality? When it comes to our emotional life, Eigen and Bion do not advocate reaching for quick solutions to emotional problems, chemical or otherwise. Eigen does not discount the use of medication, just is not in favor of its promiscuous use. Bion and Eigen highlight a different way into emotional difficulties when they speak about transformational processes that are born out of connections between waiting, patience, passivity, and faith in the context of relational communion. Most trenchantly, Levinas and Bion are concerned with what is possible when we meet insoluble problems—problems of life that can never be permanently fixed or surgically removed.

For Bion, faith, contrasted with other attitudes, is openness par excellence. He equates it with the psychoanalytic attitude, a call to be without expectation, memory, desire, and understanding (an amplification of Freud's free-floating attention). An impossible call, to be sure, but no less valuable for that. It expresses an ideal, an aspiration, a struggle to be as open as possible to the impact of experience, sensitive to the drama of impact and response. One who joins this struggle encounters transformative possibilities otherwise missed. Not exactly the other first, the primacy of the saint, as in Levinas and Wittgenstein, but a close kin.

Bion values waiting and patience, which are essential in Levinas. If in Levinas, one waits on the other, in Bion one waits on the processing of impacts, transformation of impacts, a highly complex response process involving dreamwork digesting affects. ... To let the other in and do the necessary feeling work takes time. One cannot do the other or one's response justice without time. Waiting and patience are necessary for psychic digestion.

(Eigen, 2005, p. 250)

Eigen references Ecclesiastes and offers another contrast:

> To live our lives as human, as Ecclesiastes describes, plagued by vanity, benign and malignant deceits, love and companionship, setting hands to work we can do—isn't this enough? Freud's famous association of love and work with health has this ancient book as a predecessor. In comparison with the good sense of Ecclesiastes, its modest advice to scale back, to share and care, cultivate our gardens, Levinas and Wittgenstein have an eye on the impossible. A life dedicated to the other, to doing good. What can this mean?
>
> For most, it would mean the end of life, giving oneself up, subjugation, suffocation. What about actualization of self, discovery of potential, a Goethean life? Or individuation, a Jungian life? Aren't religious principles, ideas, experiences evoked by Levinas and Wittgenstein exactly what Nietzsche called servile, crippled, crippling? How can putting the other first help us? Doesn't this last question betray our selfishness? It is as if Levinas and Wittgenstein declare sainthood a necessity, a privileged and necessary part of self-image ... they affirm or reaffirm sainthood as a necessary human direction, a fertile reality. Modern psychology gives us so many parts of selves, and now the saint takes a legitimate place in self-conception as psychic force, template, archetype, tendency.
>
> The saint in us saves us from ourselves, lifts us to new possibilities of living, gives the gift of cherishing others. Putting the other first may be the most realistic move of all. We are so used to seeing what can go wrong with this impulse—masochism, enslavement, constriction, degradation—that we fear illness when generosity moves us. What a safer, kinder, fuller world, if respectful, impassioned caring for the other were a vital nerve of living.
>
> (2005, pp. 208–9)

To my mind, Levinas is elevating ethics beyond the golden rule, beyond Kant's ethical principles, and beyond the Bhagavad Gita, when he gives meaning to the idea of returning to ethics before being, before time. A permanent questioning of being, so that in returning, one is refinding or remaking a journey of discovery related to the ethical roots of human experiencing, based on the *humanity* of humans, summarized most intensely in the appeal of the face. Thus, for Levinas, our responsibility to one another comes before existence and is inescapable.

I offer this last quote from Levinas as another expression of what Eigen and Bion refer to as *faith*. It may even touch a little of what I have tried to do with you by studying this book—stay open to new thoughts, feelings, and ideas together and allow them to grow inside us. A proximity of persons before the insoluble problem of emotional life. It's been a pleasure to be with you on this journey though Eigen's *Emotional Storm*.

A credo from Levinas to close this commentary:

> A new attitude ... the search for a proximity beyond the ideas exchanged, a proximity that lasts even after dialogue has become impossible. Beyond dialogue, a new maturity and earnestness, a new gravity and a new patience, and, if I may express it so, *maturity and patience for insoluble problems* ...
>
> Neither violence, nor guile, nor simple diplomacy, nor simple tact, nor pure tolerance, nor even simple sympathy, nor even simple friendship—that attitude before insoluble problems, what can it be, and what can it contribute?
>
> What can it be? The presence of persons before a problem. Attention and vigilance: not to sleep until the end of time, perhaps. The presence of persons who, for once, do not fade away into words, get lost in technical questions, freeze up into institutions or structures. The presence of persons in the full force of their irreplaceable identity, in the full force of their inevitable responsibility. To recognize and name those insoluble substances and keep them from exploding in violence, guile, or politics, to keep watch where conflicts tend to break out, a new religiosity and solidarity—is loving one's neighbor anything other than this? Not the facile, spontaneous élan, but the difficult working on oneself: to go toward the Other where he is truly other, in the radical contradiction of their alterity, that place from which, for an insufficiently mature soul, hatred flows naturally or is deduced with infallible logic [...] One must refuse to be caught up in the tangle of abstractions, whose principles are often evident, but who is dialectic, be it ever so rigorous, is murderous and criminal. The presence of persons, proximity between persons: what will come of this new spirituality, that proximity without definite projects, that sort of vigilance without dialogue that, devoid of all definition, all thought, may resemble sleep? To tell the truth, I don't know. But before smiling at *maturity for insoluble problems*, a pathetic formula, actually, let us think, like one of my young students, of St Exupéry's little prince, who asks the pilot stranded in the desert, who only knows how to draw a boa constrictor digesting an elephant, to draw a sheep. And I think what the little prince wants is that proverbial lamb who is as gentle as a lamb. But nothing could be more difficult. None of the sheep he draws pleases the little prince. They are either violent rams with big horns or too old. The little prince distains the gentleness that only comes with extreme age. So the pilot draws a parallelogram, the box in which the sheep is sleeping, to the little prince's great satisfaction.
>
> I do not know how to draw the solution to insoluble problems. It is still sleeping in the bottom of the box; but a box over which persons who have drawn close to each other keep watch. I have no idea other than the idea of the idea that one should have. The abstract drawing of the

parallelogram—cradle of our hopes. I have the idea of a possibility in which the impossible may be sleeping.

(Levinas, 1999, pp. 87–89; quoted in Eigen, 2005, 206–8)

Comments and Responses

Comment 1: Just in terms of doubleness of face, I was also thinking about the doubleness of being a saint. And the necessity of being selfish too, in order to live. There are people who can think too much of the other and not enough of themselves. The necessity for self-preservation and self-protection is important, necessary to live life. I guess that's what I'm trying to work out. Because what does it really mean to be a saint in this world? Being a saint, okay, but then you are not living your own life ... So, it can also be a defense. I guess I am kind of grappling with these things, individualism and collectivism and thinking about the greater good.

Response 1: Bion called those two *narcissism* and *socialism*. You point to an important double. How many people do we see in our practice who don't value themselves enough! We see very self-centric people who feel it's all about them, and we see others who are hardly able to be a whole person. Being a saint is an open question, isn't it? We can think about it our own way, and give based on who we are, or not. Nobody can be totally one way or the other. I hope that came through. We must find our own balance. In Eigen's work, doubleness can be dizzying, but ultimately it is helpful. It gives us multiple points of view from which to assess things and live more realistically. Not by holding just one point of view—that's the total or absolute stance, a bad form of wholeness. Doubleness leads us more toward multiple views and even an infinity of possibilities—a chance to see and feel life more fully, more than just one way.

References, Part Two

Bagai, R. (2021). Michael Eigen and evolution of psyche. In K. Fuchsman & K.S. Cohen (Eds), *Healing, rebirth, and the work of Michael Eigen: Collected essays on a pioneer in psychoanalysis*. Abingdon, England, & New York, NY: Routledge.

Bion, W.R. (1980). *Bion in New York and São Paulo*. F. Bion (Ed.). Perthshire, Scotland: Clunie Press.

Bion, W.R. ([1992] 2005). *Cogitations*. London, England: Karnac Books.

Bion, W.R. (1994). "Making the best of a bad job." In F. Bion (Ed.), *Clinical seminars and other works*. London, England: Karnac Books.

Bowlby, J. (1960). Grief and mourning in infancy and early childhood. *The Psychoanalytic Study of the Child, VX*, 3–39.

Bowlby, J. (1976). *Separation anxiety and anger*. New York, NY: Basic Books.

Buber, M. (1970). *I and Thou*. W. Kaufmann (Trans.). New York, NY: Charles Scribner's Sons.

Eigen, M. (1983). Dual union or undifferentiation? A critique of Marion Milner's view of the sense of psychic creativeness. *International Review of Psychoanalysis*, *10*, 415–28.

Eigen, M. (1998). *The psychoanalytic mystic*. London, England: Free Association Books.

Eigen, M. (2002). *Rage*. Middletown, CT: Wesleyan University Press.

Eigen, M. (2004). *The sensitive self*. Middleton, CT: Wesleyan University Press.

Eigen, M. (2005). *Emotional storm*. Middleton, CT: Wesleyan University Press.

Eigen, M. (2006). *Age of psychopathy*. Retrieved from https://www.psychoanalysis-and-therapy.com/human_nature/eigen/part1.html

Eigen, M. (2012). On Winnicott's clinical innovations in the analysis of adults. *International Journal of Psychoanalysis*, *93*, 1449–59.

Eigen, M. (2014). *Faith*. London, England: Karnac Books.

Eigen, M. (2016a). *Image, sense, infinities, and everyday life*. London, England: Karnac Books.

Eigen, M. (2016b). *Under the totem: In search of a path*. London, England: Karnac Books.

Eigen, M. (2018a). *The challenge of being human*. Abingdon, England, & New York, NY: Routledge.

Eigen, M. (2018b). *Damaged bonds*. Abingdon, England, & New York, NY: Routledge (original work published in 2001).

Eigen, M. (2018c). *Feeling matters*. Abingdon, England, & New York, NY: Routledge (original work published in 2007).

Eigen, M. (2018d). *Kabbalah and psychoanalysis*. Abingdon, England, & New York, NY: Routledge (original work published in 2012).

Eigen, M. (2018e). Life kills, aliveness kills. In *The challenge of being human* (pp. 77–80). Abingdon, England, & New York, NY: Routledge (original work published in *The New Therapist*, no. 76 [2012]. Retrieved from www.newtherapist.com/eigen.html).

Eigen, M. (2018f). *The psychotic core*. Abingdon, England & New York, New York: Routledge (original work published in 1986).

Eshel, O. (2019) *The emergence of analytic oneness: Into the heart of psychoanalysis*. Abingdon, England, & New York, NY: Routledge.

Freud, S. (1900). *The interpretation of dreams. Standard Edition*, 4:1–338; 5:339–625. Leipzig, Germany, & Vienna, Austria: Franz Deuticke.

Freud, S. (1923). *The ego and the id*. Vienna, Austria: Internationaler Psycho-analytischer Verlag.

Grotstein, J.S. (2000). *Who is the dreamer who dreams the dream: A study of psychic presences*. New York, NY, & London, England: Analytic Press

Heaton, J. (1999). *Introducing Wittgenstein*. J. Groves (Illus.). London, England: Icon Books.

Le Guin, U.K. (1969). *The left hand of darkness*. New York, NY: Ace Books.

Levinas, E. (1999). *Alterity and transcendence*. M.B. Smith (Trans.). New York, NY: Colombia University Press.

Milner, M. (1987). *The suppressed madness of sane men: Forty-four years of exploring psychoanalysis*. London, England & New York, NY: Tavistock.

Milner, M. (2011). *A life of one's own*. Abingdon, England: Routledge.

Rumi. (2004). *Selected poems by Rumi*. C. Barks (Trans.). New York, NY: Penguin Books.

Spitz, R.A. (1946). Anaclitic depression. *Psychoanalytic Study of the Child, 2*, 313–42.

Sullivan, H.S. (1953). *Conceptions of modern psychiatry*. New York, NY: W.W. Norton & Co.

Winnicott, D.W. (1950). Thoughts on the meaning of the word democracy. *Human Relations, 4*, 171–85.

Winnicott, D.W. (1988). *Human nature*. London, England: Free Association Books.

Wittgenstein, L. (1984). *Culture and value*. ed. G.H. von Wright in collaboration with H. Nyman (Eds). P. Winch (Trans.). Chicago, IL: The University of Chicago Press.

Index

absolutize 19, 51, 64
affective attitude 107, 114, 142
aggression 53–62, 77, 155, 156, 171
Akedah 176, 177
alpha function 122, 147
ambivalence 19, 64, 72
annihilating force 110, 117, 118, 121
anonymous "I" 69, 71, 163

Bhagavad Gita 175, 195
binaries 9, 12, 17, 67, 109, 123, 126, 147
Binswanger, Ludwig 91
Bion, Wilfred 1, 5, 10, 12, 27, 33, 41–4,
    54, 55, 66, 72, 75, 79, 91, 92, 107,
    109–11, 113, 115–17, 121, 122, 126,
    128, 133, 134, 136, 137, 146, 147, 149,
    154, 157, 162, 163, 166, 185, 191, 194,
    195, 197
blank psychosis 40
body 2, 3, 13, 17, 21, 24, 28, 32, 34–6,
    44–50, 52–4, 58, 61, 63–5, 67, 70, 71,
    74, 77, 79, 82, 85, 90, 92, 95, 101, 105,
    113, 117, 123–5, 131, 138–44, 147,
    156, 161, 166, 197
body ego 36, 45, 47, 95
body I-feeling 41, 48
bonds, bonding: binding 134, 174–81;
    legal 175; relational 78–9, 175
boundlessness 47–9, 51, 63, 85
Bowlby, John 111, 112
breakdown and recovery 89, 113
Buber, Martin 1, 109, 111, 112, 115, 116,
    189, 191

catastrophe 36, 40–4, 51, 54, 57, 104,
    116, 118, 123, 124, 177–9
cathexis 40

Clinical Case names in Part One: Alison
    63; Carl 26, 36–7, 47, 64–5, 69, 72,
    82, 91, 168; Carrie 63; Daniel Paul
    Schreber 74; Ellie 65; Frank 26, 35–7,
    47, 64–5; Pat 65; Paul 46, 63, 74; Rena
    74–80, 85; Ron 53, 54, 62, 65
Clinical Case names in Part Two:
    Amanda 143; Clea 116, 119–22; Eva
    167–73, 178; Hardy 143, 144; Leila
    130–5, 156; Pam 127; Shula 128;
    Vance 130–5
conscience 15, 29, 165, 175–6, 182
countenance 111, 115
COVID-19 pandemic 101
creative: destruction 64, 178; guilt 178;
    waiting 2, 178
creative formlessness 86
creativity 12, 62, 90, 92, 93, 111, 141, 149
cumulative resonance 121
curiosity 4–5, 52, 72–3, 128, 142–3, 164

davening 176
deadening 11, 22, 29, 37, 40, 54, 60, 83,
    147–8, 161
death drive 54–5, 60–6, 154
death instinct 40, 55, 60, 68
decathexis 22, 40
defenses 21, 23, 28, 29, 31, 34, 40,
    57, 61, 68, 89, 91, 93–4, 104, 117,
    118, 120, 124, 127, 132, 142,
    161–3, 197
deflation 28
delicate storms 104
dharma 175
disintegration 18, 85–6
distinction-union 30, 50, 70, 71, 75, 86,
    123, 132, 161, 193

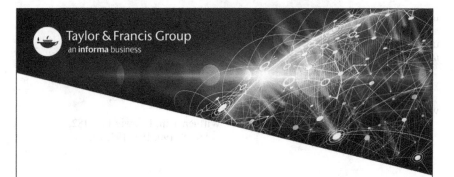